IN SEARCH OF ANCIENT NORTH AFRICA

In Search of Ancient North Africa

A History in Six Lives

BARNABY ROGERSON

For Mary and Mary

First published in 2017 by
Haus Publishing Ltd.
4 Cinnamon Row, London, SW11 3TW
www.hauspublishing.com

This first paperback edition published in 2020

Printed in the United Kingdom by Clays Ltd (Elcograf S.p.A.)

ISBN: 978-1-912208-78-4
eISBN: 978-1-909961-55-5

A CIP catalogue record for this book is available from the British Library

Typeset in Garamond by MacGuru Ltd

Contents

'Don't tell me how educated you are, tell me how much you have travelled'

Muhammad ibn Abdullah

THE ROMAN EMPIRE OF SEPTIMIUS SEVERUS, 211AD

GOTHI

Caspian Sea

DACIA

Sarmizegetusa

MOESIA SUPERIOR

MOESIA INFERIOR

Danube

Black Sea

HIBERI

Serdica

THRACIA

Byzantium

Chalcedon

Nicaea

PONTUS ET BITHYNIA

Artaxata

ARMENIA

MACEDONIA

Cyzicus

ASIA

GALATIA

CAPPADOCIA

OSRHOENE

Tigris

EPIRUS

Smyrna

Ephesus

LYCIA ET PAMPHYLIA

CILICIA

Cyrrhus

MESOPOTAMIA

PARTHIA

ACHAEA

Athens

Antioch

SYRIA COELE

Euphrates

Ctesiphon

Emesa

Palmyra

Seleucia

CYPRUS

SYRIA PHOENICE

Tyre

Bostra

CRETE

SYRIA PALAESTINA

Cyrene

Alexandria

Petra

CYRENE

ARABIA

EGYPT

Nile

Red Sea

Introduction

This is a book inspired by picnics, for I have now been loung-
ing beside the ruins of ancient North Africa for forty years.
I have always liked to affect the camp-clutter of an oriental
traveller, and so my picnics are stage-managed, with local rugs
thrown under the shade of an ancient olive tree. Food is displayed on second-hand metal trays and in brand-new Berber
pots bargained for in the souks and alongside the road. They
serve as platters for soft cheeses, juicy sliced tomatoes, piquant
olives and freshly baked flat breads. Smaller bowls can be filled
with olive oil (in which to dip hot bread), cumin (in which
to roll a boiled egg) and harissa to freshen up sardines or tuna
served from out of their own tins. Fruit, especially the honey-
dew melons available during the summer months, are gutted
of their seeds, sliced and served on the edge of a knife. Dates
are made into an additional treat by extracting the stone and
replacing it with a dried almond.

Over the last forty years, I have travelled with my family,
then student friends, then my young daughters, as well as with
journalists, artists, photographers and hundreds of fee-paying
clients. In the process, I have come to absorb an enormous
amount of North African history, which has been recycled into
guidebooks, histories and lectures. But as I come towards the
end of my working life as a picnicker abroad, I realise that there
are a handful of stories that will simply not go away. They refuse

to be pinned into tidy narratives and have become immersed in this landscape. One of the reasons they remain so restlessly interesting to me is that I have never been able to sort them out, to resolve whether they were good or bad, tragic or pathetic, selfish or heroic, malicious or noble. So this is neither a history nor a travel book, but a journey into a landscape of ruins in order to tell the stories of half a dozen individuals whose lives are now clouded with far more opinion and myth than retrievable fact. In between these life stories, we explore a few ruins that tell tales of their own.

I have not set out to present a coherent historical narrative, but the six characters are arranged in such a way that they collectively follow a rackety chronological progression through a thousand years. Queen Dido was a sacrificial refugee. Hannibal was the greatest general of all time, and is paired with Masinissa, the Berber cavalry general who helped defeat him. King Juba II was made a prisoner of war as a child and became a compliant tool of the Roman empire. Septimius Severus was an unpromising provincial from Roman North Africa, born in Leptis Magna, who not only emerged as sole emperor of Rome but brought the entire Roman empire to its dazzling apogee. Our last hero was another unpromising-looking provincial from North Africa, an intellectual careerist who became a bishop and a saint. The writings of Saint Augustine still haunt the imagination of the West.

The individual destinies of these half-dozen North Africans still speak to our time. Their descendants face the selfsame choices today. Do you try to stay pure to your own culture, to fight against the power of the West with all your might? Do you first study and assimilate this other culture, in order to use its skills in your homeland, or even to conquer it later? Or will it turn you in the end from ally to slave? There are some tragic destinies that seem to light the way: the story of the puppet king who worked hand in glove with the great power to the north; the refugee coming from out of the Holy Land; the great fighter who will at last be ground into dust. Set these against the example of three North African men who worked the existing system so well that they not only managed to prevail, but also arguably changed the system for ever.

Three of my tragic heroes (Masinissa, King Juba II and Saint Augustine) are Berber, the native inhabitants of North Africa. The Berbers can usefully be compared to the Celts of the British Isles, for they are the indigenous people, who have both kept their own language pure (in the furthest lands of the West) but have elsewhere entirely absorbed and mingled their blood with the invaders. One of my heroes, Queen Dido, was a refugee who had no Berber blood in her at all, while two others, Hannibal and Septimius Severus, were descended from Phoenician families who had intermarried with Berbers over hundreds of years.

No Arab heroes star in this collection (though Moulay Idriss and Oqba ibn Nafi make a number of appearances), because I intend to write about them in a later work. They in turn will be followed by a collective portrait of another tragic group of heroes: Omar al Mukhtar, Abdel Krim, Abdel Kader, Ahmed Arabi and Ma al-Aynayn.

This book has also been influenced by my experience of travelling with other Westerners in the North African landscape. For I have watched with annoyance, which has gradually changed into amusement, how many European tourists and archaeologists act as if they own the classical past of North Africa. Ancient history seemingly belongs all to them. This is the long shadow of public policy in the colonial era, when the French and Italians presented themselves as heirs of the Roman legions, returning to restore evidence of their monumental past. They undertook magnificent campaigns of excavation and conservation that should always be honoured, but it is time that both shores of the Mediterranean now recognise their ownership. So my six chosen heroes of this landscape have been consciously chosen to represent classical North Africa, and not the familiar drumroll of Julius Caesar, Augustus, Trajan, Hadrian, Constantine and Justinian. I have also kept my eye out for the multiple interconnections that bound the culture of this region with the wider world, particularly the spiritual traditions of the ancient Near East.

My personal exploration of North African history started in 1976, when I was seventeen years old, and has continued, with no particular order or discipline, to this day. These journeys have been broken into many fragments: a ten-day walking expedition here, a four-day journalistic assignment there, as well as a number of three-month-long road trips. Taking the year I started on this book as a random example, I spent a week in the western desert of Egypt in February, five days in Carthage in November and sixteen days taking a history tour through south-east Algeria in October. The following year I was in Morocco for the last fortnight of May and in Algeria for the first fortnight in November. I now have six blue and red passports all decorated with Moroccan, Tunisian, Algerian, Libyan and Egyptian stamps, a working knowledge of every important historical monument between Casablanca and Cairo, and some very obscure ones in between.

To help set these in some basic order it can be useful to understand the five immutable geographical building blocks of North Africa's historical landscape. There's the fish-filled but dangerous Mediterranean seashore set against the well-farmed gardens and orchards of the coastal strip. This gives way to forested Atlas mountain ranges beyond which stretch the wheat fields and olive groves of the steppeland interior. These two regions are virtually identical to what you might expect to find in any Mediterranean country, be it Greece, Spain, Italy or Turkey. But these fertile zones gradually bleed into the pure grazing lands of the arid steppe and high plateau, which once again have parallels with what you might find in the interior of Spain and Turkey. The one unmistakable landscape of North Africa is the Sahara desert, that epic wasteland of windswept black rock, eroded gravel and crescents of sand, punctuated by a galaxy of magnificently fecund oases.

In central Libya the Saharan sands reach down to the very seashore, whilst Egypt is to all intents and purposes one magnificently long oasis, formed by the Nile flowing through the eastern quarter of the Sahara desert. Tunisia, though it offers elegant instances of all five environments, has always been dominated by the culture of its coast, just as Morocco has been riven and defended by its mountain ranges, while the primary identity of Algeria is concentrated in the high steppes. I'm still surprised and delighted by this landscape, even after forty years of travelling. The year before last, I walked into an intact Roman castle in the western desert of Egypt, surrounded by what looked like a red car park, but turned out to be thousands of ceramic shards. Last year in central Algeria I finally managed to plan a picnic stop that allowed for a brisk after-lunch walk (protected by armed policemen) to an intriguing-looking Roman circular tomb on the near horizon. It turned out to have been built by an Algerian-born Roman governor-general. This Berber had conquered southern Scotland for the emperor, and by chance one of my walking companions that day had a close knowledge of the turf wall and forts he had once constructed across the Forth–Clyde frontier of Caledonia. My Algerian companions were greatly amused by this tittle-tattle of history that cast them against type in the role of the conquering colonial villain. In the evening they asked me to repeat this unlikely story to others, linking their own landscape with my own and reversing all the assumptions. For the British in those days were naked, illiterate headhunters covered in body tattoos, living in smoky communal round huts and obstinately rejecting the superior gifts of an advanced civilisation.

And though the world's population keeps expanding, the number of individuals who know the stories of their own lands diminishes every year. Many of these tales were first begun around a campfire in the evening, at the siesta end of a picnic lunch, or to kill the hours of a long coach journey or a tailback of traffic caused by military roadblocks. They offer threads of connections that often go against the imagined grain of history, linking together different ages, peoples and beliefs. They are all true, and whenever possible I have tried to connect them with an individual lifespan and some surviving monument, some touchstone that we can pat as they once did. My desire has been to entertain, and to provoke in the reader an interest in seeing the stones of Volubilis, Dougga, Djemila, Timgad, Leptis Magna, Sabratha and Ghadames for themselves one day.

1

Dido of Carthage, Princess Elissa, the Wanderer

When Purcell created the first English opera, he chose the famous story of the doomed love affair between Queen Dido, the founder of Carthage, and Aeneas, the founder of Rome. They are a pair of star-crossed lovers, both princely refugees from two ancient Asian cities of Tyre and Troy, meeting on the alien shore of North Africa. By happy chance, the first time I listened to Purcell's opera, I was in North Africa, seated in the Roman theatre at Sabratha in Libya. It was a transfixing performance, if not also touched by the bizarre, for the cast, musicians, instruments and even the audience had all been shipped out from Britain to this romantic Roman backdrop. Only the drivers and security guards were locals. We were seated in the soft light of late afternoon, but it seemed a wonderfully poignant measure of our alien nature that even the British musical instruments brought along for this, the shortest of all operas, had to be shielded from the destructive power of the North African light by sunshades.

The audience were totally entranced by the combination of music and setting, which was spell-binding. It was an instance of total art, playing with three forms and five ages simultaneously: the young musical troupe (all dressed in simple black jeans and T-shirts) performing Purcell's baroque composition which is so redolent of seventeenth-century Restoration London, all framed by the architecture of imperial Rome at its exuberant zenith, with a story-line based on Virgil's *Aeneid* that itself rested on historical legends from the Iron Age foundation of Carthage. Song interwoven with music, story, myth and the warm touch of sun-kissed ancient stones.

The Roman theatre of Sabratha is magnificent in both scale and detail, be it the fortress-like curve of its exterior wall, the marble-lined walls of its flanking green room, or the evocative details of theatrical life that have been frozen in time on the carved marble of the pulpit stage-terrace. As you sit within the theatre, the three-storey backdrop both encloses and bedazzles an audience, and also succeeds in totally removing it from the outside world, with its tiers of variegated columns rising from an undulating line of projecting porches and inverted apses that announce the various stage doors. But just as Purcell's music rested on Virgil's epic poetry, which rested on a Greek historian's understanding of the foundation legends of an Iron Age Phoenician colony, so this vast imposing architectural edifice is not the work of one time, but a curious fusion of many ages.

I still remember the shock of seeing an old photograph of the jumble of broken stone, and imagining that someone had made a mistake with the caption, before the truth gradually sank in. For the Roman theatre of Sabratha was entirely rebuilt by the Italian fascist regime, during the reign of the charismatic governor Italo Balbo. His engineers skilfully 'reassembled' the fallen stones, as graphic proof of how civilisation had finally returned to North Africa, the new Rome of fascist Italy restoring the Rome of yesterday. This great monument to Italian engineering and conservation would be turned into international propaganda when Mussolini attended the first night of *Oedipus Rex*, staged in March 1937 in the restored theatre – an Italian cast performing before an Italian audience. This was also the occasion when the famous Marble Arch, a new monument marking the old historical frontier between Tripolitania and Cyrenaica, was formally opened. These dates are known and recorded, but due to the rebuilding of the theatre, architectural historians cannot now be sure when the original Roman theatre was constructed. We do however know the last possible day on which a performance could have been staged here, which was 20 July AD 365, for the theatre was demolished by a tsunami later described in terms that will at once be familiar to those caught up in the Boxing Day tsunami of 2004.

> Slightly after daybreak ... the solidity of the whole earth was made to shake and shudder, and the sea was driven away, its waves rolled back, and the waters disappeared, so that the abyss of the depths was uncovered and every odd variety of sea-creature could be seen stuck in the slime; as well as the great wastes of those submarine valleys and mountains, which the very creation had dismissed beneath the vast ocean, at that moment were exposed to the sun's rays. Many ships were stranded as if on dry land, and people wandered at will about the paltry remains of the waters to collect fish and the like in their hands ... but then the roaring sea as if insulted by its repulse rolled back in turn, and through the teeming shoals dashed itself violently on islands and extensive tracts of the mainland, and flattened innumerable buildings in towns or wherever they were found. Thus in the raging conflict of the elements, the face of the earth was changed to reveal wondrous sights. For the mass of waters returning when least expected killed many thousands by drowning, and with the tides whipped up to a height as they rushed

back, some ships, after the anger of the watery element had grown old, were seen to have sunk, and the bodies of people killed in shipwrecks lay there, faces up or down. Other huge ships, thrust out by the mad blasts, perched on the roofs of houses, as happened at Alexandria, and others were hurled nearly two miles from the shore, like the Spartan vessel outside Methone which I saw when I passed by ...

These words of the historian Ammianus Marcellinus describe what happened to all the cities, such as Sabratha, within reach of the immediate circle of destruction of the Cretan earth-quake of 365. As I listened to Purcell and looked out over the lengthening shadows, I was not aware of any ghosts from the destruction of the theatre. For the very simple reason that plays were normally performed in the comparative cool of the late afternoon and early evening, with some evidence that sails were rigged to keep the theatre seats in the shade.

The tsunami-flattened theatre would have been very low down on the list of vital assets to be restored in the aftermath of the disaster, and any chance of this was ended when all theatres were closed by order of a Christian emperor in 391. So the ruins became a no-man's-land, squatted on by a slum of huts, and used now and then as a quarry of carved stone, especially when a necessary capital was needed, or stone required in a hurry so as to build defensive walls.

I was attending the opera as a lecturer, and was idly wondering how much of this hidden history I should share with the audience at the after-dinner talk, but held my tongue. They were so obviously relishing the belief that they were listening to Purcell's opera about the Queen of Carthage in a real Roman theatre. There is surely a limit to how much historical deconstruction anyone wants when caught up in the afterglow of opera. In just the same way I used to feel irritated when a medically trained friend would reel off the flow of hormones, rather than purely relish that other magic theatre of the bedroom. Just after listening to Purcell in Sabratha, did one want to be told that the theatre wasn't a true survival, that Virgil spun Aeneas out of nothing and added him to the old myths, or for that matter that many modern historians now doubt that Dido ever existed?

I am always in favour of the legends, but enough of a historian to be delighted by the quest for truth, and fortunately now old enough to realise that these change with the seasons and will change again.

∴

It is an ancient legend that a refugee from Syria, Princess Elissa of Tyre, established the great city of Carthage. She is also known to us as Dido, for she was saluted by the native Berbers of North Africa as *Deido* (the Wanderer) and given permission to settle on their land. Her foundation was called Carthage, which is no more than a corruption of the Phoenician for New City. The citizens of Carthage remained visiting merchants for many generations, paying rent to their Berber landlords for centuries, before this community waxed into a city that would conquer a North African empire.

Nothing remains above ground of the glory and ancient terror of this Carthage, certainly nothing that would give substance to all those dense volumes of Livy, which like some vast soap opera chronicle the bitter succession of wars that Rome fought against her one-time ally, transformed into her most dangerous rival and arch-enemy. But like many others before me I have not been deterred by the warnings of my predecessors, and have spent many weeks criss-crossing modern Carthage in the hope of catching some glimpse of its Punic past.

It has been in vain. Carthage is like Wimbledon, a suburb filled with garden villas and tarmac crescents and traversed by a commuter railway track. There are Roman ruins aplenty from the Second Foundation of Carthage, some over-enthusiastically restored and serving as an amusement park for coach tours, others remaining empty and evocative. So the elemental lesson I have learned about trying to convey Punic Carthage to a friend is that it should begin with a mid-afternoon meal of grilled fish topped by an afternoon swim. Stripping the flesh from the spine of a bream as you sip at the local wine, dunking flat bread into a saucer of olive oil and harissa, then feasting on peeled fruit is as good a communion with the passions of the past as anything built of mere masonry. And then stay as long as you can by the sea, in order to catch some of that clear dusk light that cuts through the miasma of the midday humidity of bustling greater Tunis – to catch the light from the west as it sharpens the distant horizon.

The mountain that rises to the south, Jebel Boukornine, slowly begins to stand out, growing into a sacred watchtower, with its two horns acting like a mythic beacon, signalling to distant shipping that here, clasped by the skirts of her forested slopes, lies the safe harbour of Carthage. At such moments the importance of Carthage looks to be predetermined, as the centre of a great bay in the central crossing point of the Mediterranean, defined by two great arms of land, the southern of which is the orchard- and vineyard-planted hills of the Cap Bon peninsula, so that to place a city here starts to look like elementary geography. Hence the three distinct cities that have emerged from out of this region to dominate the central Mediterranean: Punic Carthage, Romano-Byzantine Carthage and Islamic Tunis.

A special point of birth looks so necessary to the human mind in search of meaning that economic historians have questioned the truthfulness of the famous founding myth. Was Carthage–Tunis, this great commercial success story written across three thousand years of human history, really established at the whim of a refugee princess fleeing her home city of Tyre? Or was this legend, which famously ends in a spectacular suicide, much more likely to be the creation of hostile others, especially those Greek and Roman historians who chose to demean their Eastern rivals by casting them as female-ruled from day one, and like any skirt-governed group of men, destined for ultimate destruction?

For it is a truism of historical narratives that when you hear of a people led by a warrior-queen, then they must hurtle headlong down towards their final chapter. There will be the glory of a bloody first victory to come, but whether it is the revolt of the Britons led by Boudicca, queen of the Iceni (battling the Romans), or the Berber tribes of the Aurès mountains, led by their witch-queen Kahina (fighting off the Arabs), or such early Arab heroines as Kawlah or Queen Zenobia of Palmyra (fighting the Romans), the story arc ends only one way. Nor is it just the old-time women who suffer: Joan of Arc expelling the English from France or La Fraila resisting the Napoleonic invasion of Spain – they too must pay the price. For having inspired their menfolk, both Joan and La Fraila get burned alive, just like the fate recorded for Queen Dido of Carthage.

Historians label these familiar recurrent narratives as 'tropes', which is an elegant way of saying that they don't need to have actually happened, but storytellers (just like newspaper editors) have learnt to keep their audience's attention by giving them what they wanted, embroidered with variations.

What makes things even more suspicious to academic

trope-hunters is that the Elissa–Dido storyline did not seem to lead back beyond Timaeus, a Greek historian of the fourth–third century BC. Timaeus came from the Sicilian city of Taormina (though he spent most of his working life in mainland Greece), but ended his days as a pensioned historian at the big Sicilian city of Syracuse. He was a good historian, certainly good enough to be used as a principal source by all the major historians who succeeded him (such as Plutarch, Pompeius Trogus, Diodorus Siculus and Justin), who in the manner of their kind liked to gently rubbish their predecessor once they had picked his bones clean of knowledge. And that is how Timaeus' work has survived, through references and quotations from the writers who succeeded him.

Timaeus actually lived well before any of the three Punic Wars between Carthage and Rome, and yet he was the first to take the measure of the growing power of Rome. This was perceptive judgement, for he was born just after the life of Alexander the Great, at a time when everything Greek and Hellenistic was totally dominant. Timaeus lived in a world where all the great men who dominated the Mediterranean, be it the tyrant Agathocles, the master tactician King Pyrrhus of Epirus, the Ptolemaic lords of Egypt, or his own employer (King Hiero II of Syracuse) were Greek. However as a Greek born in Sicily, he absorbed with his mother's milk a certain oppositional stance to the ancient enemy of the Greeks of Sicily, namely Carthage, which ruled the western third of the island of Sicily. Carthage had repeatedly waged war and stopped the creation of a single Greek–Sicilian power. So the question is, did Timaeus put deliberate hostile spin on his history, inventing or exaggerating the Queen Dido tale, in order to soften up an old enemy? Did he denigrate Carthage as woman-led from the start, making the city into a 'pre-doomed other'? This is an exciting way of decoding history, for it corresponds with more recent fashionable themes such as Orientalism, the notion that the West has distorted and romanticised the history of its Eastern opponents as a prelude to weakening and then conquering them.

So for a long time, this was the approved and instructive way to look at Timaeus' history, as Greek propaganda aimed at undermining Carthage, for on the face of it there was small likelihood of a refugee princess personally establishing a successful trading port. This view was also backed up by the most recent excavation evidence, which seemed to rubbish all the old claims of ordered colonial settlement from a mother city. Excavations into the origins of such early trading stations as Italian Ischia, Greek Euboea and Syrian Al-Mina (which all pre-date Carthage) have revealed a much less ordered story, shorn of any prevailing ethnic identity. Instead the ancient dust has revealed a hotchpotch of Phoenician, Etruscan, Ligurian, Campanian, Cilician and Ionian craftsmen and merchants all working together, and all found buried side by side in the same small cemeteries escorted by a rich multicultural confusion of grave goods.

All the early trading centres (which numbered populations of between five and ten thousand) reveal this same foundation deposit, a rich tilth of Levantine craftsmen muddled up together, just as you would expect from the examples around us today, be it Manhattan, Singapore, London or Hong Kong. And these digs also scotched all the early attempts at creating 'linguistic divisions' between the Greeks and the Phoenicians. So typically the oldest ceramics yet found in Carthage come not from its mythical mother city of Tyre but from Greek Euboea (that long thin island hugging the coast of Greece just north of Athens). Just as the earliest deposits in Greek Euboea and Greek Corinth have been found not to be Greek but Phoenician. This was clearly a period of total cultural flux, when the Greek alphabet first emerged out of the Phoenician alphabet, as the haphazard spin-off from enterprising Greeks trading along the Syrian and Egyptian coast and of enterprising Phoenicians trading into the Aegean and up into the Black Sea. It seems that trading cities grew for the sound reason of trade, not through the political will of a colonial settlement ordained by a mother city. This is also true of Marseille (ancient Massalia), which first emerged as a melting pot of Greek, Etruscan and Carthaginian merchants all drawn to the market in tin, though the actual carrying trade was in the hands of the locals, the Ligurians and Celts.

When we read the descriptions in Homer, of the two silver belts and a pair of tripods given to Menelaus, or see how the Bible describes Jehu of Israel giving a 'golden bowl, a golden vase with a pointed bottom, golden tumblers, golden buckets, tin ingots, a staff fit for a king and spears' to his liege lord, the king of Assyria, we get a feel for the power of these early trading settlements, which alone could produce these gifts worthy of kings. They are also refreshingly modest and personal. And just now and then a sample of one of these wonderful things described in our most ancient books has managed to survive. They dominate our museums and our imagination, as they did the chroniclers and praise-singers of old. They were surely made in one of those far-flung assortment of trading towns along the Mediterranean shore.

Meanwhile the day-to-day business of a merchant tended to be far more prosaic. Preservable, transportable food has always been the backbone of Mediterranean trade – specifically the trinity of grain, olive oil and salted fish, eked out by small quantities of honey, dried fruits and wine. Bread, vegetables and meat were all part of the local economy, and were traded at the weekly marketplace. All cultures recognised the need for a fresh food market every seven or eight days, which was how long bread and vegetables can last on a kitchen shelf before becoming stale.

Now that we have (for the moment) banished Princess Dido from the process of creating a trading station, how might we better first imagine the birth of Carthage? Not with the footfall of a scented princess, but with the squalor of a seasonal fish factory, drenched in the stench of rotting fish guts, the scraping of fish skin, the drying of split fish, the squelch of marsh mud being damped up into squares. Add to that the weaving of baskets from the reeds of the marshland, and of rope for the nets, and the sifting of ever-thickening masses of sun-dried tidal mud into salt. For the place was a virtual island, a triangle of land attached by the slenderest arms of its beach front to the mainland, and separated by two great lagoons, which were once the size of an inner sea and which were themselves fed by a further network of brackish lagoons. It was a paradise for fish, offering up every degree of salinity, a home for virtually every species. And to add one further twist to nature's already abundant bounty, the largest of these lagoons connected to the sea through the narrow throat of a natural canal, which at the times of the seasonal migration of fish could be netted with ease. This also doubled in the winter months as a vast reserve of migrating birds, flying south from the cold zones of Europe, including every species of edible (and nettable) duck imaginable. And that was just landwards, for the potential tonnage of fish, including the bountiful tuna, extended ever outwards into the rich Mediterranean.

Surrounded by brackish swamps to the south – a natural breeding ground for mosquitoes – and pervaded by salt spray from the north, it was never likely to be an especially healthy place. And it would have almost certainly remained a deserted headland, a seasonal place for the fishing fleets to do their dirty work, had it not been blessed with a number of clean water springs, such as the famous one given the name of the 'fountain of 10,000 amphorae'. This was a resource indeed, especially valuable so close to the coast, which undoubtedly lured passing ships (and their trade) to stock up on fresh water. But it was not unique in this, for the Phoenician merchant captains had inherited trade-route information from their Canaanite Bronze Age ancestors, which included a lexicon of safe anchorages and watering stations, notched every 20 miles or so along the coast of North Africa. This allowed them to work their way along this shore, loaded with crude metal ingots picked up in the furthest reaches of the western Mediterranean for shipping back to the cities and empires of the Levant.

But no trader would have stopped at embryonic Carthage on any business other than fresh water and fish, for it was not a place that ever offered easy access to the agricultural trade of the hinterland. The lagoons led nowhere, and when Carthage did much later arise here, it never built any dock frontage onto any of these inner seas, for just a day's ride north-westward stood Utica, a city that was perfectly placed, with its docks on the Medjerda River mouth, to advance the North African corn trade. The Medjerda (known to the ancients as Bagrada) ran hundreds of miles due west, providing a highway right through some of the most productive regions of northern Tunisia and western Algeria. And Utica had got here first, established some hundreds of years before Carthage had been thought of, in 1100 BC.

Nor can one squeeze a drop out of any Oriental daydreams of a caravan trade into the Sahara for the youthful Carthage. If this trade existed in any tangible form, it would have been dominated by the Phoenician cities in southernmost Tunisia and westernmost Libya, settlements known as the Emporia. So just as Amsterdam was built on salted herring, it seems that Carthage slowly emerged from a long hard apprenticeship trading in dried, salted and cured fish: an unglamorous, unrecorded protohistory, almost certainly devoid of princesses. These traders shared their eating habits with their Greek and Sicilian neighbours, but it was not a universal trade, and certainly not an esteemed one. No ancient culture deemed fish a worthy sacrifice to the gods, whilst one of the major differences between the Celts of the European interior and the people of the Mediterranean shore was that the Celts resolutely refused to eat fish. This taboo was shared by the ancient Egyptians, and most of the nomad herdsmen of Asia and North Africa also looked down on fish-eaters, just as they wholeheartedly approved of meat eating and blood sacrifices.

But for those with an eye for such things, this desolate fishing anchorage had potential. The men were used to looking to the sea for their survival, their work required them to be excellent seamen, and they had no other place to run to, no hinterland of refuge. It just needed a bit of magic to fill these people with an irresistible sense of their identity.

Now we can return to Timaeus, for he tells us how this first happened. It came with the arrival of Princess Elissa–Dido, fleeing from the rule of her brother Pygmalion, who had assassinated her husband Acerbas, high priest of Hercules, for the sake of his gold. Elissa, according to this tale, escaped her brother's cupidity, sailed to Cyprus and recruited eighty young women to her venture. From there she set out towards Carthage, where the local Berber king allowed her to rent as much land as could be covered by the hide of a cow. This lease she cleverly enlarged by trimming the leather into the finest elongated lace, which stretched far enough to enclose a city-sized development plot centred on the Byrsa hill. It is an age-old wisdom tale shared among many cultures, this trickery with leather, but the detail to bear in mind is that this story recalls how the land was already owned, controlled and valued by the Berbers.

Now in the process of these land transactions, the local Berber, King Iarbas, had grown deeply impressed by this wandering princess, with all her fine manners and skills, and began to press his suit. She made her excuses, but he eventually made it clear that his demand for her hand in marriage was the price of a continued peace between landlord and seagoing tenants. She pretended to agree, but insisted that the day before her royal wedding there must be a pious sacrifice to the gods. This involved performing a hecatomb, in this case the complete consumption of the sacrificial offerings in a sacred fire. Having performed all the dedicatory rituals to perfection, complete with hymns and processions, Elissa summoned up her courage and self-belief, and threw herself onto the flames. It was said that she did not want to betray the memory of her first husband, the high priest of the god Melkarth at Tyre, with this second marriage. She may have also wanted to sanctify her new foundation with an unforgettable act that would live through eternity. So it has proved.

It is a powerful tale, made spine-chillingly gripping to my mind by the fact that it also predicts, by 650 years, the eventual fate of her city. For halfway through the Third Punic War, the Romans offered a form of peace, if the Carthaginians would agree to desert their city and move inland. In order to be spared, they must turn their back on the sea and their ancient altars. This offer they refused, and then heroically resisted, fighting the Romans street by street, house by house, until the last defenders made a funeral pyre from out of the last hilltop temple–fortress and hurled themselves into the flames. One tiny patch of Punic housing has been discovered on one of the old hill-tops, preserved from the thoroughgoing Roman destruction of Carthage by being buried under a raised Roman terrace and back-filled with rubble. These slight walls have to stand in for all of their parent city, but even in this expensive uphill quarter of the city, they stand cheek by jowl, slender, urban dwellings built around narrow courtyards, and networked with narrow alleys. Though these houses must date before the final destruction in 146 BC, it is impossible for a traveller walking among them not to be instantly reminded of the old medieval cities of North Africa, where in places such as Fez, Tunis, Algiers, Ghadames and Sefrou the old street pattern has survived intact.

Now for a paragraph's digression, a small personal confession of no historical relevance whatsoever. I have an elder sister called Dido, much admired, and was so taken by the name of her bad brother in the story that I invented a game in Pygmalion's honour whilst a young boy at boarding school. We drew straws to identify a Pygmalion, who had to turn himself into a savage beast on all fours, but who could be beaten off with sticks. No one quite got the hang of how the game should be played, so I took on the role of Pygmalion myself, who was not just a tyrant of Tyre but had something of the flesh-eating Minotaur about him, and the wild pigs in *Lord of the Flies*. Played with boyish conviction amongst the dense thickets of rhododendron that surrounded the school playing fields, the game proved an enormous success. It was banned, however, after the matron grew horrified by all the bruises and bite marks revealed at bath time – despite my friends cheerfully telling her not to worry, they were just battle wounds, earned fighting off The Pygmalion.

This wonderful name, Pygmalion (later used by Ovid and Bernard Shaw), offers intriguing internal evidence about the reliability of Timaeus, because it is a Greek transcription of a

Phoenician name, Pumayyaton, which means 'gift of the God Pumay'. Pumay can be spelled in a number of ways (Pumia, Pmy or Ipmy), and although we cannot be quite sure about him he seems to have been a metalworking war god, a fighting smith, something of a Punic Thor. He was certainly worshipped in the two great copper-producing islands of Cyprus and Sardinia. Our knowledge of him goes back to 1773, when a Phoenician inscription – the Nora stele – was found, built into a vineyard wall in southern Sardinia. It gives us our first mention of Pumay, honoured with a sanctuary above the Bay of Cagliari, and dates to about the time of Carthage's foundation.

This find provides grounds for believing that Timaeus was a serious researcher, not a myth-making early Orientalist. But further facts have emerged to enhance his reputation, for the discovery of a king list would later reveal that a King Pumayyaton, son of Mattan, grandson of Baal-Eser, ruled as king of Tyre from 831 to 785 BC. He ruled over the city when the Assyrian empire was expanding from its homeland on the borders of Syria and Iraq, formidable for its violence and confidence. Assyria's chief enemy were the Hittites in the mountains of Anatolia to their north, but its disciplined armies struck out in other directions, when not fighting the endless wars of attrition with their ancient highland enemy.

Terror was a standard Assyrian tactic, but it did not always work in its favour. Their summary execution of the king of Babylon outside the walls of his city certainly helped concentrate the minds of his fellow monarchs wonderfully. So under the leadership of Hadedezer of Damascus all the petty kingdoms of Greater Syria formed a defensive 'alliance of twelve kingdoms'. It included the Phoenician city of Byblos, Jehu (king of Israel), Gindibu (king of the Arab Bedouin, who commanded 1,000 camel-borne knights), and the city of Hama – but not the city of Aleppo, which had decided to submit. A thirty-year war brought a succession of battles, but though never defeated on the field, the allies gradually broke apart, worn down by relentless Assyrian aggression.

Tyre managed to keep out of these territorial wars, but the city fathers did not face easy choices. Should she keep to her traditional neutrality, should she join the alliance, or make an expedient early submission to Assyria? All policy options would have come at a high price, whether described as tribute, pension, war loan or ship money. And to pay for this continued independence, it is easy to imagine how King Pumayyaton might have sought to borrow the temple treasures from the city's great shrine to Melkarth–Hercules, and how this would have been opposed by High Priest Acerbas. An outsider might see such a quarrel as a mere struggle over gold between two brothers-in-law – just as Timaeus relates it. I have always imagined that High Priest Acerbas died in the manner of St Thomas a Becket or St Thomas More – a minister gradually divided by politics from his master, until some voice muttered: 'Who will rid me of this troublesome priest?'

So we now have a credible scenario, a historically viable date and a proven set of names, to account for Princess Elissa–Dido's flight from Tyre. I still doubt that she was the actual leader (she has a younger brother in some traditions), but her status as the wronged widow of the murdered high priest of Melkarth–Hercules would have made her a magnificent figurehead. It may be that Tyre could not afford civil strife in those testing times, and that a stand-off between two opposing parties within a small city-state was best settled by the bloodless decision to send one side into exile – perhaps under the face-saving pretext that they were establishing a new colony.

Elissa's voyage to Cyprus, as told by Timaeus, adds a

fascinating twist to the tale, for we now know that all the Phoenician cities along the coast of Syria were deeply involved in
Cyprus. This was partly a matter of neighbourly proximity (I
have seen the mountains of Syria from the easternmost prom-
ontory of Cyprus on a fine evening), but was also driven by the
ancient, and vital, trade in copper, mined in the interior valleys
of Cyprus but controlled through a dozen independent city-
kingdoms that ringed the coast like a crown. Kition was one
of the very oldest of them, an ancient Bronze Age city that
had seemingly been repopulated by Phoenician settlers after
the total devastation of the Dark Age anarchy of war bands.
But archaeologists have revealed that these Phoenician settlers
clearly knew their way around the old ruins, and some 200
years after their devastation, lovingly restored the heart of the
old temple to the Great Goddess, albeit in a slightly smaller
form. Which proves at the very least that Phoenicia and Cyprus
had some sort of shared spiritual experience, if not some much
deeper bond of loyalty to the old beliefs. Cyprus was a spiritual
fixture in the civilisations of the ancient world. The Cypriot
shrine of Paphos was everywhere saluted as one of the great
sanctuaries of Aphrodite, the sexualised identity of the Mother
Goddess, just as such Cypriot cities as Amathus had an ancient
temple to Melkarth–Hercules, and Kourion to the ancient cult
of horned Apollo. So it comes as no surprise that Princess Elissa
could recruit women from Cyprus to her cause, most especially
if she was espousing loyalty to the old forms of faith, against the
schemes of her modernising, maybe temple-despoiling brother.
Some commentators have pointed out that the very name Elissa
could signify 'from Cyprus' in Punic.

I like to believe that Elissa, whether we see her as a single
Tyrian princess or a collective of Cypriot temple women, must
have been formally greeted by the citizens of Utica on her

arrival on the North African shore, if not drawn at once into some form of diplomatic negotiation. For as we have heard, Utica had been the dominant Phoenician city in this region for many centuries. We do not know why the elders of Utica did not offer Elissa sanctuary within their walls. It may be that the local leadership, descended from country traders who had been intermarrying with the Berbers for generations, were wary of these refugee aristocrats and Cypriot temple women. Indeed the potential cost of hosting a high-maintenance metropolitan princess or two, attended by a retinue of Blanche du Bois, might have been disconcerting. Maybe the city fathers of Utica were also concerned about importing some of Tyre's civil strife into their home town, and with it the link to everyone's scariest foe, the Assyrians.

In that case, the decision to direct the refugees towards a nearby headland, virtually an island surrounded by salt marshes and lagoons, amounted to a tactful way out for all concerned. So Elissa would have led her refugees towards the fishing community that lay no more than four hours' ride away along the foreshore surf from Utica. It paid tribute to the local Berber king, Iarbas of the Gaetulian confederacy of tribes.

Whatever her political calculations, I envisage Dido as a passionate upholder of her religion. She had seen her husband Acerbas choose to die rather than to rob the temple of Melkarth of its treasures, had seen the downfall of many of the old city-states of the Levant, now groaning under the tyranny of Assyria. She may have been bent on creating a New City, Cart-Hadash, under the shadow of a mountain of two horns, which presented itself as a vision, a natural temple to the rain god Baal Hammon, leading up towards the two-horned Lord of the Heavens. There was a season and a rhythm to such things. We know that there was a spring sacrifice that marked the annual resurrection of

Melkarth, who is the Punic Hercules, the anointed Lord–King of the city, and who also signifies the agricultural deity Adonis–Tammuz, Lord of Renewal and Rebirth. She would also have known that it would be sheer sacrilege to substitute a female sacrifice for a young male at this season. There would be other more appropriate choices to seal her pact.

There are many folk tales associated with the Phoenician cities that hark back to the annual sacrifice of a young woman, placed out on an offshore island, or set adrift on a sacred barge, to appease the terrifying Lord of Chaos, whom the coastal-dwelling Phoenicians associated with the deep Lord of the Oceans, sender of earthquakes, and with them the tsunami devastation of their coastal cities. This would have been a par-ticularly appropriate sacrificial dedication to offer – an exiled priestess of royal lineage publicly sacrificing herself for the future safety of her new foundation. Such an action could never be forgotten. Timaeus tells us that Elissa's self-sacrifice came thirty-eight years before the first Olympic Games were celebrated, and seventy-two years before the foundation of Rome in 814 BC.

Right at the bottom of the Tophet, a walled garden filled with sacrificial urns that stood just above the beachside mar-ketplace of Carthage, a French archaeologist found a single royal tomb, a modest mud-brick cube, once crowned with a corbelled dome and encasing an urn filled with ashes. He con-siders it to be distinctly similar to the royal tombs that have survived from sixth-century BC Sidon; pottery finds suggest a date around 740 BC. It rests on the bare sandy floor, and seems to be the first thing that was built here, but around this magnet cluster thousands upon thousands of additional urns, most of them filled with the burnt bones of infants, some with the bones of kids and lambs. Originally it seems that only those of royal blood had the right to sacrifice themselves to the gods, but as the centuries passed, the bloodlines mingled, or perhaps the pride in being Carthaginian was seen to be royal enough. We have seen how the last defenders of this city would sacrifice themselves rather than surrender to the Romans. Elsewhere we hear credible tales of Carthaginian generals and admirals either sacrificing themselves, or being publicly crucified, after a defeat. The habit lapsed from time to time, but at moments of crisis the history of the city would forcefully reassert itself. In 310 BC it was recorded that five hundred youths of noble birth were publicly burned, placed in the arms of a statue of Baal that bent under their weight and dropped them into a vast fiery furnace that raged beneath.

Others have suggested that the sacrifice of children was always a private affair, as in the biblical description of Abraham walking up the mountain with Isaac at his side and a backpack of dry firewood on his shoulders. In this account, the prophet fully intends to use a knife on his son, to slice his neck open so that his blood can drench the altar, and then to burn the young body. Fortunately an angel interrupts this act and substitutes a ram – but only at the very last moment.

I once climbed to the summit of Jebel Boukornine, past a restaurant that was once used as a film set, and then up through its wooded slopes and on past the military guard post. There is no temple up here, just the remains of an ancient boundary wall that sets this ground aside as somewhere sacred, a high place for burnt offerings. It is a place for the worshipper to be alone, with only his god as his witness – no room here for false pieties before crowds of fellow citizens, no music-wreathed processions, just empty skies. In later centuries you come across carved stones, depicting a lamb or a ram being carried up to a mountain top and offered to Baal Hammon, Punic Saturn. Many of the urn markers found at the Tophet seem to suggest that the sacrifices were offered to Tanit, a specifically Carthaginian name for the Great Goddess, who serves as 'Pene Baal', the face of the Lord. Others suggest that the sacrifice was in fulfilment of a promise, a prayer that was answered. I have had well educated Tunisians in tears before my eyes, vehemently denying that their distant ancestors would ever have killed their own children. They argue that these urns held children who had died naturally or during birth and hence been placed in a special garden to be protected by the presence of the goddess.

The original Tophet of Carthage has survived, though hemmed about with the garden walls of suburban villas, and so dug over as to be totally unrecognisable, like a thrice-worked spoil heap. Still it is a weird act of chance that this, the most notorious feature of ancient Carthage, has yet survived whilst all other evidence of the ancient city has been swept away. Even for those unaware of its history, it is a moody, occasionally spooky and thoroughly confusing place, essentially a pair of archaeological pits that have been scoured clean of their layers of history, and then partly back-filled. They are often found filled with an algae-rich pool of brackish water. To add layers of further confusion, the dig site has itself been dug over a number of times, at first by treasure hunters, then by a pair of secretive amateurs, then by pseudo-professionals who never published their findings. The first thorough excavation was not until that of Pierre Cintas in 1947, repeated and refined every generation since. We still do not know the extent of the site, its shape, or the reach of its perimeter walls. Elements of a Roman-period vaulted cellar have been exposed by the dig, but despite what zealous local guides may tell you, this can have absolutely nothing to do with any temple or fiery pit. Even the fascinating collection of Punic memorial stones scattered over the site must be treated as an art installation, for none stand in the place where they were discovered, though all are real.

For not even in the Carthaginian period was the Tophet the site of a temple, let alone a brazen statue set above a funeral pyre (as you will see in many illustrations). And yet it was a holy place, an urn-field filled with thousands of buried stone boxes each holding incinerated bones, marked out with inscribed funerary stones and little altars. Every now and then, the site was partly flattened to make space for another generation of sacrifices and carved stones, but these too would later be buried beneath successive layers. So in mood, in its heyday it may have been a bit like one of those ancient graveyards in the City of London, or the Mzab valley desert oasis of Algeria. It was always highly conspicuous in the topography of ancient Carthage, seemingly right beside the main square of the town, which stood beside the two harbours. This in itself is unique in the ancient world, which otherwise drew an emphatic distinction between the cities of the dead and of the living, which were never permitted to mix. Here we see yet another strand of evidence that the Tophet of Carthage was always a place apart. From the evidence of the inscriptions on some of the stone markers, it is possible that some of the victims were believed to have entered into an arena of holiness through the ordeal of sacrifice, to have passed into the arms of the goddess Tanit – 'Pene Baal', the face of God. I think it goes too far to suggest that they had become guardian spirits of the city, but something collectively numinous clung to the Tophet of Carthage. To put it in modern parlance, it was a cemetery of spiritual martyrs, who like medieval Christian martyrs, or the contemporary martyrs of Islam, were believed to be especially and instantly rewarded. Archaeologists have found that many of the burials were so arranged that oblations of blood or wine could be offered on the little free-standing altars and would then drain away down towards the urns.

The Romans flattened the site, not with some localised fury, but as part of their thoroughgoing destruction of the entire city. In the process they spread thousands of sacrificial markers and tomb inscriptions over a wide area, but the fact that the Tophet was a mere enclosed space, not a built-up structure, meant that the heart of the site was effectively sealed in with the fallen masonry of the buildings all around it. A century and a half later, cisterns were inserted into the site, when the Romans rebuilt Carthage. Buried beneath and beside these later ruins, the Tophet slept for centuries. Of the major built structures of Carthage that dominated the city's skyline – the great temple to the Mother Goddess on the summit of Borj Jedid and the Hill of Juno, the glittering dockside temple of Reshef–Apollo with its gilded tiles, the vast sanctuary to the hero-god Melkarth–Hercules and that of the healing deity Eshmun (on the site of the Roman theatre) – not a stone remains. But the archaeologists can finger thousands and thousands of fragments of the burnt bones of children and lambs, strewn over the footprints of a refugee princess arriving on an alien shore, who with one act, made it her homeland for ever. This I believe.

2

They met at Zama: Hannibal of Carthage, Scipio of Rome and Masinissa of Numidia

It was midsummer and my travelling companions were hot and querulous. We had driven inland away from the coast of Tunisia into the baking heat of the interior. It did not help my case that I didn't really know what I was looking for. We had all shared student flats, if not beds, at some points in our lives, so my desires and map-reading limitations were known all too well. But I knew that it would be helpful to stand on the ground, even if it was not exactly the right place, and taste the smell and see the contours. Some way outside the modern town, we agreed to stop beside the road, unfurl our blanket (bought in the Tell town of Béja) and lay out a picnic under the shade of some eucalyptus. Halfway through a long drowsy lunch we were approached by boys selling coins from old crumpled brown paper bags. I admired their persistence, for visitors coming to the battlefield of Zama must be rare, but the ones who made it might well be interested in a souvenir, just as I was. Nothing polished or fake was being offered for sale here, indeed their palms were mostly filled with rusted, corrupted and clipped piles of worthless scrap. Though I could also recognise the galloping horse of Carthage on a bronze obol, looking just like the Hanoverian white horse that was the badge of my grandfather's cavalry regiment. On the other side was the worn outline of a Greek-looking head with a beard. I recognised this as Masinissa, the great Berber commander of cavalry whose role at the battle of Zama broke one empire, made another, and set him on a throne.

Our mood lifts. I start to wave my hands, filling the horizon with imaginary regiments. For somewhere on this burnt-out agricultural plain two vast armies have been nudging towards each other for weeks, criss-crossing over old lines of march and wind-blown campsites. Scouts watch scouts, they observe each other's false dust trails and count the camp fires as they are lit, so that now and then a hard-riding detachment of cavalry succeeds in observing the disposition of real columns of men and the hard evidence of the wagon trains. Neither the Roman nor the Carthaginian armies can claim any element of surprise, nor expect a display of tactical indecision, for the two opposing generals have never yet betrayed a sign of weakness. Not ever. Or if they have, then better to wear a shield on your back, and double-check every ditch and defile for an ambush.

The foot soldiers are the core of each army, and they are the veterans of the veterans, battle-hardened victors of two dozen epic battles, countless sieges, raids, massacres, night marches and sea assaults. Both armies have marched and fought each other around half the known world. The long spine of Italy, southern Gaul, Sicily, Spain, the islands and now North Africa are their testing grounds, be it coastal salt marsh, snow-clad forested mountains, desert plateaux, vast wheat-growing prairies, patchworks of fortified orchards and villages, the great walled cities or the dead lands. In experience, in confidence, they are quite evenly matched, though no one – not even the headquarters staff – can ever be quite sure about exact numbers. The head count of the regiments has been hacked about by detachments sent to garrison, to patrol the supply routes, to train new allies, to secure wellheads, seize springs, hold river crossings, then overnight abandon these potentially vital strongpoints, as the campaign sheers off elsewhere. The static of diplomacy, of rumour, of embassies, agents and delegations, is strong, for before this campaign the two armies had been at peace, locked into a two-year truce that had shown every sign of condensing into permanent peace. And then had come another round of orders, followed by counter-commands, but were these blunders or feints, were the missing detachments actually lost, or off on some secret mission known only to the chief? The vast, innate confusion of an army on the move is united by every soldier's knowledge that at any moment the boredom and irritation will give way to fear and exhilaration, victory or death.

The stakes could not be higher. The Romans led by Scipio were fighting for the mastery of the world, the Carthaginians under the command of Hannibal for their very survival.

So in October 202 the two armies drew close to one another on the fertile plain of Siliana, overlooked by the Numidian citadel of Zama, perched on the low summit of a rounded hill. The vast cornfields had long been harvested and baked dry by the North African summer. It was near-perfect cavalry country, the gentle slopes of ploughland unbroken by rocks, woodland or intervening walls.

Yet if we follow the historical script, we learn that Hannibal advanced to give battle knowing that his Roman enemy was far superior in its Numidian cavalry. Though we also know that throughout the rest of his long life, when he had fought in Spain and Italy, his superiority in the Berber cavalry of North Africa was a given which had time and time again allowed him to inflict a tactical master-stroke on the Roman enemy.

The nature of the chosen ground in Zama makes this even

more of a mystery. Why would Hannibal, one of the master tacticians of all time, advance to do battle in such a situation? For of the two generals, it was Hannibal who was under less pressure of time. He was fighting on home ground, and it was Scipio, not he, who must face the threat of guerrilla harassment; Scipio, not he, who needed to be supplied by sea and whose position could be rendered disastrous by a winter storm wrecking his supply ships or the loss of a safe North African port. It was most certainly Scipio, not Hannibal, who had the most to fear from a protracted struggle. Yet according to the traditional accounts, it was Hannibal who had marched rapidly to the north.

The day before the battle, a company of lifeguards rode out from each of the Roman and the Carthaginian marching camps. The two converging squadrons of cavalry halted at prearranged stages, so that at last just the two generals, Hannibal and Scipio, were left to ride forward and meet alone. Nothing is known of this meeting except that Hannibal proposed renewing the two-year truce that had kept the two armies at peace. The generals then returned to their armies and perfected their deployments for next day's conflict.

According to the traditional account, Hannibal ordered his own weaker force of cavalry to engage the Roman right wing, under the command of the Numidian Berber general Masinissa. They had been ordered to flee from the battlefield in order to draw the Roman cavalry away from the field of battle. This they did, and having achieved it, Hannibal ordered in his eighty-strong elephant corps to break up the Roman infantry. But Scipio had prepared for this by leaving gaps between his columns of soldiers. The unwieldy beasts took the path of least resistance down these open spaces, assailed by javelins from both sides.

Hannibal had kept his experienced veterans in reserve, but

ordered wave after wave of his light mercenary troops to attack the Roman front in order to tire the legions and blunt their weapons. When the light infantry attempted to withdraw, Hannibal ordered his veterans to lower their lances to hold them back. Faced with a certain dishonourable death if they retreated, they were forced back once more against the Roman legions. Only when the field of Zama grew slippery with blood and the Roman legions wearied of the slaughter did Hannibal order his veterans, fresh and untried, into the assault. The Roman line held, then buckled, but just before Hannibal could deal the decisive stroke, Masinissa fell upon the unprotected Carthaginian rear at the head of the Berber cavalry.

This action was vital. The moment he learned of it, Hannibal knew that the battle was lost. By the end of the day 20,000 Carthaginian corpses littered the ground. Hannibal, with his legendary energy, left the field of battle before dusk and rode night and day until he reached the safety of the coast.

I had accepted this narrative of events for years, but it made no sense once I was on the battlefield itself. Why in the steppe-land foothills of Numidia, of all places, would Hannibal have engaged a Roman army, aware that he lacked a strong enough cavalry force? All over North Africa there were other potential battlefield sites where this weakness could be alleviated, but once you stand amidst the rolling Numidian hills around Zama, you are struck by the fact that no general would willingly choose this place, unless he intended to use an advantage in cavalry.

I could not doubt any of the recorded details of Zama, and especially the fact that Masinissa's Numidian cavalry, attacking the rear of the Carthaginian army, delivered the decisive blow, and that once this happened, Hannibal knew all was lost. But I began to see that Hannibal might only have decided to fight at

Zama if he had cause to count on a very different turn of events. I began to see that the conduct of Masinissa and his Numidian cavalry was the absolute key. Hannibal's decision to fight a battle here only made sense if he thought that he either had Masinissa on his side, or at the very least could expect him to play a neutral role. Masinissa was to gallop off the field of battle, not return to stab the army of Carthage in the back.

That hot summer afternoon spent walking the likely site of the battlefield of Zama with some old student friends is now half a lifetime away, but the questions I first asked myself that day have stayed with me. As has that worn coin of Masinissa, the Berber commander of cavalry who subsequently became a king. My subsequent research will not change so much as a footnote of history about Hannibal, or prove anything one way or another about what happened that day at Zama. But it has been a very useful process, straightening out the narrative of the Second Punic War, so that the events in North Africa are given equal weight to the more famous battles in Spain and Italy. This has also allowed the story of Masinissa to emerge as one of the three fateful threads of history, interwoven with the triumphs and ultimate tragedy of both Hannibal and Scipio.

So that I can take as many readers with me as possible on this adventure, there is a fair amount of scene-setting to be done. So we will look at the city of Carthage during the boyhood of Hannibal, then move to Spain with his father, then pass in triumph through Italy with the Carthaginian army escorted by the Berber cavalry of North Africa. Scipio will emerge as the brilliant young Roman general in Spain, who is brave enough to sail the Roman army across the waters to invade North Africa. In the process he 'turns' a brilliant young Berber cavalry general, Masinissa, from his old Carthaginian loyalties to an alliance with Rome. These three destinies – of Hannibal, Scipio and Masinissa – come to a head at the decisive battle of Zama, which is the prelude to an even more tragic tale.

∴

Hannibal was born in the city of Carthage, the eldest boy of a family of six children. For the first six years of his life, his father was away fighting wars. His father was the war hero Hamilcar Barca, the toughest, most imaginative and successful of all the Carthaginian generals in the First Punic War. He alone had offered hope, and had reversed a series of defeats by pulling off a daring counter-strike. Hamilcar Barca had set up a military camp in the Sicilian interior, at the sacred mountains of Erecte and Eryx. From this base he had attempted to lead the indigenous Sicilian clans of the mountainous interior against the clenching fist of Roman dominion.

Hannibal was the spitting image of his bold father. The city of Carthage that he would know as home and explore as a boy was vast, one of the largest in the Mediterranean, with a population of a quarter of a million. This was doubled in times of emergency, when the inhabitants of all the towns and villages of the hinterland poured in to seek protection within Carthage. The walls of Carthage were one of the military wonders of the ancient world, some 33 kilometres in extent. They were at their most elaborate along the western section that defended the land frontier, for they expanded into a triple defensive line, which marched between the two tidal lagoons of Lake Tunis and Lake Ariana. So any enemy of Carthage attacking by land was first faced by a trench whose inner bank was guarded by an earth rampart, which was backed up by a narrow but deeper trench overlooked by a 40-foot wall some 5 metres thick and guarded by watchtowers every 100 feet. Vaulted casements within the thickness of the wall both strengthened the structure and provided barracks and stables so that the garrison could sally out and attack the enemy mounted on horses and elephants.

These walls enclosed not just the city and its harbours, but the Megara, a sprawling northern suburb of gardens and orchards that was fifteen times the size of the built-up inner city, so in times of need Megara could be converted into an armed camp that could house tens of thousands of men. Every inch of the shore was guarded by the sea wall, which terminated in a fortified mole that protruded out from the southern corner of the city and sheltered the most dense concentration of quays and wharfs. A pair of canals, guarded by gated archways set into the sea wall, allowed for the most precious merchandise to be taken right into a rectangular harbour basin, dug into the heart of the city, directly opposite the agora square. As every proud young Carthaginian boy knew, this open harbour was linked to the hidden circular basin of the Arsenal–harbour. This walled compound was overlooked by the admiralty tower and had its own direct access canal to the sea.

For the fortified Arsenal, out of sight from all the thousands of visiting merchants and travellers who passed through the city, was the permanent base of the battle fleet of the empire. The fleet could be drawn out of the water into the neat rows of dry dockyard sheds that encircled both the central admiralty island and the outer circumference of the circular harbour. Each of these sheds was framed by a pair of columns and housed a pair of galleys under cover. In addition there were neatly labelled timber sections, stacked flat on the rafters of these sheds, all ready to be transformed into a freshly built galley by the ships' carpenters of Carthage. So that as the full complement of 220 galleys slipped out of the Arsenal into the waters of the Mediterranean, their oars stroking the waters as one to the sound of the drums, the dockyard could at once set to work on constructing a brand-new fleet.

The keel timbers were the most vital element of a galley, and were made from the hardest, most expensive wood. These were laid down first, so that the stern-post and bow-post projected up like a skeleton of a boat, upon which a wall of interlocking planks was pegged upwards. Once this outer skin was in place, the boats were fitted with internal ribs, upon which were fixed the deck and rowing benches. The mortice-and-tenon joints used in the ship's construction were then reinforced (in belt-and-braces manner) with wooden dowel pegs. The placing of the benches was the craft secret of the shipwrights, and also one that has stayed buried with these master craftsmen. We know that it took 170 men to power a trireme, and 300 for a quinquereme, but we are still looking for structural evidence as to how these ships were rigged, the number of oars or the number of men to an oar. This navy was a drain on skilled manpower, for a squadron of a hundred triremes needed 17,000 hands to power it, whilst a full battle fleet of 220 quinqueremes required 60,000 hands. Only the richest and most powerful states, those the size of Rome, Carthage or Egypt, could afford a navy. These were hugely expensive assets, whether one measures the cost in gold, seasoned wood, or in manpower.

Hannibal had been born right at the end of the 25-year-long First Punic War in 247 BC. It was a time when there was not a family in the whole vast city of Carthage to which the sea battles of Mylae (260), Sulci (258) and Cape Ecnomus (256) had not brought grief. Tens of thousands of lives had been lost in each battle, not to mention the handful of Carthaginian admirals crucified for these failures. It was known that a Carthaginian captain could outdo a Roman one in seamanship, and could weather a storm in better shape than his rival, but the overpowering tactical weakness of the Carthaginians was that they loved their ships too much. They saw them as an investment, a sign of status, a tool for trading or for landing an army onto a foreign shore, and never learned to use them as expendable weapons in their own right.

The Romans were indifferent sailors, but had the wit to employ their Greek allies in southern Italy (especially from the city of Tarentum) to design, build and sail their fleet. Over these competent naval crews they placed one of their own aggressive young officers, who might be a useless navigator, yet who took command at the point of battle. With a stout body of marines at his back, the Roman commanding officer had little compunction about using his Greek-crewed ship as a mobile fighting platform fitted with a battering ram to send crashing into the enemy.

This was indeed how the whole protracted First Punic War ground to a final halt when Hannibal was six years old. As a boy he would have heard the news that the very last battle fleet that Carthage could afford to put to sea had been destroyed off the Aegates Islands. Fifty Carthaginian galleys had been sunk and seventy captured. It was a complete and overwhelming defeat, expressed as much by the number captured as those sunk. No one could doubt that Rome had made herself the unlikely mistress of the western Mediterranean, the Tyrrhenian Sea. Neither Hannibal, nor his father or brothers ever contemplated reviving the Carthaginian navy, nor did he rely on ships in any of his military campaigns when he came of age.

Hannibal grew up in a city whose hilltops were all crowned with temples. These shrines mirrored the topography of the Bay of Carthage, which was dominated by sacred mountains. The temples were not monumental places set apart from life, but deeply integrated into the city. Most of the shrines were architecturally modest chambers contained within large, animated sacred courtyards equipped with basins (in which the worshippers could cleanse themselves) and open-air altars. They were also galleries of Carthaginian achievement, their walls covered in votive trophies and inscriptions that proved that there was nowhere beyond their reach – that her explorer–merchants had once circumnavigated Africa by ship, crossed the Sahara by land, and had even explored the northern waters of the Atlantic with its fascinating tidal anomalies. They had established a string of colonies down the Atlantic coast of Morocco, and supported strongholds and settlements in all the islands of the western Mediterranean.

The sanctuary of Reshef–Apollo, glitteringly conspicuous with its gilded roof tiles, is thought to have been one of the sacred halls that could be used for meetings of the Carthaginian senate. Sixty steps led up through the densely packed streets at the foot of the Byrsa hill to reach the courtyard temple of Eshmun–Asclepius. Here worshippers came for instruction and advice from the priests, as well as taking part in the fasts and prayer rituals that prepared them for a propitious dream of instruction whilst they slept in the galleries of the courtyard. We can still walk through a tiny patch of housing at the foot of this hill, which survives from Hannibal's lifetime. The houses are well constructed, with internal courtyards that serve as light-wells. They were equipped with drains to dispose of used water, rain-fed cisterns (storing water used for washing), and wells for good drinking water sunk deep into the earth. Some of these houses were six stories high, with a flat roof where the washing could be put out to dry, and though modest in dimension, this maze of thin terraced homes (either 15 by 30 metres, or 15 by 10 metres) was also divided into smaller sublet apartments and shops. Steep staircases, ladders and narrow alleys completed the creation of these urban labyrinths, swarming with craftsmen and traders.

Architecturally the outer face of Carthage would have appeared rather attractively austere to our eyes, for the houses were flat-roofed and the street faces dominated by a clean façade of annually applied whitewash, with all the details of their brick and stone structure hidden beneath smooth plaster. Porches and temple pediments were visually modest, especially when compared with what their Hellenistic, Syrian and Egyptian contemporaries had achieved. But the artistic influence of those three intertwined cultures of the Eastern Mediterranean was everywhere apparent, especially in the cemeteries with monuments decorated with sphinxes, stepped pyramids, Ionic columns, crow-stepped gables with the perennially popular statues to such heroes as strapping Hercules and the squat, pot-bellied demigod Bes. The pottery tradition of Carthage was bleakly utilitarian, but the city's genius was expressed in textiles, jewelry, furniture and metalwork. So the true wealth of Carthaginian life was only revealed within the rooms off their internal courtyards, ornamented with the vivid colours of blue glass, purple-dyed cloth, painted cedarwood furniture, carved ivories and exquisitely engraved gems, chased silver and filigree-worked gold. I would further colour this lost world with bowls of ripe fruit: pomegranates, figs and dates, the smell of fresh baked unleavened bread, and the aroma of wine and olive oil.

The public spaces would have brought endless fascination to any child, for there was no industrial quarter; instead all the alleys, streets and squares of the city made up a buzzing hive of industry: packed full of forges, potteries, weaving sheds, carpenters, woodturners working with cedar. Glass-blowers, bronze engravers, jewellers and armourers worked beside their house furnaces, fuelled with charcoal and fanned by bellows. Tailors, embroiderers and highly skilled ivory and gem carvers worked in the cramped spaces of their boothlike shops. The scent, spice and incense merchants, with their links to temple worship and the secrets of the tomb, counted themselves among the most refined of trades. The sinews of this trade in scented oils and dried tree saps reached eastward to the Levant and the Yemen, the mysterious land of Punt (its whereabouts still unidentified) or to distant India. The pungent compounds of the dyers (imperial purple and royal scarlet of the Phoenicians was manufactured from crushed murex seashells) did not deprive these craftsmen of prestige, but they, as well as the reeking courtyards of the tanners (who used dog and pigeon shit as well as urine in their industrial processes) and the garum-paste makers (made from the sun-dried guts of tuna mixed in brine), tended to huddle down by the dockyard shore.

Carthage was also a vibrant commodity exchange, which had always survived by attracting Greek, Berber, Italian, Egyptian and Aramaic merchants to buy and sell, trade, exchange and loan. The carrying trade in metals had always been at the heart of the city's economy. Carthage was halfway along the sea journey between the rich mines of southern Spain and the Levantine cities, but over the centuries it had diversified to include the carriage trade in Cornish tin, Cypriot and Sardinian copper, African gold, Central Asian–Chinese steel and Parthian iron. The other solid backbone of mercantile life was the humdrum carriage of foodstuffs around the Mediterranean shore and up tidal estuaries and river valleys: the vital trinity of wine, olive oil and corn (in cargo boats rigid with hundreds of interlocking amphorae) supplemented by salted and preserved fish.

Although Hannibal did not see his father's face for the first six years of his life while Hamilcar was fighting in Sicily, his

name was known all over the city. Hamilcar means brother
of Melkarth (Hercules). We have grown so imbued with all
the classical statues of Hercules that it is almost impossible
to remember that this cult originated in the Levant, and can
be traced back for thousands of years through the Gilgamesh
storyline of the wandering hero of heroes, the king of his city,
doomed to die as all human mortals must, but who will be
turned into a demigod by his heroic adventures and the stoic
acceptance of the most appalling ordeals. Despite being a heroic
mortal (rather than an elemental sky deity), it is intriguing to
reflect that he was the chosen patron of many of the great Phoenician cities, such as Tyre and Gades (modern Cadiz), while
many of his adventures – wrestling with Antaeus at the Strait
of Gibraltar, journeying to the Atlas mountains to find the
golden apples of the Hesperides – celebrate a uniquely Phoenician achievement. To my mind it seems possible that those
who honoured such a deity were touched by a spirit of humanistic confidence in the achievements of mankind. At Gades the
priests of Melkarth wore unadorned linen, prohibited blood
sacrifice, and seem to have formed a philosophical community.

Hamilcar's surname was Barca, which means the thunder-
bolt. He was a member of the Barcid clan who claimed descent
from a nephew of Dido, the founding queen of Carthage.
They took pride in this ancestry, in the long tenuous line that
linked them back to Phoenician Tyre, which was the oldest of
all surviving cities of the Canaanites, founded in 2750 BC. She
was a brood sister to all the ancient civilisations that had first
emerged beside the banks of the Nile, Tigris, Euphrates, Indus
and Yellow rivers at this period.

The Phoenicians were proud of this heritage but were not
hamstrung by any false racial pride in being a pure-blooded
Kn'nm (Canaanite). Once settled in North Africa they had

freely married with local Berbers, islanders from Sicily, Cyprus and Sardinia, as well as exiled Greeks and allied Phoenicians. These marriage alliances rapidly extended the threads of trade and diplomacy beyond the reach of any ship or sword. For instance we know that Hannibal would himself marry a Spanish girl, while two of his sisters would marry Numidian Berbers.

So it is best to imagine Carthage not as some nascent national capital but as a rich melting pot of peoples, a typically Levantine fusion of languages, proud of their city, its ancient temples, their clan and their family. Hannibal's family owned land on the southern coast of Tunisia, probably between Acholla and Thapsus, which hints at other lines of inheritance aside from that within Carthage. For the Carthaginians, and their confederate allies, dominated the entire coast of North Africa, from the pillars of Hercules (the mountains of Gibraltar and Ceuta, which overlook the waters of the Atlantic mixing with the Mediterranean) to the Altars of the Philaeni (two mounds on the desert frontier of eastern Libya), which marked the frontier with the Greek-speaking cities of Cyrenaica.

In matters of diplomacy, in the making of peace and war, the city of Carthage acted as the single, decisive voice for its whole confederate empire. Carthage was itself a variable and composite entity. The city had evolved a polity that blended the merits of an autocracy, an aristocracy and a democracy without surrendering to any of these imperfections. It governed itself through a balanced constitution, in the manner of both Sparta and Rome, which won it the approval of both Aristotle and Polybius.

At the ruling summit of Carthaginian society were the *suffetes*, a pair of elective administrative judges whose power was deliberately curtailed by being divided between two men, and restricted to just a year of office. After their year of service, a suffete joined the council of the Adirium, 'the Mighty Ones', which was the Carthaginian name for their Senate. To stream-line business within this large and opinionated body of men, the Senate appointed specialised subcommittees of five men to consider particular issues. There was also an influential inner council of thirty – 'the summoned' – who effectively drafted new laws. This group also drew up shortlists of men capable of serving as *Rab* (chief man) of the clerks of the treasury, the marketplace inspectors and the customs men. There was also a separate council of ten to oversee the administration of sacred places and another committee of thirty to supervise the tithe tax raised from the provinces. The tithe was a proportion of the annual harvest, administered through '*Rst*', which were regional groupings of fifty Berber villages.

There was also a panel of 104 judges that was somehow kept institutionally separate from the Senate. This body had broad moral authority and continual oversight over military matters. The Carthaginians entrusted great power to their generals, who were appointed for whole campaigns as '*Rab Maharet*' – king by law. So a Carthaginian general effectively ran his own semi-independent kingdom on the march, minting coin to pay the troops. This was in the nature of the Carthaginian empire, which required most of its wars to be fought in distant islands, with no opportunity for any effective consultation with the city fathers. The offset for this bold grant of royal power to a general was the quick and savage punishment with which the panel of 104 judges habitually rewarded failure. So the public crucifixion of a general or admiral who suffered defeat was considered normal, though the judges also had the power to impose lesser penalties such as a fine or a sentence of exile. Many a defeated Carthagin-ian commander chose to commit suicide on the field of battle rather than return home and suffer the ultimate humiliation of a public crucifixion. This harsh tradition may have stopped many a Carthaginian Bonaparte or a Caesar seizing power in a military coup, but it also helped cripple any organised retreat, for the army, having just lost a battle, often then found itself leaderless after the commander committed suicide.

The Romans were much more cautious in this matter, and only appointed ex-consuls (after they had served their administrative year in Rome) to jointly command the army for just a year. But they were also much more generous about the hazards of war, and welcomed back many a defeated pro-consular commander into the ranks of the Senate.*

New laws, having been drafted by the Senate, became valid once they had been accepted by the *M'ham* (the people), who debated the proposals and then cast a simple yes or no vote. The *M'Ham* also elected the chief offices of state: the two *suffetes* and the various *Rab*, as well as generals and admirals from a shortlist of candidates. We don't know how this popular assembly was organised on the ground. We think it was first marshalled by clan, but was later based on the different quarters of the city, which each had responsibility for the upkeep of a certain section of the city's wall and the gatehouses. Wealth was always respected and honoured in Carthage, but there does not seem to have been any inherited caste system. This may have been a corollary of a city based on maritime trade, which would have often witnessed the arrival and sudden dispersal of great fortunes.

---

* The British have followed the Roman example in military matters. They delight in remembering an organised retreat, be it at Corunna, Mons or Dunkirk, in loving detail, and reward their defeated generals with a seat in the House of Lords. In naval matters they followed the Carthaginian line, as when Admiral Byng was shot on his quarterdeck in 1757 not for treason or cowardice but for 'not doing his utmost' in the opinion of the court.

What seems to have played a key role in Carthaginian social life was a web of guild associations (*Mizrehem*) that vertically bound together rich merchant-traders with craftsmen. These guilds had particular affiliations with the temples, as there were similar associations that brought clans together around shared meals at an ancestral tomb. Masses of dedicatory and tombstone inscriptions have been unearthed from the ruins of Carthage, so we know that there was a keen interest in genealogy. Some inscriptions go back six generations (which would go back 200 years), but there is also a stumbling block for historians trying to process this information. The Carthaginians invariably created their names by reference to their chief gods, which limited their palette of names. Inscriptions honouring a hundred Hamilcars and six hundred Bomilcars (servant of Melkarth) have so far been identified, alongside many a Hasdrubal (Baal be gracious), Hannibal (gift of Baal), Mago (may Baal grant), Bostar (servant of Astarte) and Saponibaal (may Baal watch over).

We do not know the exact relationship between Carthage and the various allied sister cities within her empire, though each city was self-governing, self-financing and owned its own agricultural hinterland. They contributed men, ships and money at times of war, but we doubt if they paid a fixed tribute (like the old Athenian empire) to help maintain a permanent navy in times of peace. What seems more likely is that they were all legally bound to use Carthage as a central entrepot for certain valuable categories of overseas trade, and so in this way Carthage collected a very useful customs revenue from this privileged position. The Berber villages within the empire had to surrender about a quarter of their harvest as a tithe (which helped feed the massive population of Carthage) and must furnish young men for the army in time of war. The independent-minded Numidian Berber tribes of the mountains did not pay the tithe-tax but served under their own leaders as the cavalry of Carthage. The poorer citizens of Carthage served in the navy or in the 40,000-strong home-guard militia that defended the city walls. The young nobles of Carthage were trained from youth to fight as infantry, especially within the 2,500-strong Sacred Battalion, which formed an elite of just one hundredth of the population. From out of this regiment officers could be recruited to command bands of mercenaries in wartime.

After the disastrous defeat of her navy at the battle of the Aegates Islands, Carthage was forced to make peace with Rome and end the First Punic War. The terms were not unduly onerous, for both sides were exhausted, and the army that the Romans had landed in North Africa (under the command of Regulus) had been destroyed back in 255. So neither side enjoyed a great advantage over the other, and a new frontier was straightforward to agree upon. The war had been fought for the control of Sicily. Rome had been the aggressor and Carthage had failed to defend the island. Carthage agreed to withdraw her last garrisons from Sicily, surrender all claims to the island and pay Rome a war indemnity of 1,000 talents. Rome gained her very first imperial province, which would be handed over to her ex-consuls to rule, as one of the chief rewards of political life.

Hannibal's father, General Hamilcar Barca, returned from the wars as one of the very few Carthaginian heroes. He was not alone, for some 20,000 mercenary soldiers had been employed to fight in Sicily. They were also shipped 'home' to North Africa as part of the peace agreement. They were not treated as returning heroes, indeed they were owed a lot of back pay which was not disbursed at once by the war-shattered Carthaginian treasury.

Mercenaries in the ancient world were customarily paid about a drachma a day (the same rate as a skilled labourer), which was enough to feed a whole family. The tetradrachma (a four-drachma silver coin of 16 grams weight) was the standard token of wealth that a soldier could bite his teeth on or catch the weight of in his palm. It was about the size of our present 50-pence coin, but twice as thick and heavy. After the first drink at a tavern it could be broken down into twenty-four bronze obols, coins heavy enough with which to seal the eyes of the dead. But the Carthaginian mercenaries, instead of being paid off before their regimental standards like honourable men, were marched deep into the hill country of the Tunisian interior, to the arid fortress of Sicca (modern El Kef). There they were informed that the defeated empire was strapped for cash and had an enormous war indemnity to pay off to Rome before they could be given all their back pay. There seems to have been no clear reason for sending them to Sicca, which also had the misguided side-effect of concentrating all the disaffected soldiers together, instead of dividing them up into smaller garrisons and rival ethnic groups.

The absence of leadership in distant Sicca also helped escalate an awkward situation into a revolution. The soldiers, acting on their own accord, marched back to the city of Carthage and pitched an armed camp outside the walls. They also started to add the days of their unpaid idleness in Sicca, and various expenses (such as the wages of dead comrades left to them in their will), to their original wage bill. The Senate of Carthage at last felt the incipient danger of this mass of ill-treated men and dispatched a respected old general to make a distribution of coin, but it was now too little, too late, for a group of militant soldiers had seized power. Under the leadership of a troika made up of Mathos the Libyan Berber, Antamitus the Gaul and

Spendius, a Roman deserter from Campania, the mercenaries had turned themselves into an occupying, revolutionary army. They started to mint their own coin, enlisted allies from the local Berber tribes (though not the despised landless slaves), and sought control of their own secure harbour. The leaders recruited a hand-picked bodyguard of warrior Celts and purged the ranks of any would-be peacemakers.

The atrocities and savagery of this civil war were to be the backdrop to the last stage of Hannibal's childhood. Having witnessed the well-tended villas around Carthage being pillaged, looted and then destroyed, he would also have observed how his city had become packed full of refugees and then placed under siege by the rebel soldiers based on their camp at Tunis.

Hannibal's father had been treated with suspicion by the Carthaginian Senate. As we have heard, this was not just personal rivalry, but the customary default position of Carthage with all her military leaders. But it could not be maintained. Hamilcar Barca was the only military commander with sufficient energy, experience and savagery to take on the hard-bitten mercenary enemy. He also possessed the diplomatic skills to woo some of the rebels with offers of clemency (and employment in his own army), and to win over Prince Naravas of Numidia, who brought over thousands of Berber cavalrymen to join the army of Carthage. But in the meanwhile, as in so many civil wars, the savagery escalated, and fighting spread into innumerable petty sieges and guerrilla struggles. The last battles of this three-year 'Truceless War' were to be exceptionally bloody encounters.

Hamilcar Barca had managed to isolate the army commanded by Spendius in an isolated mountain valley known as The Saw. The rebels were cut off from any water supply and were reduced to cannibalism, drinking the blood of their prisoners of war, then of their body-slaves, before they were forced to sue for a truce. Despite the most solemn oaths, the rebel leaders were arrested during the negotiations and Spendius was crucified outside the walls of Carthage, within sight of the rebel army still entrenched at Tunis. The physically exhausted and now leaderless rebel force at The Saw was massacred. When Hamilcar Barca's soldiers wearied of the slaughter, war elephants were employed to trample the remaining prisoners of war to death.

These horrors spurred the rebel army at Tunis (under the command of Mathos) to one more assault against the walls of Carthage. They were too late to rescue their comrade Spendius from dying on the cross, but they were able to turn this into a shrine before which they now proceeded to slaughter all their prisoners of war, in full view of the citizens of Carthage manning the walls. Atrocity countered atrocity. When Mathos was captured right at the end of this pitiless war, it was his fate to be dragged by the heels through the streets of Carthage and tortured by the youths of the city, in a mock triumphal procession of pain and ritual degradation.

The young Hannibal, living in besieged Carthage, must have had a ringside seat to all the horror, confusion and bloody victory of the Truceless War waged so savagely and decisively by his father from 240 to 237 BC. He would have been seven years old when the civil war started, and a ten-year-old youth when Mathos was dragged to his death. It was an education.

The Romans had been so concerned about the revolutionary anarchy of the mercenaries' rebellion that they had refused to help the rebels in any way. They were also shocked to hear that the Carthaginian garrison in Sardinia had declared in favour of the mutiny. But the rebel garrison behaved so aggressively to the locals that they were swept into the sea by an armed alliance of Sardinian hill tribes before a Carthaginian expedition could be sent to restore order.

Now, however, the Roman Senate saw its chance to intervene. On the pretext of alarm at the threat of the Carthaginian expedition to Sardinia (which had never left the harbour of Carthage), it declared war. Tactically this was a well-timed intervention, for Carthage was not only exhausted by the First Punic War but now shattered by the devastation of its civil war. It could do nothing but sue for peace. Rome imposed a crushing war-fine on Carthage of 1,200 talents, and annexed both the island of Sardinia and Corsica. Having just acquired her first province, of Sicily, only three years before, Rome's appetite for conquest had clearly been whetted, and just as quickly rewarded. She now had three island-provinces to glory over within her brand-new overseas empire.

This ruthless piece of realpolitik came with its own price. It could never be considered just, not even by expert Roman spin doctors such as Livy, busily rewriting history. It also awoke the whole Mediterranean world to the threat that Rome now posed, and roused a passionate desire among the Carthaginian leadership to defend themselves. They had more or less accepted the result of the First Punic War as a fair cop, the price of losing a war, but Rome's ruthless annexation of Sardinia and Corsica could never be accepted. There was no hope of peaceful coexistence with such a people. They faced a simple choice: learn to be strong or be destroyed.

Hamilcar Barca had a plan. In 237 he shipped the Carthaginian army to southern Spain. He made good use of the existing Phoenician cities along this coast (such as ancient Gades, Malaga and Abdera) as allies before leading his army to conquer the rich silver mines of the interior. With these resources at his disposal he was able to establish Acra Leuce, 'the white fort', near modern Alicante, as his personal naval base. And just as the Carthaginian empire had organised itself in North Africa, so did he in Spain. The tough Iberian tribes of the Spanish mountains yielded soldiers, the conquered tribes in the agricultural plains paid the tithe-tax, while in the Carthaginian style, Hamilcar Barca commanded his army like a king, minting coins, making alliances and judgements. Once he was certain that the expedition had been a success, he summoned his boys from the city of Carthage to join the camp.

Hannibal would have been twelve when he left the docks of Carthage. His father's army was his school and his university. He and his two younger brothers, Hasdrubal and Mago, were trained up in all the arts of war and diplomacy under his father's watchful eye for the next six years. The famous oath sworn by Hannibal, never to be a friend to Rome, probably took place at this time in the ancient temple of Melkarth–Hercules in the island-city of Gades. Remembering the derivation of the word Hamilcar, it would have been a most suitable place.

The military authority of Hamilcar Barca had now grown so absolute that when the Micatani, a Numidian Berber tribe, revolted against Carthage the Senate asked him to crush this new rebellion on their behalf. Other Numidian tribes were befriended by the great general, and sent their young men to fight as cavalry in his army. The Berbers were treated as social equals, for he married one of his three daughters to his chief Numidian ally, Prince Naravas.

Hamilcar Barca was caught by an ambush in the Spanish mountains during the winter of 229, when one of his tribal allies suddenly turned against him. He proved himself a hero to the last, sacrificing himself (he drowned on his horse in the Jucar River) so that his sons might escape. After eight years of war, he had succeeded in carving out a whole new empire for Carthage. It was entirely self-financing, fed by his control of the famous silver mines of Tartessos, unknown to modern history, but somewhere in modern Andalusia.

Hannibal was eighteen when he watched his father drown, and too young to take over command. This was exercised by his brother-in-law Hasdrubal the Fair, who was given the supreme command of the army. Hasdrubal the Fair was a fighter, but he was also a diplomat. He arranged for the allied Spanish tribes to acclaim him their leader, not just the distant vote of the popular assembly at Carthage. He also decided to create a new city, so that his regime operated independent of the Phoenician cities on the Spanish coast. He turned the Spanish port of Mastia into Cartagena, the New City, which began to outstrip the motherland in wealth and power, for his rule was upheld by a standing army of 60,000 soldiers, backed by 8,000 Numidian cavalry, which he kept well occupied, extending the frontiers ever north and west into central Spain. He also carried on the training of his young brothers-in-law. Hannibal was married to a local Spanish girl, which must have been popular with his tribal allies. By the age of twenty-two he had earned his first independent military command.

Hasdrubal the Fair had dealt tactfully with the Romans. Lest they be alarmed by this burgeoning new empire, he repeated earlier protestations that the Carthaginians were merely securing the Spanish silver mines so that they could pay off the war indemnities that Rome had imposed upon them, one after their victory at the end of the First Punic War, the second after they had seized Sardinia and Corsica. To avoid any accidental conflict, Hasdrubal also agreed to the Roman proposal that the Ebro River was to form a frontier line that neither side would cross.

He knew that the Romans would come, but also that he had little to fear from them at the moment, as they had their work cut out on other frontiers. Their annexation of Sardinia and Corsica had not been peaceful, because the hill tribes had risen up in rebellion against their new masters. Rome was also deeply embroiled in Illyria, fighting the Dalmatian tribes on the eastern coast of the Adriatic, which it wished to annex. But most promising of all, in the eyes of a Carthaginian strategist, was the series of raids launched into central Italy by Celtic tribes. These had begun during the First Punic War, but reached their peak in 226 BC, for the Carthaginians were not the only people to feel threatened by the waxing power of Rome. Under this mounting pressure, when an assassin struck down Hasdrubal in 221 there was no doubt, either in the city of Carthage or among the well-paid soldiers in Spain, that they had need of another strong imaginative commander.

Hannibal, the son of Hamilcar Barca, had been fighting in Spain for half his life: twelve years as a junior officer and three as a commander. He was twenty-six years old, married, and experienced enough to be trusted with total command. He was also the spitting image of his father Hamilcar, whose veterans recognised the same keen eyes and the fire that burned there. Hannibal was acclaimed both by the popular assembly back in the city of Carthage and by the 60,000 men he commanded in Spain.

The recently subdued mountain tribes of Spain seized this chance to strike for their independence, so that Hannibal spent the next two years consolidating and then expanding his inheritance. He led an attack on the Olcades tribe, stormed their citadel of Alithia, then crushed the Vaccaei tribe further westward, expanding his control over the Tagus valley. On his return to meet with a delegation of Roman envoys, he was forced into battle against a second coalition of tribes. In his absence the Roman ambassadors placed the city of Saguntum under their protection. It was a consciously aggressive act, for Saguntum was south of the previously agreed frontier of the Ebro River that divided the Roman sphere of influence from the Carthaginian. Hannibal at once laid siege to the city, which was not a large one, but seven months passed before he could storm its walls. The Carthaginian army, even when commanded by Hannibal, never stood out for the methodical skills of siege warfare. Rome could have assisted her new ally in this period, for seven months gave plenty of time to react. Instead she sent a delegation to the city of Carthage demanding that they hand over their general to Rome for punishment. When this was refused, they declared war. The timing of the Second Punic War was Rome's, not Carthage's.

Rome was already immeasurably more powerful than Carthage. It had complete naval command of the Western Mediterranean, a vast reservoir of manpower from the valleys and mountains of Central Italy, and was allied with the sophisticated Greek cities of southern Italy. Its army was at least twice the size of its opponent's, and made up of loyal citizen soldiers, not a polyglot mixture of mercenaries. It also had the advantage of a compact homeland, while the Carthaginian empire was split into disjointed portions: the North African homeland, torn by civil war, separated from the new conquests in Spain.

Hannibal, on his side, had a battle-tested professional army under his absolute command. The Carthaginian army in Spain had been his entire identity since the age of twelve, he would have known every officer personally, and they trusted and obeyed him. This was echoed by Hannibal's complete trust in his two younger brothers, who held command of independent armies. The Roman military was formidable, motivated and well disciplined, but as we shall see its command structure was weakened by the legal tradition of dividing command of the army between two (potentially rival) ex-consuls, appointed for just one year at a time.

Hannibal had developed a daring tactical plan, linked to a coherent strategy. He believed that it was not just Carthage that feared Rome, and that once he could defeat the Roman field armies on an Italian battlefield he would be able to rapidly build up a grand alliance, uniting the Gauls of southern France and northern Italy with the Greek cities of southern Italy. He had no grand ambition to destroy Rome, but rather to put it back into its Latin box, and in the process recover the old island empire of Carthage: Sicily, Sardinia and Corsica. This revived Carthaginian empire would dominate the Western Mediterranean, just as the Eastern Mediterranean was dominated by the powerful Hellenistic kingdoms: together they would keep Rome in check. Rome would pose in the future as the true heir to the classical culture of ancient Greece. At the time of the Second Punic War this was not true. The empire of Carthage was the ally of the Greeks, and Rome the expansionist enemy.

Hannibal moved with lightning speed once war was inevitable. By the time the Roman ambassadors had returned from their filibustering mission to Carthage, his scouts had already crossed the river Ebro. A series of forced marches took his army of 60,000 men across unconquered north-eastern Spain and southern France. The Celtic tribes nearest Rome (in the Alps and the Po valley) were potential allies, but those who had watched the rapid emergence of the Carthaginian empire in Spain had every reason to fear Hannibal, so his army had to fight its way across the Pyrenees. It was well trained in these sort of operations, constantly bifurcating into fast-moving columns that outflanked the disorganised opposition by picketing the commanding heights, and shielding a difficult river crossing by sending detachments upstream.

The march was fast, and its objective distant, but in the eyes of the local tribes Hannibal was also extending his empire over north-eastern Spain, leaving a sizeable force of 10,000 men to hold the Pyrenean passes. Nor was he concerned that the garrisons he left behind (as well as the desertion of various tribal allies) were rapidly reducing the number of men in his army. The forced march condensed his army, so that it consisted of only the leanest, toughest and most motivated of his soldiers. However, he was racing against time, for he needed to cross the Alpine passes before winter could close them. This he achieved, despite the added peril of an October storm that tested his army with wintery conditions, though anyone who had spent a decade campaigning in the Spanish mountains would have been inured to snow, sleet, ice and lethal winds.

Yet the crossing of the Alps has passed into legend, and generations of historians and travel writers have focused on which route may have been taken. The Roman historian Livy stresses the heroic nature of the march, and describes the way the invading army had to carve its path through the mountains, cutting one passage by heating the rocks with fire and cracking them with vinegar. The Greek historian Polybius was less impressed, for he knew that the army had simply used the well established routes of Celtic herdsmen who moved their herds every year up into high midsummer pastures, and then down again before autumn. Hannibal's famous corps of war elephants may have been used as nothing more glamorous than an edible packhorse, and as only one survived the march into Italy, they offered no tactical edge. What mattered far more were the tough columns of Berber cavalry from the mountains of North Africa. Six thousand Numidian cavalry poured down from the Alps into northern Italy to give Hannibal complete dominance in this vital element of ancient warfare. They served in units of five hundred men under the command of their own tribal leaders, such as Prince Maharbal.

They would prove their prowess at the very first engagement, at the battle of Ticinus. The Roman general had imagined that his disciplined legions, bristling with lances like a porcupine, could hold any position, especially as the men carried javelins, and could loose off a shower of these light spears as the enemy came close to their line. However, the Roman infantry folded under the frontal assault of the North African cavalry, who had developed a battlefield technique of galloping up to a line of infantry and hurling their lances just as their horses pirouetted around to return to a safe range. The Roman infantry fell back to seek the support of their own cavalry, which had been held in reserve, but the confusion of this manoeuvre gave the North African cavalry the opportunity to outflank the Roman positions. When the Roman cavalry tried to break out, they caused panic among the infantry, and so the whole army broke and fled the field. They were hunted down until nightfall by the victorious Berber cavalry. The Roman commander, an ex-consul called Scipio, owed his escape from the slaughter to the bravery of his seventeen-year-old son, one Publius Scipio, whom we will meet again.

News of this Roman defeat spread like wildfire, for we must bear in mind that northern Italy was not then filled with industrious cities and beautiful villas. Instead the flatlands of the Po valley were covered with marshes and pastures dispersed through wild woods that were threaded with braided streams. The region was not even considered to be part of Italy, but was part of that wild Celtic hinterland that stretched across all of Europe. It was labelled Cisalpine Gaul, and as recently as 225 BC two of the Celtic tribal confederations, the Boii and Insubres, had joined forces to raid central Italy. These tribes had only been subdued by the Roman army just seven years before Hannibal's arrival. Within this recently conquered territory the Romans had installed two fortified settlements, Cremona and Piacenza.

After the Roman defeat at the river Ticinus, all of Cisalpine Gaul rose in rebellion. Hannibal's army was doubled at once, with thousands of new allies, while the surrender of the Roman stronghold of Clastidium, complete with its grain silos packed full of recently harvested corn, solved any immediate worry about his supply line. In order to try and halt the collapse of Roman authority across northern Italy, the Senate instructed a second consul to march urgently north. He would reinforce the remnants of the first army, which after the river Ticinus was sheltering behind defensive positions. The new commanding general, ex-consul Sempronius Longus, was eager to achieve a victory before his year of command was over.

It was in the battle of the river Trebia (which drains into the river Po near the modern town of Piacenza, ancient Placentia) that Hannibal first revealed his extraordinary tactical genius, backed by detailed knowledge of the ground, totally obedient junior officers and good intelligence.

On the morning of the winter solstice, the new Roman army (composed of legions shipped north from Sicily) stumbled across what seemed to be the disorganised enemy. They had been allowed to win a number of previous skirmishes and were feeling increasingly confident, so when a Carthaginian counter-attack failed and was followed by a retreat (really an organised feint) it encouraged the Roman army to advance from their well-defended camp and cross the river Trebia in pursuit. They never spotted that the young Carthaginian general Mago (one of Hannibal's younger brothers) was hidden in the deep bush with a thousand soldiers and another thousand Numidian cavalrymen under his command.

The Roman army proceeded to cross the river Trebia in good order, so that the two armies, with their vast lines of disciplined infantry (there were possibly 40,000 men on each side), clashed that morning. Once again the superiority of the Numidian cavalry meant that the Roman cavalry was brushed aside and that both wings of the Roman infantry were in danger of being turned. It was at this critical moment that Mago launched his surprise attack on the Roman rear. Attacked from all sides, the Roman army panicked and broke ranks. They were virtually annihilated, except for a body of troops who formed a disciplined square of 10,000 men who fought their way back to the safety of the other riverbank.

After the battle was over, Hannibal made certain that all the Celtic, Ligurian and Italian prisoners of war that had fallen into his hands were treated well. They were told that the Carthaginians came not to conquer but to free them from the oppression of the land-grabbing Romans, and they were then set free.

Hannibal's greatest enemy that winter was not the Romans but the rain and the mud. He lost the use of an eye from swamp fever, but this made him seem like an avatar of Odin–Lugus, the fearsome war god of the northern Celts, who was also known as Belenus, though the Romans equated him with Mercury (rather than their beloved Mars) due to his mystical wisdom and role as a trickster messenger between earth and heaven. The superstitious noticed that Hannibal's Punic surname 'Barca' had the same meaning as the god Lugus. It was also widely believed that the Barcid family's long devotion to the ancient Tyrian cult of Melkarth–Hercules had secured them his divine support. As we have already noticed, the very name of Hannibal's father, 'Hamilcar', means brother of Melkarth–Hercules. Hannibal's line of march also followed an ancient mythical droveway associated with Hercules.

It is a perpetual challenge for modern readers to reach back beyond the glories of the classical artistic tradition and remind themselves of the cult practices that interconnected the ancient world. Tacitus wrote that the northern Celts remembered:

that Hercules, too, once visited them; and when going into battle, they sang of him first of all heroes. They have also those songs of theirs, by the recital of this battle-cry as they call it, they rouse their courage, while from the note they augur the result of the approaching conflict. For, as their line shouts, they inspire or feel alarm.

The Romans for their part also began to fear that the Goddess had turned against them. They looked back over their recent triumphs (such as the conquest of Sicily, Sardinia and Corsica) and recalled that they had defiled many of the shrines of the Mother Goddess.

Hannibal had won Trebia at the time of the winter solstice. The next triumph would coincide with that of the summer solstice. In the spring he marched south into Tuscany, his Carthaginian army now massively reinforced with Celtic allies, who once more raided the rich farmland of this province. The new commander, consul Gaius Flaminius, wished to be seen as the defender of Italy. He advanced to expel the invaders, but the superb discipline of the Carthaginian army (assisted by the lighting of distant campfires to indicate a phantom army) allowed it to remain hidden. They lay in wait as the advancing column of Roman legions blundered into a trap. On the muddy shore of Lake Trasimene, overlooked by wooded gullies, Hannibal sprang his ambush on 24 June, 217 BC. Fifteen thousand Roman soldiers were slaughtered, including their commander – Flaminius had been identified by a Gallic warrior whose family had suffered from his hands in a previous war with Rome and he was determined to avenge his clansmen with the blood of the consul. A few days later, the Roman cavalry (under the command of Gnaeus Servilius Geminus) was caught in a second surprise attack and slaughtered by the Berber cavalry. A little stream that feeds into Lake Trasimene still bears the name *Sanguineto*, 'Blood River'. At the sacred spring of Hercules at Caere, blood appeared.

This third consecutive defeat convinced the Romans of the folly of opposing Hannibal on the battlefield. Quintus Fabius Maximus was chosen to act as dictator, both to unify the command structure and to organise the recruitment of new forces. Fabius refused to be drawn into battle, but used his four legions to shadow Hannibal's army, to garrison strong points, picket the mountain passes and pick off straggling columns when the opportunity presented itself. It was patient, unglamorous work, but it was the right tactic, though the devastation of central and southern Italy by Hannibal's armed columns caused enormous suffering.

Fabius was also determined to lessen the spell of misfortune, by calling on the aid of the gods, especially those that might have been accidentally slighted by Rome. So a new temple was consecrated to the great Mother Goddess Venus, especially in her Sicilian identity as the mistress of Mount Eryx, long assimilated with the Carthaginian cult of Astarte. On a more pragmatic level he also gave honour to 'gritty determined resolution', the virtue the Romans called *Mens*.

By the following summer the Romans had recovered their confidence and were anxious to maintain their authority over central Italy. They had been hard at work creating a mammoth new army of eight legions, four under each of the two consuls, which may have numbered as many as 80,000 men. There was no chance of ambush in the flat farmlands of Apulia, or so they thought, so on 2 August 216, after a number of days of lumbering opportunity, the two armies converged for battle at Cannae. Hannibal and his brother Mago were in command of the Carthaginian centre, with one of his trusted nephews, Hanno, in command of one of the two cavalry wings.

Hannibal had deliberately placed his light infantry, his Spanish and Celtic tribal allies, in an arrowhead formation in the van of his army. He knew that they would be brushed aside by the advancing Roman legions, who did indeed surge forward to exploit their victory. His heavy North African infantry (under his direct command) now stood their ground – no mean test of discipline, when they had just witnessed the rout of their advance force. But a salient had now developed, into which the Roman army advanced with confidence, for it seemed they were about to snap the Carthaginian army in two. But instead they found that two flanking wings of Carthaginian infantry had transformed themselves into horns that now attacked their exposed flanks.

The last element of the trap was completed when the Numidian cavalry under the command of Hannibal's nephew returned to the battlefield. They had first destroyed the Roman cavalry on the left wing, then swept down on the rear of the Roman cavalry on the right wing. Having destroyed both these divisions, they were free to assault the great block of Roman infantry. The Roman legions, fighting on their native Italian soil with the advantage of much greater numbers, were trapped. The grain fields of Cannae became a killing ground, with casualties so vast that seventy thousand may have been slaughtered, including a consul, twenty-nine commanding officers, and eighty men who wore the senatorial stripe. The gold rings worn by the nobility, and the silver rings worn by the knights, were harvested from the corpses to fill a heavy sack that accompanied Hannibal's brother Mago as he sailed south as a herald of victory. Mago poured its contents on to the floor of the Carthaginian Senate in a graphic illustration of the scale of the victory.

The defeat at Cannae, succeeding those at Ticinus, Trebia and Trasimene, was the nadir of Rome's fortune. It was her gravest hour and her greatest test. For Hannibal's grand strategy now also bore fruit, as various Samnite hill towns, alongside such great Greek cities as Capua, Tarentum and Syracuse, defected to the Carthaginian alliance. This league was completed when King Philip V of Macedon joined the allies, having been promised the recent Roman conquests in Illyria as his reward. Hannibal for his part offered Rome very moderate peace terms and the promise of the speedy evacuation of his army from the war-devastated countryside of Italy. There was never the slightest chance that he could have seized the city of Rome, which would have required a vast army and the sort of logistical back-up and engineering skills that his Carthaginian army never possessed. For even such isolated cities as Nola, Neapolis and Cumae successfully resisted the Carthaginian sieges that were laid against their walls in the aftermath of Cannae.

Rome remained implacable, and despite the devastating fourth military defeat of its armies in Italy, refused to even listen to Hannibal's mild terms for a new peace. Instead it set plans afoot to raise an army of twenty-five legions (more than 100,000 men) that would allow the Roman empire to wage war on three fronts. They would attack the Carthaginian empire in Spain, whilst simultaneously besieging such rebel cities as Capua (near Naples in southern Italy) and Syracuse in Sicily. In central Italy Rome would revert to the unglamorous but sound Fabian tactics of holding all the strong points and shadowing and harassing the enemy.

It was to be total war, and one that would have to be waged for another decade, but in fact just before its defeat at Cannae, news of a decisive turn in the wheel of fortune had already bolstered the Roman position. For the resources of Rome were such that even while raising army after army for destruction by Hannibal in Italy, it had yet been in a position to also send an army to invade Carthaginian Spain. The supremacy of the Roman navy had never been challenged in battle, and so it was free to raid the coasts and such remaining Carthaginian strongholds as the Balearic isles. A fledgling Carthaginian flotilla was based in Spain, but this had been destroyed in a battle fought on the Ebro River in 217, which had been followed by a military victory in Spain in the spring of 215. Two young brothers, Gnaeus and Publius Scipio (each in command of a legion but lacking any adequate cavalry), had defeated the Carthaginian army commanded by Hannibal's brother Hasdrubal at the battle of Dertosa. This not only symbolically extended Roman authority south of the Ebro for the first time, but blocked Hasdrubal from marching west to reinforce Hannibal. Which was one of the reasons that his other brother, Mago, had been sent with that diplomatic bagful of gold rings to pour with a flourish onto the floor of the Carthaginian Senate. For to prosecute the war further, Hannibal needed many more men and a navy.

Just three years after Cannae, Rome had expanded its army to twenty legions. It was free to send two legions to hold on to Sicily, two to police Sardinia and Corsica, while two garrisoned the walls of Rome and another two legions camped in the Po valley to secure Cisalpine Gaul. This left it with ten legions free to engage in offensive actions.

The Carthage homeland would respond to Mago's appeal for aid, but of the two armies it could raise, neither could be sent to reinforce Hannibal. One was sent to Sicily in an attempt to foster rebellion against Rome, whilst Mago led the other to Spain in order to prop up the already endangered Carthaginian position there.

So after Cannae the Second Punic War settled down to the nitty-gritty graft of besieging a city. Hannibal tried to bolster his position in southern Italy by capturing more cities for his alliance, but failed in practically all these efforts, while Rome succeeded in all its ventures. It stifled a revolt in Sardinia, then crushed the uprising against its authority in Sicily, before going on to capture the city stronghold of Syracuse itself. The fall of Capua in 211, followed by Tarentum in 209, proved just how methodical the Roman army had grown in the engineering skills required for successful siegecraft. The series of Roman victories against the stout walls of Syracuse, Capua and Tarentum could be set in the balance against the tens of thousands of slaughtered men on the fields of Ticinus, Trebia, Trasimene and Cannae.

Such was the background for the famous cavalry raid of Hannibal, which in 211 saw him ride at the head of two thousand Numidian horsemen to hurl a lance at Rome's Colline Gate. It was a grand gesture but nothing more. The tactical point of it had been to distract the Roman army from completing the siege of Capua. In this it failed.

The fatal flaw in Hannibal's grand strategy was also now slowly emerging. His brilliant manipulation of the Celtic alliance had protected his back, equipped him with armies of light infantry, and given him the grand air of a liberator. However the annual devastation of the herds and fields by Hannibal's composite army, complete with all its Celtic regional allies (recruited from Spain, the Po valley and the Alps), had emphatically reminded every town and city in Italy just why they needed Rome. For they had all become subordinate allies of the city of Rome for the very good reason that it was the only power capable of protecting Italy from the recurring menace of Gallic raids and Celtic invasions. So the continual presence of the army of Hannibal in Italy had the curious side-effect of increasing loyalty to Rome, not sapping it. A wise Carthaginian senator had asked Mago (flushed with the victory of Cannae) if he could identify a single Latin village which had left the Roman alliance for that of Carthage, or name a single man, from any of the thirty-five military tribes of the city of Rome, who had deserted to Hannibal's army. Mago could only answer in the negative.

The control of Spain proved to be the key barometer of the war. As we have seen, the Romans had won the first round of fighting (at the battle of Dertosa, fought near the Ebro River in 215), but this was reversed four years later by the destruction of the Roman army in Spain in 211.

A charismatic young leader, Publius Scipio, was then selected to be the next military commander. This was the man who had saved his father's life at the battle of Ticinus, and he had gained useful tactical experience in the subsequent years. As a member of the powerful Cornelia *gens*, or clan, within the Roman Senate, Publius Scipio was also assured support of a large faction within the Roman leadership.

Now he displayed his flair by leading a sudden assault on Cartagena, the capital of Carthaginian Spain, having ascertained that the defending armies were a ten-day march away. His men rapidly threw up earthworks against the eastern walls in order to assault this section of the city, which allowed Scipio to secretly instruct 500 marines (armed with light scaling ladders) to ford the lagoon at low tide in order to ascend the weakly garrisoned western walls. It was a bold move, full of risk but also reward. His men seized control of a city whose treasury was filled with 600 talents of silver ready to be minted into coin that assured the loyalty of their soldiers. This fell into his hands.

In the spring of 208 Scipio's army clashed with Hasdrubal's at the battle of Baecula. Hasdrubal was worsted, but cut his losses in order to fight his way north, determined to then march east and reinforce his brother Hannibal in Italy. He left two other commanders in Spain to continue the fight against Scipio, who was now the dominant military power. Indeed, and much to his embarrassment, the young Roman general found himself acclaimed king by his allies among the free tribes of Spain. This was bound to cause him trouble back in the staunchly republican Senate of Rome, for his charismatic style of command had already won him favourable comparison with Hannibal and the envy of his peers. But Scipio's skills were irreplaceable.

In the spring of 206 the two Carthaginian commanders in Spain joined their forces and advanced on Scipio's numerically weaker force. The subsequent battle of Ilipa was to be Cannae in reverse, for Scipio adapted Hannibal's tactics (deploying a weak centre and strong infantry wings) to engulf and then crush his opponents. Overnight the Carthaginian empire imploded, with the remnant forces retreating to a few strongholds on the coast, such as the ancient island city of Gades, from where they shipped their men out, either returning home or making a last-ditch attempt to reinforce Hannibal.

The Romans were triumphant everywhere but in Italy, and they were aware that Hannibal and his army were the one factor that could yet lose them the war. They had intercepted a number of the messengers who were communicating between the various Carthaginian armies. One of these allowed the consular commander Claudius Nero to ambush Hasdrubal, who had safely crossed the Alps and was but a few weeks away from reinforcing his brother. He was killed and his army destroyed.

Once the corpse of Hasdrubal had been positively identified, his head was cut off and packed in salt in a leather bag. A few days later this bag was thrown into the advance lines of the Carthaginian camp, grim and conclusive evidence that Hannibal's army was now alone in the world. His army remained a potent force, but the wind was now strongly blowing in favour of Rome, and his Greek and Celtic allies gradually melted away, leaving him increasingly bottled up in his base camp of Bruttium, in present-day Calabria.

In 205 Hannibal's most powerful ally, Philip of Macedon, made his peace with Rome. There were other Hellenistic powers that could have come to Hannibal's aid (most especially with their strong navies), but Rome played it soft with Greece in this period, heaping such sanctuaries as Delphi with gifts and victory trophies and flattering other rulers with subtle attentions. Hannibal's potential to damage Rome had been further weakened by the destruction of a fleet of eighty transport ships dispatched to him from Carthage. His one hope of reinforcement was that his surviving brother, Mago, would succeed in leading a 12,000-strong Carthaginian army from out of the wreck of their Spanish empire and march across the Alps (like his two brothers before him). He did break into northern Italy, but the road south was barred by the legions.

Scipio had meanwhile returned from the conquest of Carthaginian Spain to a heroic welcome in Rome. He had defeated the enemy and also doubled the size of the Roman empire. The Roman Senate was divided about their next move. Should they once again risk confronting Hannibal on the field of battle in Italy, or should they strike at his homeland of Carthage? Scipio championed the latter policy, but a compromise was agreed. Sufficient forces were to remain in Italy to hold Hannibal in check in the south and coop up Mago's army in the north.

So Scipio spent the next year building up the Roman army in Sicily to be ready for the invasion of North Africa. This force comprised two legions, essentially formed from the troops that had survived the battle of Cannae. Scipio needed to be absolutely confident that they were well enough trained to operate as an independent force in the hostile environment of North Africa. And there was further ground for delay, for a central plank in Scipio's strategy was that Rome should only invade North Africa once it had a reliable local ally in place.

Scipio had long identified Syphax, the Berber king who ruled what is now Western Algeria from the citadel of Siga, as his most likely candidate. Syphax was far enough away from the city of Carthage to feel independent, while the entire coastline of southern Spain, northward across the Mediterranean, now lay in Roman hands – the Roman fleet was free to operate wherever it wished. Syphax had been courted by Roman agents for many years, but he preferred to keep a friendly relationship with both Rome and Carthage, playing the two powers off against each other, while subtly extending his own kingdom.

So Scipio decided to travel to the Berber citadel of Siga to see if he might clinch the deal himself. The same thought had occurred to one of the Carthaginian generals, who had also travelled to Siga to talk politics. So this was how the two men who had commanded opposing armies at the decisive battle of Ilipa found themselves meeting as guests around the peaceful table of King Syphax. The Carthaginian general, Hasdrubal Gisco, left the court of King Syphax deeply impressed by the energy and intelligence of his Roman opponent. Publius Scipio left the court convinced that he had sewn up a tactical alliance between Rome and Syphax's North African kingdom. Indeed this may well have been the case for a while, for soon afterwards Syphax succeeded in doubling the size of his kingdom. He expanded deep into the eastern region of modern Algeria, and established Cirta as his eastern capital; he now ruled over a vast and powerful Berber state. But Hasdrubal Gisco had a trump card up his sleeve. His daughter, the beautiful and intelligent Sophonisba, was offered in marriage to King Syphax. Carthage now had a powerful ambassador and agent sharing the same bed and destiny as the king. In due course, Syphax switched his alliance from Rome to Carthage, or rather kept to his old policy of steering his own course through the two powers.

This meant that Scipio was forced to look elsewhere for a local ally within North Africa. Until then he returned to his task of training up his men for the invasion. In the spring of 204 a fleet of two hundred broad-bottomed transport craft left Sicily and sailed south. Such was Rome's naval supremacy that this vast body of ships only needed to be guarded by a squadron of twenty galleys. However, the risk of bad weather prompted Scipio to land his forces just north of Carthage, though he had planned on setting up a more distant (and secure base) further to the south. That winter the Roman invasion army rested in its military camp, for it had failed in its first attempts to storm the walls of any Carthaginian city with a decent port. Scipio now launched another diplomatic offensive to try and win Syphax round.

At the same time, he was using these embassies to intensively reconnoitre the land, so that when he saw that the talks were about to stall, he was ready with his military option. This he pursued with his customary energy and dispatch. First he ambushed the camp of Syphax's Berber army, firing its winter quarters (wooden huts clad in leather) and causing panic. Then he attacked the Carthaginian army, which was a second-rate militia force (all the best men had been sent abroad). Then in a dazzlingly successful series of battles fought outside the walls of Utica and Carthage (which is sometimes called the Battle of the Great Plains and sometimes the Battle of the Bagradas River) these two demoralised forces were defeated and then destroyed.

The Carthaginian Senate sent a delegation to speak words of peace to Scipio, while another was dispatched to Hannibal, begging him to return and defend his homeland. The terms dictated by Scipio were harsh, but not unreasonable. Carthage would abandon all its possessions outside North Africa, evacuate its last island possessions, pay a war indemnity of 5,000 talents, feed the Roman army and limit its navy to just twenty galleys. The Carthaginian ambassadors accepted these terms in order to confirm a truce with Scipio in North Africa, then crossed over the sea to ratify them with the Roman Senate. In Rome they soon learned that Scipio, so beloved by the people of Rome, had many jealous rivals in the Senate. They scented an opportunity to split the general from the Roman Senate, arguing in parallel that the city of Carthage was the innocent victim of the reckless military ambition of Hannibal and his brothers, those reckless sons of Hamilcar Barca.

The truce was confirmed, though it was agreed that the final peace treaty could only be signed after all the invading armies had quit the soil of Italy. So it was under a flag of truce that Hannibal and his brother Mago separately left their camps in northern and southern Italy and sailed home to North Africa. To make doubly certain, Mago's army was shadowed by a powerful Roman fleet as it passed such dangerous lures as the old Carthaginian possessions of Corsica, Sardinia and Sicily. He died of his wounds before he reached home.

Hannibal had meanwhile discharged those of his soldiers who did not feel that their homeland was in North Africa, and appointed garrisons to guard those Greek cities within southern Italy that still remained his allies. The tale of the heartless massacre of his own allies is retroactive Roman propaganda, glossing over the unpalatable fact that Hannibal had made many loyal allies in southern Italy. At this point in his career he still had every hope of beating the Roman army in his North African homeland and swiftly returning to improve the Carthaginian position in southern Italy. The pots and caches of coins that have been discovered by archaeologists at Bruttium are not evidence of a massacre of his men. They were buried by his well-paid veterans anticipating their return to southern Italy, which had been their base for ten years. In a similar way Hannibal had left his own offerings. At the inviolate temple of the Italian Mother Goddess, which stood at Cape Licinium, surrounded by an Arcadian parkland–sanctuary of wild woods and virgin meadows, he offered up trophies of his past victories to Juno and a solid column of gold, accompanied by bronze inscriptions that commemorated the achievement of his army. Wild herds of cattle and deer freely grazed the paddocks of the sanctuary, which had been first raised in honour of the goddess by Melkarth–Hercules – the selfsame god at whose sanctuary he had vowed eternal enmity to Rome as a young boy, and whom his father Hamilcar had been named for.

So for a curious two years, between 204 and 202, there was a truce in force between Rome and Carthage. Hannibal, in order to keep his distance from any accidental conflict with Scipio's Roman army (encamped outside Carthage), had landed his army of 20,000 veterans far down the southern coast, at Hadrumetum. He may also have been able to use his own family's landed estates in which to house and feed his army. There is a tradition that during the period of truce they were kept busy planting vast new orchards of olive trees in the steppeland.

It was a good call, for the presence of the Roman army had

grown vexatious, and while the Carthaginian armies had com-pleted the evacuation of Italy, there was no sign of the Roman army quitting the suburbs of Carthage. When some Roman supply ships were wrecked on the coast, then pillaged (in the time-honoured manner with which wrecked shipping has always been treated), it proved to be the unexpected flashpoint that revived the war.

So it was that in October 202 the two armies, after a two-year truce, drew close to one another outside the Numidian citadel of Zama. As we have heard, Hannibal was defeated that day, in a battle that showed no evidence of either his or Scipio's tactical brilliance. The two armies met, and the issue was not decided by either the battle-hardened veterans of the Roman or Carthaginian legions, or by their brilliant commanders, but by the actions of the Berber cavalry allied to Rome that day. Something has surely been lost in the telling. Why would Han-nibal have advanced to give battle, knowing that his opponents were superior to him in Numidian cavalry? He above all men knew from what happened at Ticinus, at Trebia, and at Cannae itself, not to mention a decade of wars fought in Spain, what a decisive advantage this gave his opponents.

I believe that in order to understand why Hannibal fought at Zama, seemingly walking directly into his one and only mili-tary defeat, we must turn our eyes to the arcane world of Berber tribal politics.

∴

When we last looked in this direction, Scipio had been trying to woo King Syphax (based on his citadel capital of Siga in the far west of Algeria) into a Roman alliance. In the process King Syphax and his son Prince Vermina used the opportunities of this two-power rivalry to expand their rule over Berber Numidia. They had eventually been won over to the Punic cause, though the marriage of Sophonisba, the daughter of a Carthaginian general, to King Syphax may have been not so much the cause of this policy as a public seal on the alliance. The Berber army of King Syphax then fought alongside Carthage's homegrown militia in an attempt to oppose Scipio's Roman invasion of North Africa. This alliance did not prosper, and the two armies were defeated by Scipio in a series of battles called (among other names) the Battle of the Great Plains.

These victories allowed Scipio to send a column of Roman troops to assist his brand-new Berber ally, General Masinissa, in seizing control of Eastern Numidia. The Roman he trusted with this special task was Gaius Laelius, who was not a general but one of Scipio's closest friends and most trusted confidants. He was a childhood friend of Scipio who came from a poor and undistinguished background, though he was neither a slave nor a freedman. He was a companion, somewhere between a page, a valet and a bodyguard (maybe even a lover), in the Scipio household. So although Gaius Laelius had no official rank, he fought beside Scipio at every major battle. Together they saved the life of Scipio's elderly father (Consul Publius Cornelius Scipio) at the battle of Ticinius, and they also survived the killing fields of Cannae together. Gaius Laelius accompanied Scipio to Spain in 211 and took a leading role in that first dashing campaign which saw him lead a picked squad of marines through the tidal surf to seize the walls of Cartagena. Indeed he was the only man apart from Scipio who knew what was being planned that triumphant day. It was also Gaius who first made direct contact with King Syphax in order to arrange for Scipio's personal mission to visit him at Siga. Later Gaius Laelius led a number of armed raids on the North African coast, collecting experience and intelligence whilst Scipio was training the Roman field army in Sicily up to battlefield readiness.

So Gaius Laelius was no stuffed shirt. He knew exactly what he was doing when he rode beside Masinissa in a long raid deep into central Numidia. Between them they seized control of Cirta and captured King Syphax and Queen Sophonisba. This was no mean achievement, for Cirta was a fortress formed by nature. The city sits atop a mountain plateau, almost entirely encircled by the coils of a fantastically steep canyon whose near-vertical rock walls are filled with the roaring waters of a living moat. (In 1836 a French military column attempted to storm this citadel with all the advantages of nineteenth-century technology. It failed.)

We are not certain, but it seems likely that Cirta fell to this raid not by siege, but because it was Masinissa's ancient homeland. This Berber kingdom had been ruled by his father Gala until 206 BC. After his death, his brother Oezalces seized control of the throne in some sort of alliance with Syphax, so Gaius Laelius was fully aware of the potential political ramifications of this bold dash into the wild tribal mountains of Numidia. It was a tactical risk, demanded by the long-term strategic gains. Scipio had helped Masinissa recover his homeland. It was the reward for his help in the recent campaign, aiding the Roman invasion of North Africa and fighting beside Scipio as one of his cavalry commanders. Nevertheless Gaius Laelius insisted that the defeated King Syphax be spared any vengeance at the hand of Masinissa. He was safely escorted to the distant coast to become a prisoner–guest of the Roman republic back in Italy.

Gaius Laelius also forbade another of the spoils of war, which was the marriage of Sophonisba with Masinissa. She could not become one of his wives or concubines, which was a polite way of saying that Masinissa could not be trusted with the daughter of a leading Carthaginian noble, whispering ideas into his ear every night. Famously, Sophonisba chose to take poison rather than accept a life of captivity without Masinissa, if we follow Livy's narration of events. Though when composers re-create this operatic story they often forget to mention that her husband, King Syphax, was not dead but was living a life of comfortable, if forcible, exile.

For this is where things grow even more complicated, and sometimes our sources conflict. Masinissa was not a natural ally of Rome. He had been brought up in the city of Carthage, a son of one of the great Berber lords of Numidia (King Gala or Gia), who was an honoured ally of the Carthaginian empire. So aside from his Berber Numidian identity, he spoke Punic like a native, and knew the city of Carthage as his childhood homeland. Indeed it is claimed that he was in love with Sophonisba as a young man, and may even have been betrothed to her, before she was given to King Syphax. Masinissa was just ten years younger than Hannibal, whose entire family, especially his younger brothers Mago and Hasdrubal, he would have known intimately. For Masinissa, like them, had also been trained in the arts of war in the great army of the Barcids in Spain. Indeed we know that he fought in the battles of Castulo and Ilorca as a junior commander of cavalry, and that from 208 to 207 he was effectively in command of a guerrilla campaign fought against the Roman legions in Spain. It was a vital role with far-reaching implications, for Masinissa had been trusted to wage war against the otherwise victorious Roman army, so that Hasdrubal could be free to rapidly march and join his brother in the Carthaginian army of conquest in Italy.

We also know that Masinissa was one of the two Carthaginian cavalry commanders at the battle of Ilipa in 206, where the Carthaginian generals managed to unite three separate armies in a last bid to overwhelm Scipio. So although novelists, film-makers and even some historians often depict him as a rough tribal lord of the mountains, Masinissa was part of the inner circle of the Numidian–Punic military elite. As we have heard already, the battle of Ilipa in 206 BC shattered the final remnants of the Carthaginian empire in Spain, and in the aftermath various junior commanders either retreated home to North Africa or tried to join Hannibal in southern Italy.

It was Masinissa's double misfortune to come back home to North Africa in the year that his ageing father died. His brother Oezalces had seized control of their inheritance, probably with the connivance of King Syphax. For a while (maybe two years but no longer) Masinissa was a refugee in his own homeland. This was the period when he travelled south into the edges of the Sahara to escape the agents of his brother and Syphax. If the great royal tomb at Medracen belonged to his grandfather or great-uncle, we must imagine that his tribal homeland was south-eastern Algeria. It was in this period of his life that he was 'turned' and became a Roman ally. One of the great cavalry generals of the Carthaginian empire turned his life and whole career against his own comrades, his family, his language and childhood friends to make himself an ally of the hereditary enemy. To put it into an American perspective, Jeb Stuart decided to become a Yankee; Prince Rupert crossed over to Cromwell.

It was part of the genius of Scipio and his trusted friend Gaius Laelius that they managed to discern that this battle-hardened cavalry general, of Numidian royal blood and impeccable Carthaginian culture, was ready to become a sworn ally of Rome. Gaius Laelius' reconnaissance raids from Sicily would have been the most likely opportunity for the first contact to have happened, as it could not have taken place deep in the Sahara. Indeed it probably occurred at the port of Hippo Regius. But there must have been many Roman staff officers who wondered exactly how much trust you should put in a man such as Masinissa. Scipio and Gaius Laelius clearly went the whole way. They employed Masinissa as their commander of Numidian cavalry in the Roman service from the point of their first invasion in 204, and the triple victories that they won over Syphax and the Carthaginian militia may have owed much to his assistance. The decision to send Gaius Laelius, and a Roman army with him, to allow him to recover his kingdom in central Numidia was reckless but was also inspired. Scipio was the same age as Masinissa, and was offering not only friendship, but the chance to create his own kingdom as an ally of Rome. Scipio was also personally charming, brave, intelligent and of impeccably noble blood. It looks a perfect match.

However, with the hindsight of history we are in a position to know much more of the inner workings of Masinissa's mind than Scipio did. We know that Masinissa never stopped being a Carthaginian, for many years later, even though he was cherished as a Roman ally, he would turn Cirta into a little Carthage in the mountains, packing it full of Carthaginian exiles working in his employment, complete with its own murderously busy Tophet sanctuary, the Hodna. No one who has seen the massed sacrificial stones recovered from the Hodna can doubt the degree of his attachment to the old gods of Carthage. A royal tomb that stands on a hillside outside Cirta, belonging either to him or to his son Micipsa, looks totally Hellenistic in its furnishings.

We also know that in his middle age he would pursue a policy that attempted to unite Berber Numidia with the remnant of the Carthaginian empire, backing both a political party within the city of Carthage and a hard-edged foreign policy that relentlessly annexed bits of the old Carthaginian empire to his Numidian–Punic kingdom. It was as if Masinissa had studied how Phillip II had struggled to unite the militant power of the Macedonian highlands with the civilised cities of Greece to incubate the superpower achieved by his son Alexander the Great. So (unlike Scipio) we know exactly what was going on at the back of Masinissa's mind as he worked as an outward ally of Rome. He desired to create a strong, independent North African state resting securely on its own cultural traditions. So it would not have been impossible in those two years of truce between Rome and Carthage (when both Scipio, Hannibal and Masinissa were all in North Africa and their three armies all at peace) for Hannibal to have been offering Masinissa the very same thing that we know he also desired. Especially after King Syphax had been deposed, and the lovely Sophonisba was dead by her own hand, like a politicised Juliet. There was every window of opportunity for those talks to have progressed in the two-year truce, indeed they didn't even have to be deniably secret, for both Scipio and Hannibal were in command of armies confined peacefully to their barracks.

Ambitious maps of the extent of the two Numidian kingdoms, of Masinissa's Massyli and Syphax's Masaesyli, are often drawn up. I used to like to imagine that these two rival tribal confederations represented the two different Berber highland confederations, separated by different dialects, that still underwrite political rivalry in Algeria – the Kabyle of the northern coast and the Shawia of such south-central mountains as the Aurès. Though this is all guesswork, for the two tribal names of Massyli and Masaesyli are simply two different transliterations of the same Berber word meaning the Noble or Powerful People, just as the name Masinissa is derived from the Berber word 'Msnsn' – our Lord. An inscription from Dougga names Masinissa as the son of Aguellid (King) Gaia (obviously a version of Gala) and grandson of the suffete Zilasan.

This all conspires to allow me to imagine that the battle of Zama was not just an encounter between the two master tacticians Scipio and Hannibal. It was also the epicentre of a protracted diplomatic competition between the two of them. Scipio had been actively pursuing an alliance with a regional power in North Africa for years. He could offer recent bold deeds, an inspiring sense of trust, maybe a personal friendship, and an alliance with the rising Great Power. Hannibal could offer generations of shared cultural loyalty, the same gods, the same language, and decades of shared military service in the great Barcid army. They also shared the same ultimate vision.

Which would have given that meeting on the eve of the battle of Zama more than just a casual interest, as each general watched the other's face for some tell-tale sign. Had Hannibal offered Masinissa a share in the creation of a powerful Punic–Numidian empire of North Africa, which they could both cherish and defend? Or had Scipio encouraged Masinissa to act as a double agent, in order to lure Hannibal into a decisive battleground, rather than pursue a long guerrilla campaign against the Romans?

We know that the intervention of Masinissa's cavalry, attacking the rear of the Carthaginian army, was utterly decisive, and that when Hannibal saw it he knew for sure that the battle was lost. To my mind the charge of Masinissa's Numidian cavalry into the rear of the Carthaginian army was one of those critical choices that change the fate of nations but that tilt on a knife-edge of chance. I think that Hannibal and Scipio may have been tinged with the same apprehension as that on Bosworth Field, when both the Duke of Richmond and Richard III watched to see which side Lord Stanley would fight for. Or like Robert Clive's secret negotiations with Mir Jafar, in which money had changed hands and promises had been made, but not until the last moment could one tell on which side the coin would fall, and who would win the day and an empire at Plassey. We will never know, but if you ever get the chance to walk around the fields of Zama, I now expect you to share my sense of wonder.

At the very least you must ask yourself what on earth was Hannibal doing here? For he of all people knew exactly what an overwhelming edge the Berber Numidian cavalry had given him in Italy, and this force no longer stood behind him, but fought beside the Romans. If, however, Masinissa had decided to side with his old comrades, Zama would have been an even greater bloodbath for Rome than Cannae.

Hannibal escaped from the defeat at Zama, riding back towards the military camp he had established at Hadrumetum (modern Sousse). From there he travelled to Carthage for a meeting with the Senate. He told them that the war was now completely lost, and that they had only one option, which was to sue for peace. In his camp at Tunis, Scipio dictated the harsher clauses of a new settlement. Carthage was forbidden any territory outside North Africa, the use of war elephants, or to possess more than ten warships. From now on she could wage war only with the permission of Rome, and was charged with an indemnity of 10,000 talents of silver to be paid off over the next fifty years.

Once her ambassadors had travelled to Rome to sign this treaty and then returned, Scipio received all the Roman prisoners of war into his camp. Italian 'deserters' found to have served Carthage in her wars were publicly executed, and a vast funeral pyre of thwarted imperial ambition was made out of all the ships of the Carthaginian navy.

⁙

On the western horizon, Scipio confirmed the frontiers of a greatly expanded kingdom for Masinissa. This Numidian kingdom now reached into central Tunisia, to include such cities as Thugga (Dougga), Makhtar and Bulla Regia within its boundaries. We do not know where his western frontier marched, but it seems likely that Prince Vermina, Syphax's son and heir, was permitted to rule over the western third of Algeria from Siga. Only then did Scipio return to Rome to be acclaimed in a great triumph and saluted as 'Africanus'.

His friend and colleague Gaius Laelius, having helped win two wars for Rome, was also rewarded. This confidential agent and king-maker was made a quaestor, the very lowest administrative office in Rome, usually filled by young aristocrats. It might appear a humble enough reward, but it was one that allowed this man from a poor landless family to eventually make it into the Senate and serve as an ambassador. Right at the end of his life, Gaius Laelius would be interviewed by a Greek writer, and so became a major eyewitness source for Polybius' history. His master would also do well, but his eminence had also procured him many false friends, biding their time for his eventual downfall. Twenty years after Zama, Scipio Africanus would be prosecuted for corruption and treason in the courts of Rome, for he had accepted a vast gift from a Hellenistic monarch. He would die in disgrace, albeit in the comfortable exile of his own estate.

Hannibal spent the first six years after Zama in busy retirement, employing his surviving veterans in planting the southern steppelands with olive groves that would enrich their descendants. Then in 196 BC he stood for the office of one of the suffetes of Carthage, and won the election. He began a wholesale overhaul of public administration, revealing the corruption, jobbery and embezzlement that had blocked the arteries of the Carthaginian state. To confirm the clarity of his new administration he boosted the powers of the Tribunal of 104, which down the centuries had watched over the powers of generals and admirals. In this new era of peace, membership of the Tribunal of 104 was opened up to annual election, and it was decreed that no member should serve consecutive terms. So at a stroke it was no longer a shadow Senate, selected by co-option within the elite, but became a powerful ombudsman for the inspection of public accounts and administrators. Public finances were revolutionised, but Rome had no tolerance for the idea of a wealthy, peaceful, democratic Carthage.

Roman envoys were sent to Carthage the next year and interviewed some of the disgraced officials so as to be able to bring a case of treason against Hannibal. He was forced to flee the city of his birth to escape arrest, after which the Roman envoys insisted that his house be demolished. He escaped to the Kerkennah Islands, off his country's east coast, where he was feasted by so many of his old veterans, who thoughtfully requisitioned all the island's sails to make a great banqueting tent, that when Roman officials arrived in pursuit of their old general there was not a boat fit for action.

Like the Barcid he was, Hannibal's first landfall in the East had to include a visit to the ancestral altars of Tyre and the city's ancient temple to Melkarth. From there he travelled to the great metropolitan city of Antioch, before moving to the elegant, well-watered city of Ephesus (on the west coast of modern Turkey). This was then serving as the capital of Antiochus III, an able Hellenistic monarch who had become fully aware of how dangerous a power Rome had now become. Antiochus III had succeeded in restoring the Seleucid empire to its old dimensions, and aspired to reunite the old empire of Alexander the Great. This set him on a collision course with Rome, which could not suffer any state to equal its power. Which meant that Hannibal, with all his experience of fighting Rome, was a very welcome guest at the Seleucid court. Indeed Hannibal was fated to have one more bizarre military adventure, for he was made the admiral of the Seleucid fleet at the same time that a Seleucid army invaded Greece in 192 BC.

The subsequent victory of Rome on both land and sea (the fleet under Hannibal's command was blockaded in the harbour of Side) effectively expelled the Seleucid empire not just from Greece but out of Anatolia (modern Turkey). Antiochus III now tasted the humiliation that had been forced upon Carthage by the peace treaty that Rome forced upon him at his new capital of Apamea (in central Syria) in 188.

Hannibal was no longer employable. He moved out of the Seleucid domains and worked as a consultant on a number of different projects, such as designing a new city for the king of Armenia and an improvement to the naval arsenal of the king of Bithynia. He was also writing pamphlets that explained how Rome operated and how relentless its ambitions were. Hannibal explained how a rival power to Rome would be isolated and neutralised as its various neighbours were placed under Roman 'protection'. These subordinate allies would then be encouraged to strangle this independent state, by seizing its trade and its most useful ports. By the time the Roman victim was ready to strike back, it would have been sapped and surrounded by the dependent allies of Rome. These would be given territorial pickings as their reward, but would in due course be annexed once they were no longer of any further use.

The end came for Hannibal in 183 BC. In a curt little interview, a Roman general had ordered Prusias, king of Bithynia (which occupied the north-west corner of Turkey), to deal with this local problem or lose the friendship of Rome. So one night Hannibal found that his seaside villa had been surrounded by Bithynian troops. They had been briefed about the escape route that the old general always prepared from each of his temporary homes. Hannibal had just one move left, which was to swallow the poison that he now always travelled with.

He had been right of course, but a generation too early, a Cassandra in the political wilderness. The full range and violence of Rome had not yet been unleashed on the world, but soon it would be. The kingdom of Macedonia was the first of the civilised Greek states to pass under the Roman heel. It had been relentlessly hedged in by Rome's subordinate allies, such quisling states as Pergamon and Rhodes, and then shattered, despoiled, humiliated and conquered in a series of four brutal wars. At the conclusion of this 'liberation' the tombs of the family of Alexander the Great were looted by Roman soldiers and the kingdom subdivided into four small provinces.

By then it was far too late for the world to pay any attention to Hannibal's old warnings. So in 146 BC Rome no longer needed to hide its appetite for relentless growth, for that was the year when it destroyed two of the largest cities in the Mediterranean. Carthage and Corinth were not just conquered by the Roman legions, they were completely flattened. The only way to express this in modern terms is to imagine a European state deciding to obliterate both London and Paris in the same year, to unveil a power that now knew no limits.

∴

After the flight of Hannibal, the political momentum in North Africa swung to Masinissa. His first task had been to pacify the tribes within his enormous Numidian kingdom, then to encourage agriculture in his lands, alongside the payment of the royal tithe. This policy was enabled by his employment of Punic officials who took the culture of Carthage into these new lands. At the same time he pursued an aggressively expansionist policy towards Carthage by exploiting a clause in the peace treaty that gave him the right to claim his ancestral heritage, even if it lay within the Punic frontier. Rome, as we have just learnt, was fully preoccupied by its wars in Greece in this period, against the Seleucids and then the Macedonians.

Roman policy was to back its regional ally against the local power, whatever the justice of the case. Such was the decision in 162, which not only gave Roman support to one of Masinissa's land grabs but then fined Carthage 500 talents for having dared defend its own territory. Masinissa absorbed these new provinces into his kingdom of Numidia, but ten years later was prepared for another coup. In 152 BC he seized the cities known as the Emporia, which controlled the lucrative trans-Saharan trade. A Roman commission of inquiry, faced with this cast-iron case of Numidian annexation of Carthaginian territory, decided to suspend its decision, but the trial was actually a turning point in Roman policy. The elderly Cato had been included in this embassy, and had been shocked to find how vigorous, populous and commercially dynamic the city of Carthage had remained. He may also have spotted the danger of a union between this dynamic city and Numidia, for the second prong to Masinissa's foreign policy had been to sponsor a political party within Carthage, which actively campaigned for union with Numidia. There was a third prong too, for he also pursued the more traditional royal diplomacy of bestowing dowry-laden daughters on various key Carthaginian nobles.

So now, almost certainly for the first time, the Roman Senate realised that its Numidian ally Masinissa was aspiring to unite all North Africa under his control, with Carthage as his potential capital. It was a far-sighted vision, and one that would have raised the fusion of Berber and Punic culture to a new level.

But first a violent swing to the left in Carthaginian politics in 155 BC turned Masinissa's friendly policy on its head. Supporters of the Numidian king were expelled from Carthage, and Carthalo, the democratically elected general for that year, gave military backing to Agasis and Soubas, two Berber rebels who led a peasants' revolt against Masinissa. This revolt had little impact, except to provide an excuse for Masinissa to annex the rest of the Emporia and the two Carthaginian districts (groups of fifty Berber villages) that were centred on Beja and Makhtar. Masinissa, the great Berber king, the veteran of a hundred battles, was eighty-eight in 150 BC. It seemed that he was on the brink of achieving his life's ambition of presiding over a unified Punic North Africa.

Rome had different plans. Ancient historians wasted much energy explaining why the Roman republic needed to assault a defenceless democratic city of Carthage completely shorn of all its empire. They seldom cared to face up to the fact that the Roman republic was led by factions of profiteering aristocrats who made vast fortunes from war, diplomatic kickbacks and the administration of conquered territories. These were just the type of men who would be most suspicious of Carthage's popular democracy and most interested in the profits of another conquest. A Roman senator was legally barred from all engagement with trade and finance, so that he was totally dependent on the income of his farm and the rewards of serving the state.

So the real question is not 'Why?' but 'When?', and this is what the Roman senator Cato understood so well when he made the famous gesture of shaking out a rich cluster of Punic figs from the folds of his toga onto the floor of the Senate. Cato, who was rabidly pro-war and habitually finished each speech with the words '*Delenda est Carthago*' (Carthage must be destroyed), sought to attract the special attention of his colleagues. The senators knew from boyhood the strength of the stalk of an unripe fig, but how when the fruit is ripe it drops effortlessly into the harvester's hand. Carthage, one of the juiciest prizes of the Mediterranean, was now considered ripe for the picking. The brutality and thoroughness of the destruction of Carthage by Rome is a bitter tale, and one that can still send a shudder down through the centuries.

It was while defending their territories from yet another one of Masinissa's territorial annexations, in 150 BC, that the Carthaginians first heard the news that Rome was mobilising for war. They did everything they could to avoid this monstrous threat. Carthalo and Hasdrubal, the leaders of the popular party, were first deposed and then condemned to death. An impeccably aristocratic embassy was meanwhile dispatched to plea directly to their fellow plutocrats sitting in the Roman Senate. The delegation was listened to, but only for the number of months it took Rome to complete its preparations for war.

In the spring of 149 BC the Roman army was ready. It was led, as was traditional, by the two proconsuls. The legions were able to disembark peacefully on to the North African shore, for Utica had opened its walls to this overpowering armada. As the Roman army slowly marched towards the walls of Carthage, the Carthaginians hurriedly agreed to their every new request in an effort to placate the superpower.

First they ceded hostages (300 noble children), after which they surrendered their military arsenal, before at last, in sheer desperation, unreservedly placing the city's future in the hands of the Roman state. It was only when the Carthaginians heard that it was the implacable intention of Rome to plunder and level the entire city, and to forbid them to establish a new one within ten miles of the sea, that they understood the awful logic of appeasement.

As one, the Carthaginians then rose up to defend their homes, their temples, their livelihood and their honour. The surviving members of the democratic leadership were summoned back to power by the vote of the popular assembly. The entire population mobilised for war, labouring day and night to replace the arsenal so naively surrendered to the Roman army just a few weeks before. The women cut off their long locks of hair, which were woven to form catapult rope and bow strings. The smiths' forges laboured day and night, and achieved staggering heights of production: 100 shields, 500 javelins and 1,000 catapult darts manufactured every twenty-four hours. The Roman legions delayed their first assault, and when at length they advanced, the city was ready. The Romans were repulsed from the long line of triple walls, bordered by a 60-foot moat, that defended the western, landward face of Carthage. The consuls made camp (roughly on the site of today's Tunis–Carthage airport) and settled down to the intricacies of a long siege. They had a vast professional army of 80,000 men under their command.

For two years the Roman army became bogged down, literally, for the walls of Carthage were reinforced by salt marshes and brackish lagoons. They were also harassed by Punic forces operating from the hill country, assisted by volunteers from Numidia who included members of Masinissa's own family. We know that Masinissa must have been secretly appalled at the turn of events, but he kept up appearances by dispatching one of his sons, Gulusa, to command the Numidian cavalry in the service of his old Roman allies.

In 147 BC the precocious military talent of Scipio Aemilianus was recognised. He bore a fateful name, for this young man was the adopted grandson of Scipio Africanus. The legal constraints on his youth were waived. He was first elected consul and then, like some new Achilles, placed in sole command of the Roman siege. Carthage's Punic sister cities, most of which had sued for peace in 150 BC, watched in silence as Scipio slowly tightened the noose. One must not heap blame on these cities, for they had merely followed Carthage in that first desperate attempt at appeasement.

Scipio's first act was to hunt down the Punic bands waging guerrilla warfare from the hills. Next he established a maritime blockade of the city, after which he launched a series of marine assaults on the sea walls that protected the two harbours. It was during the spring of 146 BC that one of Scipio's repeated assaults finally forced its way through these battered sea walls. He rushed further troops into this breach, and seized control of the nearby Agora, the public heart of Carthage. His men were now free to fan out and loot the surrounding temples of their glittering treasures, collected over the last 700 years. The Carthaginians, starved and exhausted by three years of fighting, fell back onto the high points from which they continued to defend their falling city, contesting each street, each alley, each house. The citadel on the Byrsa hill, occupied today by the colonial Cathedral of St Louis, held out for another six days. Here Scipio at last showed some compassion, accepting the surrender of the 50,000 starved and embattled citizens who had defended this hill against his legions. He spared their lives, but that was the full extent of his mercy, for these captives would later be auctioned off into lifetimes of slavery.

The temple of Eshmun (on the hill later to be occupied by a Roman theatre) was the last stronghold to fall, defended by Hasdrubal the Democrat with 900 zealots. Having exhausted every last resource of war, they turned the temple into a furnace, an ultimate Moloch, and sacrificed themselves to its flames. Hasdrubal begged for mercy at Scipio's knee, while his wife, disgusted at his behaviour, hurled insults at his stooped back. She returned to the roaring fire that was consuming the sanctuary and, grasping her young children to her breast, hurled herself into the flames. A second Dido.

The historian Polybius had been tutor to Scipio Aemilianus when he was a boy, and had subsequently been included in his staff. He was an eyewitness to the siege. So just as Wellington huddled beneath a cloak on the field of Waterloo, Polybius witnessed the young general weeping in the aftermath of victory. For in the flames of Carthage's destruction he foresaw that one day Rome, too, would fall, and quoted the *Iliad*: 'Holy Troy will perish also, and Priam and the people of Priam.' Polybius was outwardly a pro-Roman Greek who had successfully assimilated into the Roman ruling class. He had first arrived in Rome as a political pawn, one of a thousand influential hostages, after the Roman Senate had become concerned that perhaps its old ally, the Achaean League, did not love it well enough. In his old age, Polybius was able to examine the ruins of Corinth, as well as to watch the death throes of Carthage. In Greece he was able to personally help those refugees who had survived the obliteration of ancient Corinth by the Romans. Although outwardly pro-Roman in all his writings (but a much fairer observer than Livy, that spin master of Latin propaganda), it may have brought him secret consolation to think that one day this fate would also overtake Rome.

Not even the smoking walls of Carthage, soaked in the blood of the slaughtered, were permitted to stand. The first task of the enslaved citizens was to level their city under the direction of Roman military engineers. The ruins were solemnly cursed and the administration moved to Utica. The boundary of the new province of Africa remained the old Carthaginian frontier, the *Fossa Regia*. The other Punic cities, such as Hadrumetum, which had surrendered to Rome at the start of the war, were confirmed in their status as self-governing city-states (*civitates liberae et immunes*) and remained free from tax and judicial oversight. The landholdings of all the Carthaginians and those towns and villages that were judged to have fought for Carthage in the war were surveyed, confiscated, and the population enslaved. A portion was set aside to reward various local allies, but the majority of this vast landholding was sold at public auction to a carpetbagging confederacy of Roman speculators. The administration of the conquered province, which was essentially confined to the supervising of the annual tribute due to the Roman state, was bestowed upon a senator for just one year at a time. It was a licence to extort money from a defenceless province, given to reward a man after he had held some public office in Rome. He brought with him his personal staff, but was inevitably dependent on the local tax farmers, usually resident Italian merchants and settlers.

This republican period of Roman rule was a pitiless epoch. No trace of any constructive building or concerted policy survives. The one recorded act, the roasting alive of the Roman governor by the irate citizens of Utica, casts a single ghastly glow.

The Romans had a reward in store for their ally Masinissa. He died during the siege of Carthage in 148 BC, and so Scipio Aemilianus was at hand to process his will. His kingdom of Numidia was to be divided into three parts, between his sons Micipsa, Gulusa and Mastanbal. It was standard Roman policy to weaken an ally by dividing the inheritance between rival heirs, once they were no longer of any use. The same fate would befall the next generation (after Micipsa had reunited Numidia), which would once again be divided between three princes, just as Herod the Great, their ally in Palestine, would have his state divided into the three tetrarchies. Divide then rule.

When Prince Jugurtha, Masinissa's talented grandson, succeeded in reuniting these three broken portions of Numidia back into a single kingdom, he became an enemy of Rome. Army after army was sent into Numidia in the six-year Jugurthine War (118–105 BC). He was defeated in the end, and Numidia split once more into three parts, one given to Rome's new ally, King Bocchus of Mauretania, one to Jugurtha's half-brother King Gauda of Numidia (105–81 BC), the other third annexed to the Roman conquest colony of Africa, with its frontier held down by a string of Roman military colonies. Divide then rule.

3

The Tomb of the Christian Woman and King Juba II

It was our first day in Algeria. The road was dense with mist, we had lost our police escort back at the last roadblock, and we were now twisting up a single track into the hills. A single car stood rather menacingly in the far corner of an empty car park with its lights stabbing into some pine trees. My job was to educate but also to reassure this group of travellers. None of them had cancelled from the tour, even though just a month before an experienced French traveller had been abducted while out walking in the mountains. His kidnappers had beheaded him and posted this barbarity on a website. It is in times like these that my technical illiteracy is an advantage, for it keeps me innocent of such scenes and made me much better at my job of looking cheerful and relaxed whilst abroad. I also explained to my group that we were all British, internally bolstered by the presence of a few Australians, and so it was most unlikely that we would be targeted by any Islamist terrorists in Algeria, who would be much keener on the old proven enemy of France.

To further reassure them, I told them about the equality-of-age law, with reference to travellers. A friend of mine called Jason had discovered this rule while travelling with his erudite old hippy father in the Balkans. Just before approaching a border post he reminded his father to jettison any illegal sub-stances before they reached the frontier post. The father agreed that his son should certainly empty his pockets of any stash of grass about his person, but there was absolutely no need for him, Jason's father, to do so. This frontier post would be guarded by young men. He had watched human males, so he knew that we are only driven to assert ourselves amongst our own age group. This is instantly calculated by all males, of whatever age, taken down in one gulp like the prevailing weather. These are both your team and your competitors, the only ones that you innately 'rate', while the rest of the world can be scorned or charmed to taste. So true enough, my friend was stopped, questioned and searched by machine-gun-toting frontier guards of his own age, but his father was waved straight on through.

It was not that it was beneath their dignity to hassle an old man, it would just have been boring. The reverse would have been true if an old colonel approaching retirement age had been in charge, for he would have wanted to measure himself up against the tall, grey-haired stranger in the long coat, and find out the story of this man from his own time. So using this logic, our group of culture-hungry travellers with an average age of seventy-plus would be almost invisible to any bearded young terrorists. And to prove my point, I reminded them that only last year some Islamist terrorists had attacked a gas plant deep in south-eastern Algeria, and had kidnapped thirty-nine foreigners, but they had all been working technicians of their own age. It was a fair debating point, but it did not help lift the mood of our group.

But then it was our first day out, when no one had devel-oped a sense of what is normal. The dense morning mist and the silence had certainly brought a chill to this harmless day trip out from the capital. And then having walked out in the weather, with no sense of where we were, or our destination, the wind shifted, and they caught a first glimpse of what we had come so far to experience. And like a child playing in grand-mother's footsteps, we were a little shocked at how close we had come, without being aware of this mass of ancient stone that now rose like some slain giant right before us.

The tomb of the Kubr-er-Rumia (the Christian Woman) is a circular pyramid of ancient stone. In the misty half-light that we approached it in that morning, it appeared to be a grey for-tress whose strong outer wall was buttressed by a line of Ionic columns. As we walked around this structure, we passed a suc-cession of four monumental doorways, the wooden details of crossbar and door-frame seemingly metamorphosed into stone. They were real enough to the touch, but these massive stone portals had been built never to be opened. As proof of their strength, they had been subjected to artillery bombardments which had blown cavern-like holes into the masonry, without ever revealing an interior.

For a hoard of gold, the loot from the fall of the Visigothic kingdom of Spain, was believed to be buried somewhere in the middle of this circular pyramid. The cross-struts of the stone gates, designed to look like ossified wood, do create the sign of the cross. This is considered to be the origin of its confusing name, the tomb of the Christian Woman, Al Kubr-er-Rumia. Otherwise there is nothing about the place that has any Chris-tian or medieval resonance. To our eyes it was triumphantly classical, a piece of the ancient civilisation that underwrites our British culture, first made in Rome, stamped all over us. And that bizarrely was what most of us were here to see – better frag-ments of the Roman empire than our own island could offer up.

And then the sun finally burnt its way through the trails of morning mist, and we were given shafts of deeply satisfying

Mediterranean colour, bright blue skies, and the tomb became a pyramid of golden stone. We also found ourselves not beside an old city wall, but perched on the summit of a hill. Below and behind us, still half obscured by remaining banks of mist, was the neat level floor of a well-farmed valley. The horizon now marched off to distant forested mountains to the south with the great sea to the north. I have been to this place many times, but this unveiling of the great monument by the weather was the most satisfying of all. Each and every time that I come, it reveals a bit more of itself, but without answering any direct inquiries about its age or identity, like a beautiful old woman at the dinner table, brimful of experiences, and fully prepared to ward off questions with stories.

∴

This splendid age-defying classical pyramid is the final resting place of a famous pair of star-crossed royal lovers, King Juba II and Queen Cleopatra. This is not just my fancy, but has been entombed as a fact in countless history books and encyclopedias on and off the web. For the so-called tomb of the Christian Woman stands within a day's ride of Cherchel, the capital city of a Berber kingdom that was ruled by Queen Cleopatra Selene (the child of Mark Anthony and Cleopatra) and King Juba II (the child heir to the ancient Berber kingdom of Numidia). Even today the tomb remains highly visible from the sea, the road of choice for the ancient world, standing above the coast just east of the busy port of Tipaza. It would have been even more conspicuous in the ancient past, when the stones of this vast mausoleum were sheathed in a limewash, the details picked out in red and blue capped with something gold that twinkled with radiant glory on the summit. This could have been an eagle perched on a golden globe, a four-horse chariot (often used to represent the ascent of the soul), or – following the example of the Mausoleum of Halicarnassus – it may have been topped by a pair of statues of the royal orphans, seated side by side on equal thrones, the hand of one raised affectionately to the shoulder of the other, in that endearing gesture of marital love used by the Egyptians.

Juba II had been created king of Mauretania by fiat of his powerful patron, the Emperor Octavian Augustus, when he became a man. A few years later Augustus gave him a wife, the last Ptolemaic princess of Egypt, Cleopatra Selene. She came with a magnificent dowry, which enabled this perfect pair of client monarchs to choose the port of Iol as their capital, and to embellish it with a palace, a library, a lighthouse, an amphitheatre, an aqueduct and a temple to Isis, all laid out on an efficient gridlike plan, making of it a little glowing model of Romano-Greek civilisation with wafts of Ptolemaic Alexandria about it. They modestly named it Caesarea, in honour of their imperial patron, the same name that another client monarch, King Herod of Judaea, had thought suitable for his own newly built port. But unlike other examples of fawning supplication to the source of power, such as Leningrad and Stalingrad, the name Caesarea somehow survived. The Arabs pronounced it 'Sharsal', which evolved into present-day Cherchell.

So from their city of Caesarea in Mauretania, Juba and Cleopatra spread the gifts of civilisation among their barbaric subjects, preparing them to one day join that commonwealth of culture, and become a fledgling province of the Roman empire. To round off this dream, King Juba was classed by Plutarch, no less, as 'the most learned of all kings'. He is also respectfully cited by Pliny as a major source of geographical knowledge.

King Juba assembled a great library in his new capital,

and assisted by an expert staff of researchers is credited with fifty completed works. These include books on music theory, theatre studies, linguistics, applied arts and Roman archaeology, though his two greatest works were acknowledged to be a geographical summary of all the knowledge relating to Africa and Arabia, including its varied fauna and flora. In his research on the latter he was assisted by the scholarly enthusiasm of his personal physician, Euphorbus (who was brother to the emperor's own physician, Antonius Musa). Juba honoured Euphorbus by assigning his name to his botanical researches amongst the spurge family. Euphorbia is the genus of a group of some two hundred plants that thrive in arid lands and have developed complex white saps to make themselves distasteful to grazing animals, but which also give them a range of medicinal uses as both emetic and laxative. Another intriguing etymological trail that leads us back to the learned court of King Juba is the name of the Canary Isles, which are not named after the yellow songbird, but the savage island dogs kept by the indigenous Berber inhabitants, observed by an exploration party sent out by this ever-inquiring scholar–monarch. These hounds were compared to the famous Molossian hounds that were bred in the Greek highlands, and to the Agassian hunting dogs exported from the British Isles.

Over the last hundred and fifty years, thousands and thousands of European travellers have delighted in this romantic story of a pair of enlightened monarchs ruling over their perfect private kingdom as exiles. It sounded a perfectly pitched ancient note to the colonial concept of extending Western standards of civilisation to uncouth Barbary. It also helped that a visit to Cherchell provided a near-perfect day trip out from Algiers, which throughout the late nineteenth and early twentieth centuries was a popular resort for expatriate settlers and ship-borne winter visitors. None of these travellers missed out on the opportunity of visiting Cherchell, gazing in admiration at the fine edifices, a classical temple turned into a church, a forum-like piazza with a fine arcaded colonnade, before being stunned by the astonishing exhibits in the rich little museum. The labels on the portrait busts and heads, of Ptolemy this and Cleopatra that, the sublime carving of the gods and some exquisite mosaics, transported the visitor to the palace of Juba and Cleopatra, which must have overlooked the harbour from a fine colonnaded terrace abutted by libraries, gardens and shrines to Isis and Artemis.

To add to this vision of antique glory, it become customary for visitors to Cherchell to also explore the ruins of Roman-era Tipaza, assisted by a delicious meal of fresh-caught fish. So only a miserable pedant would miss out on the chilled rosé served with the prawns, and so have a clear enough head to question the fine historical maps of the city for precise dates, look for the exact provenance of each find, and whether the identification was based on an inscription, associated ceramic debris, or an art historian looking at the shape of the curls of hair on a brow. On a third visit, I found out that I could do both. And though one might at first diminish the experience, one could also help excavate something rather darker and more chilling.

∴

So I began to look at Cherchell with fresh eyes. The lovely-looking classical church (now a mosque) in the town square turns out to be an entirely nineteenth-century colonial creation, as is the charming harbour-front piazza, decorated with resurrected bits of classical carving. It remains a very elegant approach to the museum, but nothing more, a monument to

French town planning, not to any found evidence of an ancient forum, agora or palace courtyard. Next to go was an elegant classical colonnade (spotted in old black and white photographs), which is inaccessible (because within the grounds of the military staff college), but was also revealed to be another exercise in constructive colonial Roman-romanticism. My next discovery was that not a fragment of the royal palace, let alone King Juba's library or Queen Cleopatra's temple to Isis, has ever been found. But no matter, not a stone from King Solomon's temple has ever been found in Jerusalem, and that has clearly not diminished the passions of migrants from Brooklyn. So I was not too put out to find that none of the fine royal statues on display in the museum came from any first-century BC ruins, but had all been unearthed in the Roman public baths, built 200 years after the death of Juba and Cleopatra.*

So it began to appear likely that the royal city of Juba had been completely swept away by the Mauretanian revolt (which we will look at later) and replaced by a Roman military colony established here during the reign of the Emperor Claudius. This new city was formally renamed Colonia Claudia Caesarea, with not a whiff of reference to being a capital of King Juba, unlike other North African cities such as Bulla Regia (Bulla of the King) or Hippo Regius (Port of the King), which proudly continued their association with the native Numidian kings.

To throw in an English memory peg (and a possible comparison), the Mauretanian revolt happened in the same period that Boudicca's revolt burnt down Roman Colchester and

---

* Though a scholar later told me not to be too quick to throw the baby out with the bathwater in this case, because the bathhouse culture (although a product of the golden middle age of the empire) also had antiquarian tendencies, which could suck in genuinely old statues to ornament these new spaces.

London, which were both speedily reconquered and rebuilt. So apart from pleasing myths like Boudicca's barrow tomb on Parliament Hill, her secret burial chamber below platform 9½ of King's Cross station, or a Roman temple buried beneath the foundations of Colchester's castle, there is nothing tangibly from the period of Boudicca that you can touch either. I began to wonder if this might be the same for King Juba. I kept these researches to myself, for I was not interested in spoiling any holiday or destroying the myths fanned by local historians and proud museum curators.

It was much more rewarding to concentrate on finding the real pieces of antiquity, to stroke the stonework of the bits of Roman Caesarea that still stand, and have always stood. These included the remnants of the theatre (a popular place to drink an illegal beer out of the sight of the wife – and then smash the bottle) and a fine stretch of aqueduct, outside the town. However, in conversation with archaeologists I learned that with even these monuments it was 'virtually impossible to distinguish between the construction programme of the client kingdom, before AD 40, and that of the Roman province thereafter'. Even the excavation maps (loyally printed in every history of Roman North Africa) became insubstantial. The forum turns out to be a supposition, the amphitheatre has disappeared (quarried into rubble by the French over the nineteenth century) but the grid plan of streets (five blocks extending inland from the harbour) does at least rest on found evidence.

∴

So although his library, his palace, even his city, had started to melt away on close inspection, I became ever more fascinated with the life of Juba II, the scholar-king. I had also begun to notice that he was never listed among the ancient heroes of Algeria, unlike such martial ancestors as Masinissa and Jugurtha. Juba's face never appeared on a poster, his name never commemorated a hotel or a café. Collective zones of silence have always fascinated me, so I began to flesh out the life of this North African client king working for the Roman empire.

Juba II was aged but four when he fell into the hands of 'enemy Romans' after his father (King Juba I) had been defeated by Julius Caesar. The boy prince was packed off as a prisoner to Rome in order to play a starring role in the quadruple triumph of Julius Caesar – over the Celts of Gaul, Juba I of Numidia, Ptolemy XIV of Egypt and Pharnaces II of Pontus. It must have been an extraordinary personal experience for the boy. By tradition the captive princes, laden with gold chains, led the whole vast victory parade, which included army-sized columns of unarmed soldiers, senators, officers, painted billboards of the highlights of the campaign, vast effigies, bejewelled portrait busts, wagons loaded with booty, two flawless white oxen (destined for sacrifice), and of course the conquering general riding a four-horse chariot. So the boy prince of Numidia represented his conquered North African homeland before thousands and thousands of Roman citizens drunk with wine, victory and pomp. They lined every step of the three-mile processional route that began in the Field of Mars, then passed through the city's triumphal gate, before twisting up through the Roman streets to reach the Capitoline Temple.

After the triumph was over, the usual fate of the prize human trophies was to be consigned to some dungeon and then quietly done away with, an inglorious obscure death either by slow starvation or suffocation, but far removed from public martyrdom. This was the fate that befell Juba's own great-uncle, King Jugurtha of Numidia, a hero to his people, now and then, who led an eight-year struggle against the Roman conquest of North Africa. Other, less political, prisoners of war could meet their end in bloody exhibitions staged in the aftermath of the triumph, either in the amphitheatre games or in staged show-piece set battles.

Juba was not only spared this fate but entered Caesar's household as a guest, a graphic symbol of the *Clementia* that marked the end of the civil wars. His status fluctuated between that of an exotic pageboy and an adopted nephew. We don't know for certain, but it seems likely that this actual household was run by Caesar's sister Julia, and after her death by Octavia – who was known to have cared for all the children of Mark Antony, as well as her own.

It was in this extraordinary household that Juba made the most important friendship of his life, with Octavian, ten years his senior. Octavian was also in many ways just another adopted orphan. Juba became a squire-like personal assistant to the serious young Octavian, who was impressed by the young man's scholarship and familiarity with Latin and Greek literature. Neither of them was physically cut out to be a warrior, but they both did their best, and would share the adventure of a military campaign in Spain, as well as witnessing the decisive naval battle of Actium. Juba's decision to concentrate on literary pursuits may also have been informed by an understanding that this was the best, if not the only, chance of survival. He must keep his head down and cling tightly to the friendship of Octavian, as the only way to avoid the next batch of murderous proscriptions that punctuated each next round of Roman civil wars. For whatever secret pride he may have felt about his royal blood, he would also have learned how deeply involved his family had been in Roman politics, and the faction fights of the civil wars. But always on the wrong side, the side of the enemies of his patron Octavian.

Juba II's grandfather King Hiempsal II had ruled as one of the kings of Numidia. He was also a close ally of Sulla, the ultra-conservative leader of the blue-blooded senatorial party of Rome. Juba's own father, Juba I, had grown up within the strong bonds of this client-like allegiance, and so became a close confederate of Pompey, Sulla's political heir. Although Juba I was a frequent visitor to the city of Rome, he nevertheless remained every inch a Berber king, who wore a magnificent beard and traditional dress and carried himself with a proud martial bearing. The vast resources of corn from the kingdom of Numidia and its crop of young men serving as the auxiliary cavalry of the Roman army also made him a man of great consequence.

However, Juba I's loyal support for Pompey had brought him, even as a young man, into direct confrontation with Julius Caesar. In a celebrated court case held in Rome, Prince Juba I was physically assaulted by Julius Caesar, who playfully tugged at the prince's royal beard. But threat was added to this insult when one of Caesar's Populist allies proposed that all the royal lands of Juba I's Numidian kingdom should be confiscated and sold at public auction, both to feed the people and also to destroy a known enemy, this rich foreign ally of the right-wing aristocrats within the Senate. So when it finally came to the civil war that broke out between Pompey and Julius Caesar, there was absolutely no doubt which side King Juba I would be on, or what would become of his throne, his beard and his lands if that side lost.

King Juba I's army proved itself to be a decisive force in the first round of the Roman civil war, for Caesar's Populist ally Curio managed to overthrow the official Roman governor of Africa in a battle fought beside the Bagradas River. But then Curio pushed his luck and marched inland. He was caught in an ambush by the Numidian army under the command of General Saburra. Juba I now had his revenge for all the insults he had had to swallow as a young man in Rome, for the Populist senators taken prisoner after the battle were brought in chains to the royal capital and publicly executed there. The role of Numidia in this Roman civil war had always been important, but the stakes now grew even higher.

The next round of fighting within North Africa in this Roman civil war was to be even more complicated. The senatorial party, defeated at the battle of Pharsalus in central Greece, had scattered to the four winds. Some had taken refuge in the independent kingdom of Egypt, while others had fled to the Roman province of Spain. But most of the key figures of the senatorial party decided to take refuge in the Roman province of North Africa, which had been in their hands ever since Juba I's general had destroyed the Roman Populist army under Curio.

Caesar had started to weaken this stronghold of his enemies. First he encouraged Bocchus II, the Berber king of Mauretania, to attack King Juba I of Numidia from the west. Then he sent an unscrupulous but energetic Roman mercenary called Publius Sittius to make a landing on the Numidian coast. Juba I promptly marched inland to defend his homeland from this dual assault, which allowed Caesar to land unopposed on the North African shore, at Thapsus in central Tunisia.

Juba I was then summoned back by his Roman senatorial allies Metellus Scipio and Faustus Cornelius Sulla, so that he could reinforce them and together they would outnumber Julius Caesar's comparatively small invasion force. Had they moved fast and caught Caesar off guard, the whole fate of the civil war might have been reversed in an hour, but there were reasons for their reticence.

Julius Caesar was a charismatic commander who was known to be extremely generous to his troops. As the leader of the Populist party he was known to be well disposed to the ordinary citizen–soldiers of Rome. By contrast the rank-and-file soldiers serving in the army of the blue-blooded senatorial party were not so much in love with their leaders, who were known to be stingy and arrogant, and who also lacked a single decisive commander, and were allied to bearded foreign kings.

So aside from the actual fighting on the battlefield of Thapsus, there was an intense propaganda war being fought between the two political camps, in which Julius Caesar held all the winning cards. To lessen their public dependence on the military might of King Juba I of Numidia, his army had been ordered to camp away from the senatorial army. But Roman soldiers continued to defect from the senatorial army to Caesar's camp in numbers that ultimately sapped their ability to fight with any confidence. The tension of these secret negotiations, and the capacity for deceit and doubt, may help explain why the normally mercifully inclined Caesar behaved so violently, even after he had won the battle of Thapsus. He gave orders to massacre 10,000 Roman prisoners of war in the aftermath, even though many of these were supposed to have been anxious to enlist under his command.

Although Juba I's Numidian army (which may have numbered as many as 16,000 men) was virtually untouched by the actual fighting of the battle of Thapsus, he realised that it was not just a battle, but the entire war, that had been lost. The destruction of the army of his senatorial allies left him totally exposed. He could have little doubt what humiliating fate awaited him, so he made a legendary compact with General Marcus Petreius, his remaining Roman ally from the old senatorial party. These two colleagues fought a duel to the death, watched by an audience of just one, a gladiator–slave who had received solemn instructions from both men to kill whoever survived.

It was a legend for any son to be proud of, but one that Juba the young historian would have had to brood on in absolute silence. The fate of his homeland did not make such an edifying tale. The kingdom of Numidia was annexed by Julius Caesar to become the new province of Africa Nova, and its farmlands either auctioned off or given to soldier settlers. The semi-independent port-cities along the shore of North Africa were subjected to enormous fines at the whim of Caesar, though they had taken no part in the war.

Julius Caesar's mercenary ally Publius Sittius proved himself a useful ally in the subjugation of the interior. He not only defeated the Numidian general Saburra, but organised manhunts that tracked down all the various senatorial leaders who had taken refuge in North Africa. So it was Publius Sittius who was responsible for the death of young Faustus Cornelius Sulla, the dictator's dashing young son, while his men also succeeded in tracking down Metellus Scipio just as he was about to leave the Numidian port of Hippo Regius (modern Annaba) for Spain. Though once again we find that a defeated senatorial leader chose suicide rather than to sue for mercy from Caesar. They died better than they fought.

Sittius was rewarded with the Numidian capital city of Cirta and its surrounding territory as his personal domain, which he settled with his troops and named Colonia Cirta Sittianorum Cognomine. It was a brutal act, to give the ancient proud capital of the Berber kingdom as a personal fief to a mercenary chief.

Sallust, an old political ally of Caesar's from the Populist party, would also be rewarded with North African spoils. He had come in useful by organising the ships, supplies and coin that had enabled Caesar's lightning-fast invasion of Tunisia, so his reward was the first governorship of the newly conquered province of Africa Nova, the old Numidian kingdom of Juba I. Sallust proved himself the very model of the worst aspects of the Roman empire, an extortionate, greedy, deeply corrupt governor, who amassed such a vast fortune that he was able to buy up one of the hills of Rome on his return home, and lay it out as a splendid garden–palace, complete with a fabulous library.

Indeed, not the least of the many confusing and contradictory trails within the life of young Juba II is the strong possibility that he, in his role as a historical researcher, must have consulted Sallust's library, from the legacy of the rape of his Numidian homeland. But it would have been difficult not to have been charmed by old Sallust in retirement, for the artistic creator of Rome's most famous garden stood outside the charmed circle of Roman nobles. Sallust always remained proud of his Sabine ancestry, and its highland culture. He was also interested in collecting the old archaic vocabulary of Latin and chronicling all the old Populist heroes, looking backwards from Julius Caesar to the Populist general Marius and thence to the murdered Gracchi brothers (the Jack and Bobby Kennedy of ancient Rome). It is also highly likely that some of the remnants of the ancient library of Carthage might have physically been found on the shelves of Sallust's library, for we know that after Scipio's sack of Carthage in 146 BC the library of Carthage was given to Prince Hiempsal, son of Masinissa, as his reward for assisting the Romans as commander of the allied Numidian cavalry. This library must have been carried back to the Numidian capital of Cirta, and if it survived the various sieges and sacks of the Jugurthine Wars, one can be certain that the extortionate but book-loving Sallust would have wanted to lay hands on what was left of it. He looked after his books until his death, around 35 BC, when Juba might have been seventeen years old. His garden and library subsequently fell to Octavian.

Two years later, aged nineteen, Juba was serving on the staff of his childhood friend Octavian, so he witnessed the naval battle of Actium (31 BC) at first hand, which turned his patron into the master of the world. The vast army and navy that served Octavian was under the authority of the battle-hardened soldier Agrippa. Here, if not before, Juba would have noticed that Octavian was wise enough to know what he was good at, and what was not for him.

Octavian was a man of the most extraordinary talents, but with the hindsight of history it is easy to forget that he was not destined to win. In fact he must have looked a rank outsider. He did not belong to the old nobility of Rome, despite his father's marriage to a niece of Julius Caesar. Octavian's father had been a new man, the very first of his family to enter the Senate, for his own father (Octavian's grandfather) had been a despised but very successful money-lender, the child of a slave who had set himself up as a rope-maker once he gained his freedom. I think this paternal line of inheritance may have helped Octavian to deal in realities such as the delicate political art of 'negotiation', which was perhaps the most decisive element in what happened at the battle of Actium. Certainly the defection of one of Mark Antony's admirals (complete with his battle plans) was a vital element in Octavian's victory. So too was the decision of the Egyptian navy to sail home halfway through the battle. These two defections have never been adequately explained, but I have always imagined that Octavian succeeded in 'turning' two enemy admirals into allies that day through the arts of negotiation. He knew that most men have a price, no matter how noble their blood line.

Behind all the bizarre diplomatic manoeuvres of this last campaign of the Roman civil war, fought between Octavian and Mark Antony, two old allies, cousins and brothers-in-law, there was something else for the young Juba to observe. For the war between Octavian and Mark Antony was also fought over the fate of a thirteen-year-old boy about to become a man. Caesarion, the son of Julius Caesar and Queen Cleopatra VII, could have united the cultures of all the Mediterranean: Italy, Greece and the Levant. Indeed this was Mark Antony's plan, that Caesar's only son would reign as Caesar–Ptolemy XV, King of Kings, and merge the intellectual renewal of Roman Populism with Hellenistic autocracy and Egyptian spirituality. But once Octavian won the war against Mark Antony, his first action was to secure control of this teenager and have him killed. It was an odd way for the loyal heir of the legacy of Julius Caesar to behave, to murder his only son, but it was yet another lesson in palace realpolitik for a young prince such as Juba to absorb.

A year after Actium, Juba had finished his first book. He was now aged twenty. He had done well to survive that long, but his ever-busy patron Octavian now had a specific task for him. He was plucked out of the study, confirmed with the title of king (but given no kingdom), and sent on a potentially awkward mission off to his Numidian homeland. He was not being made governor of his father's old kingdom, which was a maelstrom of activity. Octavian was merging the two provinces of Africa Vetus and Africa Nova into one, which was going to be ruled from a rebuilt Carthage. In the meanwhile, all the fertile ploughlands of the African provinces were being resurveyed, some proportion of this land confiscated (maybe a third, maybe a half), and then drafts of discharged veteran soldiers were being given lands, re-energising all the military colonies first established by such Populist heroes as Marius and Julius Caesar. In addition Octavian was establishing seventeen brand-new towns, mostly sited along the well-watered lands along the Bagradas River. It seems likely that these were old crown lands that had once belonged to King Juba I and his ancestors. King Juba II was sent to the southern frontiers of the new province of Africa Proconsularis to do what he was good at, which was research, using his exceptional command of all the relevant languages: Berber, Punic, Greek and Latin. For if the lie of the land looked promising, the Emperor Octavian was toying with expanding south.

In order to make sense of this appointment, it is helpful to know that at exactly the same period, Octavian was pursuing an expansionist frontier policy on another southern boundary of his empire. He had pushed the frontier of Egypt south of its historic Aswan border and there set up a formal client kingdom. At the same time he was ramping up the Roman diplomatic representation in Aksum (northern Ethiopia), which was being groomed towards becoming another Roman protectorate–ally. This was not some quixotic venture into the unknown spaces of the world, but a methodical policy that was trying to tighten control over a pair of ancient and very prosperous trade routes that connected Egypt with the incense trade of Yemen and the maritime spice and silk trade to India.

Just like King Juba II, Octavian employed a native prince of a client kingdom (Nabatea – ancient Jordan) as his researcher–guide, who identified the well-known Arabian ports of Leuke Kome and Aden as the vital forward supply bases. So by 25 BC Octavian was ready to order the Roman governor of Egypt, the prefect Aelius Gallus, to lead a Roman army of 10,000 men into southern Arabia. It would later be written off as just a survey, but it was undoubtedly intended to be a conquest.

The Roman army succeeded in marching the whole way south through Arabia, passing through such future cities as Medina and Mecca, to reach Marib in central Yemen. This could not have been achieved without the close support of a navy, but it came very close to fiasco, as the army was far from prepared for an arduous march through such bleak deserts and mountains. Rome was not the first empire, nor would it be the last, to blunt its teeth on the arid mountains of the Yemen and the hardy tribes who held them.

Octavian soon found out that his grand strategy had been watched by an even more cunning operator. Queen Amanirenas, the one-eyed warrior monarch of the kingdom of Meroe, also had her spies on the ground. She pushed an army north into Roman Egypt from the Sudan, but only after she knew for certain that the Roman army had already got stuck fast in Arabia. She was able to sweep all before her, and at one point seemed on the point of annexing all of southern Egypt south of Thebes to her Sudanese empire, before a combination of Roman military success and diplomacy gradually re-established the frontier. Nearly two thousand years later, the severed bronze head of Octavian, seized during the sack of Aswan, would be found by archaeologists where the queen had buried it, as a victory offering to her gods.

Juba's researches into the landscape, resources and animals of southern Numidia seem to have occupied him for at least two years, around 29–27 BC. He was examining territory that had been known to Carthaginian merchants for centuries, and had once been ruled by his ancestors. The Emperor Octavian was too distracted to make immediate use of his findings, but these years of work on the ground were vital for his books on the flora and fauna of North Africa, which would later be mined and praised by Pliny.

Seven years later, the Emperor Octavian would indeed order a reconnaissance in force of this area. This southern advance of the Roman empire was much better planned than the disastrous Arabian campaign. In 21 BC Augustus proposed that Lucius Cornelius Balbus be made proconsul of Africa, and take on the task of crushing the Berber tribes on the southern frontier. Balbus came from a Jewish family of bankers based in Gades (Cadiz), the ancient Phoenician port at the centre of the metal trade. His uncle, Lucius Cornelius Balbus the elder, had risen to very high office, indeed he may have been the first non-Roman provincial to have achieved the office of consul. He did this by winning the gratitude of Julius Caesar, and then Octavian, as a reliable banker. This skill was matched by discretion, based on a natural modesty and a role so studiously apolitical that he would be appealed to by both sides as a conduit of mercy during some of the worst moments of the civil war proscriptions. His eponymous nephew had become much more embedded in the Roman establishment than his banker uncle, for he had received a thorough education in the army as a young legate, seeing action in both Spain and North Africa. He also continued the strong links that his family enjoyed with both the bullion traders of Gades and the household of the Caesars.

All these skills combined during Balbus's proconsulship of Africa, for he would succeed in taking a Roman army deep into the Sahara desert, where advance preparation and detailed knowledge of the landscape were vital. King Juba had contributed to this – call it staff work or espionage – so all the oasis communities on the route south, such as Cydamus (now Ghadames), were garrisoned well in advance of the progress of the main army. This enabled the Roman legions to move swiftly across the vast expanse of the Libyan Sahara, occupy the Fezzan oasis and storm the hitherto invulnerable hilltop kasbahs of the

Garamantian kingdom. On his return to Rome Balbus would be given a triumph by Octavian – the last one ever to be granted to a general who was not a member of the imperial family. As he was a provincial, a Jew, a banker and a second-generation Roman citizen, to give him this honour may have delighted Octavian – a chance to humiliate the old ruling senatorial class and remind them that their days were over. The emperor's own paternal ancestry, the son of a senator, grandson of a banker, great-grandson of a slave turned rope-maker, might have made him look favourably on such a meritocrat as Balbus, while Juba II, the son of a king, appears to have worked as his spy.

In 26 BC Juba II had been recalled to Rome, where the emperor once again had need of his services. Octavian had decided to personally lead the military campaign against the last group of Iberian tribes that was resisting Roman rule, lodged in the high mountains of Galicia, 'the cliffs to the west of the Pyrenees'. Although encircled by eight legions and five auxiliary cavalry regiments, and with Roman ships patrolling their coast, the free Cantabrian and Astures tribes maintained a steadfast resistance from their mountain-top fortresses. They had served as mercenary soldiers for the Carthaginian empire and the Berber kings for hundreds of years. Their young men were accustomed to dying in foreign wars, but they had never once permitted an enemy into their own homeland.

For Rome to defeat these tribes, the procedure was first to divide them, split up the clans, and make local allies who could be promised the lands of the defeated. This kind of work required men of respect with proven language skills, as well as historians who could analyse the tribal histories and spot ancient blood rivalries and feuds that could be usefully manipulated. Even so, it was a brutal campaign, for in bloody encounter after encounter, the warriors preferred to die rather than surrender. They saw glorious death as a form of union with their deity, which one can try to imagine as something like the warrior cult of the Vikings, who imagined the Valkyries taking only the very bravest of the brave up to heaven, to join the band of immortal warriors gathered around the god Odin. The yew tree that is sacred to Odin, or any of the other names of the Celtic–Germanic god of battles, certainly provided these Spanish warriors with their chosen suicide potion, which was fashioned from yew seeds. The whole episode reminds one of an adventure of Asterix and Obelix – but in reverse, for the good guys' magic potion is poison and the Romans win.

This war had been planned as a quick and easy conquest, which would round out Roman territory and reduce the size of the permanent garrison. It became a campaign of attrition so exhausting and dispiriting that the Emperor Octavian refused to celebrate his ultimate victory with a triumph, and seems to have caused him some sort of physical collapse – he was never a very convincing soldier. But he did not forget his coterie of reliable old friends. Sometime towards the end of this war, he decided to give Juba II a wife and a kingdom of his own. Our knowledge of the date is shaky, but between the years 26 and 20 BC Juba II was made king of Mauretania and given Cleopatra Selene, one of the daughters of Cleopatra and Mark Antony, as his wife. She came equipped with an enormous dowry. She, like Juba, had done well to survive thus far, and probably owed this to the fact that she had grown up in the household of Octavia, Augustus' beloved elder sister. Even so, it helped enormously that she was a woman. Neither her twin brother, Alexander Helios (who was aged ten when his father and mother lost the battle of Actium), nor her younger brother, Philadelphus, reached manhood. They may have been permitted their child-hood, but as male heirs of the Ptolemaic dynasty, blended with the warrior blood of Mark Antony, and half-brothers of Caesarion, it was not expedient for them to survive. They were far too much of a risk to be allowed out into the political world.

But now at last textual history and traveller's myth do seem to connect. For twenty years Juba II and Cleopatra Selene did indeed rule their own client kingdom from their own capital city. There were some bizarre elements behind Octavian's decision. Juba II, the heir of the Numidian kings, was ruling over the territory and people of their most ancient rivals, who in war after war down several centuries had done all they could to harm and hurt each other. No modern parallel will serve, but you could try thinking how well an American might be regarded as a presidential candidate in Mexico, or a Turk as a prime minister in Athens or Armenia. Nor do we know what happened to the dynasty of real Mauretanian kings, the grandchildren of Bocchus I, the sons and cousins of Bocchus II, who may have been of the line of Syphax. They had served as useful allies of Rome for the last 150 years, and Bocchus II had willed his kingdom to Octavian after his death. By the spread of coin finds in the area around Cherchell, one can hazard a guess that Juba II's authority was supported by Spanish auxiliaries, maybe veterans of that gruelling war of attrition in the far north. Certainly that is the axis of connection that is suggested by the inscriptions that were raised to Juba II in the Spanish ports of Gades and Cartagena – both cities that also looked back to a Phoenician past. One can also hazard a guess that Octavian was less interested in the rough Berber hinterland of Mauretania than in any light that Juba II could shed about the old lucrative trade routes of the Carthaginians – especially the gold trade of the Western Atlantic seaboard. This would also explain why it was that Juba II is recorded as mounting costly naval expeditions into the Western Atlantic, and discovering and reporting on the Canary Islands.

There was a lot to sort out. The whole region of Mauretania existed in a form of legal limbo. None of the port-cities of this most western part of North Africa, or the inland marketplaces that sat astride wide river estuaries, had ever been formally conquered by any Roman legion. Most of them had existed in some form of treaty relationship with ancient Carthage for hundreds of years, but by the end of the Second Punic War this had either slipped into independence or some sort of relationship with the Berber Mauretanian kings, themselves allies of Rome. As we have already heard, in 33 BC the last of these kings had 'bequeathed' his kingdom to Octavian, well before his victory over Mark Antony.

All the Mauretanian ports had a tradition of looking for cultural leadership to Gades (an even older city than Carthage), which had long practised a much more humane version of the Canaanite–Phoenician belief system. No child sacrifices to the Mother Goddess have yet been found in Gades (or any of the Phoenician cities of westernmost Mauretania). Indeed, Gades was famous for its great ancient temple–shrine to Hercules, which did not permit any blood sacrifices at all, and which was controlled by a remarkably ascetic-sounding body of priests. Hercules is also an intriguing figure to choose as the central spiritual patron of a city. He is a doomed wanderer who grew out of the Phoenician cult of Melkarth, the King of the City, mixed up with ancient Semitic elements of the story of Gilgamesh, the questing hero who despite his great qualities proves to be a mere doomed mortal, fated to die a horrible, almost self-sacrificial, death before he is reborn.

Gades was physically isolated from the Spanish hinterland, a low-lying lagoon sitting in the centre of a vast shallow bay. So despite the evidence of our maps, imaginatively shaded with different colours for the different Roman provinces in this region, the real active connections were ones that criss-crossed these provincial frontiers. The ports were in conversation, and the Spanish and North African coastal cities had much more in common with each other than with their own hinterlands. The coastal geography of southern Spain, northern Morocco and western Algeria is remarkably similar. They all possess a narrow fringe of cultivated Mediterranean agriculture along their coast, and behind it vast stretches of highland. So each port along the coast of North Africa flourished by exporting from its hinterland the common currencies of Mediterranean life, primarily the great staples of the interior such as grain and olive oil, bolstered by other goods – metals, wax, honey, wild animals, slaves. In exchange the city merchants could offer such things as salt, fish, salted fish, and such imports as fine wine, metalware and textiles.

All this is written in the reality of Juba II's city of Cherchell, defended by walls that did not date back to the Punic or Roman civil wars, but were built to keep the potentially hostile Berber tribes of the interior from sacking the rich city on the coast. The next-door port city of Tipaza is similarly well equipped with strong walls: a stone-and-mortar illustration of how much a Mediterranean city might safely trust the hinterland above it.

Juba II would have discovered this for himself, but the Roman governors who succeeded him also made little impact on the basic political geography. In terms of large-scale transport, roads in Mauretania never became as important as coastal shipping. We still have found no evidence that a road was ever constructed to connect the two halves of Roman Mauretania, between northern Morocco (Mauretania Tingitana) and western Algeria (Mauretania Caesariensis). In times of trouble, the Mauretanian cities did not look to the North African legion for support, but received reinforcements from the Spanish garrisons. You would find soldiers from the IX Hispana (Spanish) Legion, not the III Augusta, in these cities.

So this is the world that Juba II would have tried to rule as the client king of Mauretania. He was not, like his ancestors, the lord of the vast interior and commander of a hundred thousand horses. He was a city-dwelling intellectual, loyally occupying an administrative post at the direction of his master, the first emperor of Rome. From the evidence of inscriptions we can tell that this city of Cherchell was occupied by a large number of citizens descended from Greek slaves and Greek freedmen. This is the only such instance in all the cities of North Africa (which normally exported slaves and did not import them). There are two schools of thought about this: is it evidence of a naval garrison (for the Roman navy was effectively recruited from such Greek-speaking cities as Tarentum), or were they loyal palace staff from the court of Juba and Cleopatra, recruited from Alexandria?

Caesarea in this period was one of the four naval bases of the empire, alongside Classe (near Ravenna), Misenum (near Naples) and Forum Julii (present-day Fréjus) in the south of France. The Roman navy was never the senior service; indeed it was the reverse, recruited entirely from ex-slaves, Greeks, Syrians and Egyptians. A galley crew comprised a hundred rowers (25 oars on each side of a galley with two men to an oar) who could achieve 7 knots on a calm day or 14 when they were under sail. A dozen petty-officer sailors ran the boat, among them the helmsman (*gubernator*), a supervisor of rowers (*celeusta*), the lookout (*proreta*) and *iatros* (ship's doctor), under the command of the captain (*trierarchus*).

A squadron was formed from ten galleys under the command of a *navarchus*, and so it is thought that the harbour at Caesarea might at times have housed a fleet of three squadrons under a *navarchus princeps* – an admiral. Their primary task was to keep a lid on piracy (especially against the unconquered tribes along the Mauretanian coast), so that the sea lanes remained safe for the eight hundred grain ships that every year poured 40 million measures of corn into the granaries of Rome. When Octavian was planning a war, the various naval bases would be stripped to a skeleton force in order to provide an operating fleet, such as the 130 ships that supported his Arabian adventure. On other occasions, such as for Juba's exploration of the Atlantic coast of Morocco, and south down to the Canary Islands, the Caesarea fleet might have itself been augmented.

Juba II would have been powerless in terms of the practical military authority he wielded in the interior (the historic lands of his dynasty's oldest enemy). He remained completely dependent on Rome for his military security, and so had no temptation to even dream of establishing himself as the true Berber monarch of North Africa. Instead his designated task seems to have been to sort out the relationship between the various port cities of this region, using the fleet in his harbour. Juba II clearly played many different roles as the agent of Octavian, for in inscriptions raised to him in both Gades and Cartagena he is referred to not as *rex*, but as *duumvir*, not king but city consul. I have already suggested that his master Octavian was probably interested to learn if there was any chance of opening up Carthage's former gold trade with West Africa, via merchant-venturers working the trade routes of the Western Sahara. This would tie in with what the emperor had been up to on the other edge of Africa, exploring the Red Sea trade routes that led to the spices of the Indies and the silks of China.

Octavian, ever the man to learn from his mistakes, had shed the desire to conquer Arabia. On the south-eastern edge of his empire he had resumed the expedient of an annual fleet of merchant ships (100–200 strong) working the monsoon seasons. It is not impossible that Juba II was in command, or helped oversee a similar policy on the south-western edge of the empire. Archaeologists have found evidence that during the reign of Octavian drafts of Roman colonists were inserted into many of the small trading towns and ports on Morocco's Atlantic coast, as suggested by those charmingly neglected excavations in north-west Morocco, Banassa and Thamusida, converted from a mire of riverine silt, and which both had access to the sea through their riverine ports. There was clearly a very skilful diplomat–administrator at work on the edge of this empire, for ports such as Sala and Lixus (again associated with river-front harbours not directly perched on the coast) remained in legal terms just an 'ally' of the Roman empire and were not yet included in the provincial administration. They too show evidence of enthusiastic Romanisation during this period, constructing their own amphitheatre, forum and Capitoline temples, architectural showpieces directly connected to what was being built at Rome at this time.

In Cherchell, Juba II's wife gave birth to a child, who was named Ptolemy. Once again we cannot be certain of a date, but some time between 10 and 5 BC seems most likely. All the males in her mother's family had been named Ptolemy, which gave them a direct link to the youthful companion of Alexander the Great who would rise through the ranks to become one of his most powerful generals. Much has been made of this Hellenistic identity, rather than the selection of any of the names of Juba's own Numidian royal family. 'Cleopatra' is not of course an Egyptian word, but Greek, combining *kleo* and *patra* – 'father's glory'. Queen Cleopatra's father was one of Julius Caesar's greatest generals and also his second cousin, so despite her Ptolemaic blood she also had lots of important relations in Rome. Naming her son Mark Antony after his grandfather would not have been a politic thing to do during the reign of Octavian.

A couple of years later, a message came from Octavian (now renamed Augustus Caesar) giving Juba II a new task. He was to drop his work as the licensed king of Mauretania, leave his young family and sail at once for Rome. Augustus wanted Juba (who would then have been about forty-eight years old) to travel with his grandson, Gaius Caesar, to the East. It was intended to be an apprenticeship in the arts of governing a great empire for this young man who had already been anointed heir to his grandfather. His young brother was to remain in the western half of the empire. Gaius was one of the two sons of the marriage between Julia (only daughter of Octavian) and General Agrippa – his ever-loyal ally.

It was a personal honour for Juba II that the Emperor Octavian retained such implicit trust in him. We don't know Juba's function, but he was probably one of a handful of wise older men who formed a body of counsellors for young Gaius Caesar. Octavian may also have thought that in the East, which was still dominated by hereditary monarchies, it would look impressive for the young Gaius Caesar to be seen to be employing kings in his court – literally to be a King of Kings. The tour was open-ended. It has attracted much speculative attention over the years, as it coincides with the birth of Jesus. It seems that Gaius Caesar and his entourage sailed to Antioch then marched through the Syrian frontier before proceeding further east in order to secure the Parthian frontier. A peace treaty was signed with Phraates V, the young Parthian monarch of the same age as Gaius, on an island in the Euphrates. With this most troublesome of all frontiers secure, the Roman army was free to turn its attention to Eastern Anatolia, and imposed its preferred candidate as the new king of Armenia.

During this period, presumably as part of a diplomatic campaign to win over local allies, Juba II acquired a second wife, Princess Glaphyra, daughter of King Archelaus of Cappadocia. Like his first wife, she was proud of her royal ancestors, who included the kings of Pontus and half a dozen of the great Hellenistic dynasties. Indeed we know that her blood pride had already made her a rather taxing presence for the Herodian princesses at Jerusalem when she had dwelt among them as a daughter-in-law of Herod the Great.

On 9 September AD 2, Gaius Caesar was stabbed during negotiations held outside the siege of the fortress of Artagira (near Ararat), and eighteen months later he died of these wounds whilst being nursed on the coast of Lycia, on 21 February AD 4. Juba II no doubt made his own personal report to the grief-stricken Octavian, who had already lost his other younger grandson and designated heir (Lucius). Juba II left his second wife in the East (she later married a third husband), but he may have brought home a daughter from this relationship, perhaps the Princess Drusilla of Mauretania whom we hear about in inscriptions.

Now aged over fifty, Juba II was at last free to return to Cherchell. His wife had ruled as regent in his long absence, and it may have been in this period that she ordered the striking of her own coinage. Historians consider that a charming epigraph composed in her honour, which links her death to an eclipse of the moon, will give us the exact date of her death:

The moon herself grew dark, rising at sunset,
Covering her suffering in the night,
Because she saw her beautiful namesake, Selene,
Breathless, descending to Hades,
With her she had had the beauty of her light in common,

And mingled her own darkness with her death.

But from my own experience of the time-keeping habits of poets, I think they are almost certainly torturing this metaphor (which plays on the meaning of her name, Selene – the moon) to produce a date for an exact lunar eclipse (such as in AD 5 or 8) that it was never intended to reveal. Certainly a hoard of silver coins struck with the image of Queen Cleopatra of Mauretania has been securely dated to AD 17. This date would suggest that Juba II and Cleopatra Selene enjoyed fifteen years of companionship together in Cherchell.

This is the period that most readily frees one's imagination to wander and build cities in the air, for it is essentially the only time when they could have been ornamenting their capital city with their own seaside palace, a royal library and a theatre, as well as contriving the route of the splendid aqueduct that would enable the city's fountains to gush with spectacular flows of sparkling-fresh spring-water, wetting the marbles and mosaics into life. Juba II had finished all his travels. He had seen Arabia, Anatolia, the Sahara, the Pillars of Hercules, northern Spain, western Greece, Armenia and Syria for himself, and would have had the time to pull together all his travel notes and complete his various histories and geographies. There would have been a full-time library staff at hand to help with summaries and then write up fine copies, to be sent to the scholars and chief libraries of the empire. I long for a sealed jar to be discovered in a desert cave packed full of scrolls, and his works to return to our shelves, sitting beside Pliny and Tacitus.

Their son Ptolemy saw service with the various auxiliary regiments that guarded Mauretania, and may also have been given a spell as an honorary legate (a junior trainee officer) in the official Roman legions that were stationed in nearby Numidia. For there was trouble on the southern frontier and the army was continually being beefed up in this period. In AD 21, the thirty-year-old Prince Ptolemy was officially appointed heir and co-monarch of Mauretania. Two years later he was on hand to escort his royal father to his grave. Juba II had achieved the ripe old age of seventy-five.

I have imagined Juba II's death.

He was first laid out in his palace with his feet facing the main gate, wrapped in a purple toga picked out with thread of gold. The votive crowns and honours he had been awarded in his life were lovingly placed around him, with the secret jewel-like totems that would assist him in his journey through the after-life. The palace courtyards rang with the mourners' shrill cries. When his cortege was ready, he would be taken to the central square of his capital, where his son and heir would mount a rostral platform and deliver the long eulogy. Then the body would be removed from the city of the living and make its solemn way out towards the city of the dead, which stretched beyond the walls. Accompanying the cortege would be the faces of his ancestors, their masks worn by honoured members of his court and tribal chiefs, attended by marble busts draped in royal purple carried by magistrates and the chief officers of the urban guilds. So a complete genealogy of walking ancestral spirits escorted him to the Elysian Fields, their pace directed by the funeral drones of bronze horns. A vast funeral pyre orna-mented with rare woods would consume his body, the fires quickened with scented and precious oils. Sacrifices would be made there, mostly of pigs, to appease the deities of the Under-world, the gathered spirits, and to feed the vast crowd with a form of last communion. Nine days later his ashes, gathered in a silver casket chased with gold, were conveyed up to the magnificent mausoleum that stood on a hill a day's ride outside the city. The doors of the mausoleum were resealed.

Some thought that the great mausoleum that he and his queen constructed had been consciously modelled on the circular mausoleum that Augustus had built for himself outside the city walls of Rome, looking out over the Field of Mars and the altar of peace. Others saw echoes of the great tomb of Mausolus, whilst only the tribal lords of the interior would know that it was virtually a carbon copy of the great ancestral tomb of the Numidian kings that lay on the frontiers of the great desert. These vast circular tombs were an intensely potent element of the Berber culture of North Africa that was never allowed to die. Six hundred years later (the same period that separates us from Agincourt) a renascent dynasty of Berber lords, recovering their freedom from the embers of the Byzantine empire, would build their royal tombs on exactly the same architectural model.

On the forty-second day after his death, a vast and dangerous crowd would have assembled, drawn by another great round of sacrifices. Oxen would have been slaughtered, butchered and cooked on great open-air altars. Tribal chieftains and Berber clansmen drawn from the vast interior would have been included in this festival crowd, which mixed the Mediterranean culture of the coastal cities with something much more elemental and popular, Berber and African. The mausoleum would have shone bright with a fresh coat of stained lime, a vast, empty temple that stood at the centre of a sea of thousands of tents and huts. Behind the rituals, the chants, the scent of burning fat, the corrals of horses, the separate enclosures for the 463 Berber tribes, something else hung in the air. Which according to your viewpoint contained the exhilarating sharp essence of freedom or the stink of treachery.

Or so I hope. We don't know for certain that Juba II and his queen built the structure that we now know as the Tomb of the Christian Woman. Some scholars have started to argue that it is actually a much older structure, built by one of their political predecessors, such as Bocchus or Syphax. However we can be reasonably sure that they made use of it, for a few decades after Juba II's death the tomb would be described by a Roman travel writer.

Pomponius Mela was a geographer, born into a small Romano-Phoenician fishing port that stood in the Bay of Algeciras, in the lee of Mons Calpe, the great Pillar of Hercules that we now know as Gibraltar. He was a diligent scholar, touched with something of the pedant. He collected together all the old sailing itineraries, cross-checked them with his own travels and assembled them all to make a hundred-page geographical description of the known world, fanning out from his home, beside the Mons Calpe. Certainly the closer his geography is to the sea routes out from Gibraltar, the more accurate he becomes. He is one of our best sources for the obscure trade routes that snake their way north along the Bay of Biscay towards the British Isles, and he was the first to name the Orkney Isles.

In about AD 43 (he died in 45) Pomponius describes the mausoleum on his maritime route along the North African coast, by briefly mentioning that east of Iol–Caesarea, 'on its far side is the common tomb of the royal family'. It is a terse enough phrase, but is evidence that places Queen Cleopatra Selene and King Juba II within this structure, and also provides room to speculate that earlier rulers may also have been placed here.

The Berbers were renowned for the respect with which they treated their heroic dead, whom they venerated as deified ancestor spirits. These powerful spirits of the dead (known to the Romans as *Manes*) communicated with the living through dreams and divination rituals that took place in the shadow of their tombs. They may have given advice to the living about how best to appease the Great God, or merely have been fed with praise and offerings so that they did not maliciously haunt the living. There is consistent evidence of pilgrim-like rituals that involved circumlocution (prayerful holy walks around tombs) while fasts, vigils and sacrifices prepared the pilgrim for the holy sleep that might produce a propitious dream. Celebrating the anniversary of an honoured ancestor was also the occasion for a family gathering, and the more revered the ancestor, the bigger this communal feast, so it could grow into an annual clan gathering that was the spiritual linchpin behind a great gathering of the tribes. For a revered spirit-ancestor could provide the authority for a truce from blood feuds, the security of merchandise, and also watch over fair dealing among the traders. The great popularity of these tomb-centred ritual gatherings would also explain why the royal tomb was not placed outside the capital city (like that of Augustus just outside the walls of Rome, or Alexander within Alexandria) but at a safe 20-kilometre distance, allowing vast tribal crowds to gather without endangering the life of the city.

The collective cult of the royal ancestors may also have upheld the authority of the Berber kingdoms. Tithes of the annual harvests, be they assessed in the gathered corn, or a percentage of the newborn from the great herds or horses and cattle, may have been collected on behalf of these powerful dead ancestors, who in return worked for the fertility of the land. We have tiny fragments of evidence, partial inscriptions not conclusively dated, that suggest that Juba II's son, King Ptolemy of Mauretania, was working within these deep-rooted Berber traditions. He appears to have added his great-grandfather, King Hiempsal of Numidia, to the royal ancestral cult, and allowed himself to be seen as the priestlike intercessor with the Great God Saturn, who throughout North Africa was revered before all others as the true manifestation of the Father of Gods.

King Ptolemy had also greatly increased his personal standing in North Africa by his involvement in the last military campaign against the rebel Tacfarinas. A nine-year guerrilla war had been smouldering away in the southern mountains of Numidia, spearheaded by Tacfarinas' Musulamii tribe. Ptolemy's old father, Juba II, had not involved himself in any of the military campaigns waged by a succession of Roman governors against this tribe. In the very first year of his reign, King Ptolemy (perhaps aged thirty-six at the time) had commanded a cavalry army that worked beside the Roman legions to hunt down this rebel leader, who was finally caught and killed at Auzia (modern Sour el-Ghozlane, which lies about 100 kilometres south-east of Algiers). The young king became the hero of the hour, and a Roman senator was dispatched from Rome to dub him with the title of '*Rex, Socius et Amicus Populi Romani*' (King, Ally and Friend of the People of Rome) and invest him with an ivory sceptre of authority and the purple toga of a king. His father would have swelled with pride for his boy, whose authority over the Berber tribes of the hinterland would have been much enhanced by this military victory. King Ptolemy ruled his kingdom for a further fourteen years.

King Ptolemy was summoned to Rome by the Emperor Caligula in AD 40. We know that Caligula had plans to visit Alexandria and the eastern empire. He might have thought to continue a tradition, so that having King Ptolemy in his suite would be much like Juba II serving as the adviser to Gaius Caesar. They were also cousins.

Instead he had him murdered. It is said that Caligula grew envious after the crowd in the amphitheatre of Rome roared out a greeting to King Ptolemy, dressed in his magnificent purple toga, that was louder than his own applause. The kingdom of Mauretania was annexed, divided into two halves and placed under direct Roman imperial administration.

We have no idea of Caligula's motives. He may have simply wished to add a new province to the empire. He may have taken fright at the growth of King Ptolemy's prestige in North Africa, and decided to nip any potential rebellion in the bud by a brutal act of realpolitik that at least spared the region another round of seven years of war, such as Rome had waged against both Tacfarinas and Jugurtha.

Caligula's upbringing as a powerless seven-year house guest of the Emperor Tiberius may have infected his psyche. He alone had survived (through his mild-mannered charm) whilst all the rest of his talented family (including his mother) had been either executed or assassinated. He would repeat these actions, culling his cousins out of paranoia muddled up with fears about his own worth. Caligula had had no military or administrative experience before he became emperor. Ptolemy, a fifty-year-old king with military experience and twenty years of ruling, would have elicited all of Caligula's fears, rational or not. They were cousins who shared Mark Antony as a grandfather, but there were important differences. Ptolemy, through his other grandparents, was descended from two royal dynasties, while Caligula loathed the memory of his plebeian grandfather Agrippa, that brilliant general and loyal ally of Augustus, purely because he was a new man. So probably for all these reasons, the emperor had his cousin and guest cut down by his personal German bodyguards without trial and then annexed the last independent kingdom of North Africa to the empire.

I hope that Ptolemy's ashes were sent back across the ocean

on board a galley dressed with black sails, cruising in the wake of an official squadron filled with Roman officers ready to annex his kingdom and clerks dispatched to make an inventory of all his lands and possessions. I am certainly tempted to place such an urn in the third niche in the modest tomb room that archaeologists have discovered in the centre of the royal mausoleum, approached through a long internal corridor that almost describes a complete circle of the massive stonework of the monument before heading for its centre. But those with an understanding of the ritual importance of number will have already counted the sixty engaged columns that encircle the mausoleum. They will know that sixty is the base figure for the oldest spiritual reckoning of the universe, how the sages of ancient Sumeria had divided the sky into six houses of sixty degrees, how they also proportioned time on this same sacred scale of sixty seconds within a minute, just as sixty minutes made an hour; how sixty was also a symbol for the eternal one, just as their notation for 1 was a simple wedge and sixty marked with a great wedge. They will also have been intrigued by the number of niches that have been set into the internal corridor that winds within the mausoleum. It might be just chance that there are forty-two, or it might be a conscious playing with the sacred resonance of that number in Egypt. Not only was the great kingdom astride the Nile divided into forty-two parts, but the great hall of death was governed by forty-two judges, and the dead soul was expected to be able to make forty-two confessions based on the forty-two moral codes of Maat, the ancient personification of justice.

Caligula did not long outlive his crime, for he was killed just six months after the murder of his cousin Ptolemy. The throne was then passed to his uncle Claudius, in January AD 41, at the insistence of the Praetorian Guard. Claudius, like Juba II, had survived the murderous jealousies of the royal court by keeping his head down and writing histories.

There had however been a reaction to the injustice of Ptolemy's murder. An official of the royal Mauretanian court, a Greek named Aedemon, led a revolt against the Roman usurpation. But now it was Claudius' turn to make history, not just record it. In AD 41 he sent a promising young Roman official, Caius Suetonius Paulinus, who ruled as the first governor of the new province of Mauretania. He had just served his term as praetor, one of the dozen administrative judges in Rome. Paulinus also came from just the sort of middle-ranking Italian provincial family that the imperial court tended to favour. We think he came from Pesaro, a Roman colony on the Adriatic shore of northern Italy. Young men from the old senatorial families of Rome were seldom trusted with military commands. Most of the port cities on the coast of Mauretania had remained obedient, as did the dozen or so towns of the interior, whose loyalty had been beefed up with discharged veterans over the last forty years.

Aedemon's brave gesture of revolt did not last long, but his example stirred the Berber tribes of the interior into rebellion. We do not know if they rode to war in support of the murdered Prince Ptolemy or for the very good reason that their lands would now be assessed and taxed like every other conquered province of the Roman empire. The decision as to which side each tribe would take was crucial, so Tangier (Roman Tingis), one of the key ports of the area, was sacked, though the city of Volubilis, locked deep in the interior of Morocco and overlooked by a spur of the Rif mountains, survived. The leadership of a local Berber magistrate, Marcus Valerius Severus, played a key part, but he must surely have had a close relationship with the powerful Baquates tribe for the city to have survived, for the scale and ferocity of the Berber rebellion took the emperor and his governors by surprise, as did the reports of the vast mountain ranges and depth of Mauretania.

Their decision was a wise one, which was to divide the province in two, make peace with the tribes in the eastern half of Mauretania (by keeping the Roman occupation to the coastal strip) and concentrate all their military energy on the western half. The frontier of the two new provinces was sensibly placed on the river Moulouya, an ancient boundary that for centuries had divided the Berber kingdoms. Four legions assisted by auxiliary cavalry were rushed into northern Morocco, which was now renamed as the new province of Mauretania Tingitana. The towns were defended by forts and watchtowers, while mobile columns tracked down concentrations of the enemy. Gaius Hosidius Geta was one of the legionary commanders operating under Suetonius Paulinus' authority. He had been given command of the IX Hispana Legion, which had served in Augustus' rather brutal subjection of northern Spain, but was now sent south across the Strait of Gibraltar to fight in Morocco.

Geta managed to engage one of the Berber warrior chieftains, Sabalus, in two pitched battles and then led his legion in pursuit, marching south into a desert region. But at one point it became clear that the pursuers were about to become the pursued, as the fast-moving Roman force ran out of water. Sabalus' scouts observed the sufferings of the Romans and each day reported the situation to their master, who was biding his time to mount his counter-attack. As the noose tightened around the embattled Romans, Sabalus crept forward with his scouts to make his own observation, but at the eleventh hour the pious Roman general ordered his troops to follow the advice of his Berber auxiliaries and propitiate their gods with a rain ritual, with offerings of prayer, dedication and sacrifices which included their last reserves of water and wine. When that evening it began to rain on the Roman camp, Sabalus was so impressed by the way the gods had favoured the Romans that he rode up to their camp and offered his surrender. We cannot tie this story to any specific geographical region, but the following description that Pliny gives us clearly ties in with a crossing of the Middle and High Atlas passes by the Roman army and a descent into the Sahara.

Suetonius Paulinus, whom we have seen Consul in our own time, was the first Roman general who advanced a distance of some miles beyond Mount Atlas. He has given us the same information as we have received from other sources with reference to the extraordinary height of this mountain, and at the same time he has stated that all the lower parts about the foot of it are covered with dense and lofty forests composed of trees of species hitherto unknown. The height of these trees, he says, is remarkable; the trunks are without knots, and of a smooth and glossy surface; the foliage is like that of the cypress, and besides sending forth a powerful odour, they are covered with a flossy down, from which, with skill, a fine cloth might easily be manufactured, similar to the textures made from the produce of the silkworm. He informs us that the summit of this mountain is covered with snow even in summer, and says that having arrived there after a march of ten days, he proceeded some distance beyond it as far as a river that bears the name of Ger; the road being through deserts covered with a black sand, from which rocks that bore the appearance of having been exposed to the action of fire protruded every here and there; localities rendered quite uninhabitable by the intensity of the heat, as he himself experienced, although it was in the winter season that he visited them.

From these two accounts of the victorious achievements of the Roman military columns led by Paulinus and Geta, which succeeded in plunging deep into southern Morocco, to the edge of the Sahara, one might expect a vastly enlarged new province of Mauretania. But the reality on the ground is very different from that purveyed by literary propaganda. The Romans never conquered the rich agrarian plateau of south–central Morocco, never built forts to watch over the Rif mountains, the Middle Atlas, the High Atlas or Anti-Atlas mountains. Instead their rule focused on just the coastal plain of the north-western coast, which to put it into a British context is like being content with occupying Kent and Essex but ignoring the rest of the country. In modern Moroccan terms, all the great centres of power and wealth, such as Fez, Meknes, Marrakesh, Agadir and Casablanca, remained beyond the Roman frontier.

Nowhere is the limited nature of the Roman occupation more apparent than in the city of Volubilis. This commercial centre of the interior, with a population of 20,000, was only held secure by a circle of five cavalry forts that surrounded the city like a suburban ring on the near horizon, beyond which stretched the unsubdued mountains. Clearly something had gone wrong with this three-year military operation, which had tied up four legions out of the total twenty-five that held down the entire empire. Perhaps the great military expeditions had proved to the generals on the ground that although the Berber tribes of Morocco could be defeated in battle, the empire didn't have the resources to conquer this land composed of four mountain chains. Perhaps the traditional society of the Berber tribes remained too nomadic for a land tax on crops ever to be worth collecting. Perhaps the casualty rate of this disorganised guerrilla war, which had begun as a rebellion, had simply been too high. And perhaps the war had not been nearly as successful as we were told. Powerful tribal units such as the Baquates of central Morocco were confirmed in their total independence. It is hardly conceivable that the rich lands they occupied were not at the centre of the old Berber kingdom of Mauretania ruled over by Bocchus, while the Roman governor and his four legionary commanders seem to have been left in control of only what they could hold with troops on the ground.

A truce was made, for the legions had also been ordered out – they were needed elsewhere. The unglamorous suppression of a revolt in the south-western corner province of an old client kingdom was set aside. It had never been a planned operation, just the disorderly outcome of a crime in the last months of Caligula's reign.

Claudius, the new emperor, now wanted to concentrate on a conquest that he could call his own, and had fixed his eye on another westernmost corner of the empire, the island of Britain. It also had useful associations with Julius Caesar. So Geta and his IX Hispana Legion were recalled from the Moroccan campaign and summoned to the beachheads of France, where they drilled alongside the XX Valeria Victrix, XIV Gemina and II Augusta legions – the latter under the command of a promising young general called Vespasian. They invaded Britain in AD 43. Geta would nearly be killed at the crossing of the river Medway, but he survived and turned that day into a victory. He would retire in honour to Rome, serve as consul, and father noble children (his granddaughter Vitoria would marry Lucius Septimius Severus, of whose family we will hear more later). His legion, the IX Hispana, remained in Britain, and the forts they built would one day blossom into the cities of Lincoln and York.

This regiment was twice nearly obliterated, at Colchester and north of the Forth, before falling in AD 108 – if, like me, you remain bewitched by Rosemary Sutcliff's story of *The Eagle of the Ninth*. His old colleague from the Mauretanian campaign, Caius Suetonius Paulinus, would also serve on this bloody northern front when his orderly campaign of conquest erupted into the nightmare of another uprising, that of Boudicca's revolt. There never was a time when this conquering army of four legions in the British Isles could be reduced in number to a tidy garrison, so they were never free to return and finish off the job of conquering Morocco.

Rome never completed its campaign for the conquest in Mauretania. The truncated little province of Mauretania Tingitana sat completely unconnected to the rest of North Africa, surrounded in every direction by free Berber tribes, and the lines of its frontier based on the reach of the Ninth's old campaign. But there were no longer four legions to enforce even this. Instead there was just a junior governor based on the port of Tangier (who was not an ex-consul but an ex-praetor). They served in this post for three years at a time, borrowing a scratch garrison from spare cohorts lent by the legions in Spain. It worked for a while, but during the reign of Marcus Aurelius this rudimentary presence was tested by a widespread Mauretanian revolt that encouraged the cities to look to their own defence. This was the period when both the cities of Volubilis and Cherchell wrapped themselves up in a strong ring of Roman-era walls. A hundred years later, in around 281, the Baquates tribe stormed the defences of Volubilis and the other cities of the interior. General Maximian, the soldier son of a Serbian shopkeeper, chosen by Diocletian as his hard-hitting military co-emperor, set up his headquarters in Tangier, but was wise enough not to take on tribes that even in the heyday of the empire had never been subdued. Instead he 'restored' the empire in Mauretania to the defensible ports of Tangier and Septem (Ceuta), just the northern hub of Morocco – in British terms this is a bit like holding on to just Dover and Ramsgate.

And this was how things endured into the Middle Ages, albeit with the tattered silk robes of imperium now maintained by no troops on the ground and a polite fiction. For it seems that the Berber lord of the Ghomara tribe (who have always occupied the western Rif mountains) was raised above his peers by being invested by the Byzantine emperor as a military count. They liked this dignity. We know the name of one of these local lords, Julian, while another might be listed very grandly as Urban, Exarch of Africa. In exchange for the formal robes of office, the folding ivory diploma and tapestry slippers shipped from the court of Constantinople, he acted as a sort of honorary consul for the distant empire. From his position of power in the Berber highlands, he managed to deny the port of Tangier to the invading Arabs. But it is as Count Julian of the ancient Phoenician–Roman port of Septem that he is remembered by the storytellers. They tell how he sent his daughter Florinda to the court of good King Witiza the Visigoth at Toledo, where she received the finest education, and also served as both ambassador and hostage for her father's good behaviour. But after the king's death, Roderick (the Visigothic duke of Baetica, more or less modern Andalusia) seized control of half the kingdom and then compounded his crime of usurpation by seducing Count Julian's daughter and sending her back home, pregnant and dishonoured.

She is the aggrieved 'Kubr er-Rumia' of Arab legend, the vengeful La Cavia Rumia of the Spaniards, endowed with the evil eye, who is destined to bring down a whole kingdom. For her father, Count Julian, became obsessed with the idea of vengeance against Roderick. His ships were dispatched to scout out the coast of Spain for weak spots while his agents started talking to the partisans of Prince Achila (who ruled north-east Spain as the legitimate Visigothic heir) in order to foment further discord among the Visigoths. And having done his best to prevent the Arab armies from conquering his homeland, he now sent an ambassador to their headquarters in Kairouan, offering a military alliance. Musa ben Nasser seized the opportunity and appointed Tariq ibn Ziyad, one of his trusted Berber deputies (from an ancient Zenata lineage within the Nefzawi tribe), to set up a garrison in Tangier. Once this was safely achieved, he gave him licence to lead a small raiding force across the Strait of Gibraltar, and report back on the state of the Spanish kingdom. But Tariq was also advised and encouraged by Count Julian, who had ships, safe anchorages and allies already in place, so Tariq was able to increase his army from a raiding force of 1,000 men to an army of 7,000 Berber cavalry. This force of very recent Berber converts to Islam left from the Byzantine docks of Ceuta cheered on by its Berber Christian inhabitants. They landed at Algeciras (one of Count Julian's possessions) and then advanced to make their own base, by occupying the fortress peninsula of Gibraltar that stood across the Bay – subsequently named, from this event, Jebel Tariq, Tariq's mountain. His enemies whispered that it was here that Tariq set up court like an independent monarch, advised by his ambitious young concubine, the slave girl Umm Hakim. I hope that came about.

Roderick, the ruler of the Visigoths, had been campaigning against the Basques in the north of Spain, and now sped south to confront this new threat. The actual site of the battle of Guadelete River is not known for certain, but was somewhere in the region of those two austerely beautiful towns Medina

Sidonia and Jerez de la Frontera. The battle was hard-fought and bloody, but Roderick had been doomed from the start by the defection of the two commanders of his right and left wings, Sigbert and Osbert, which allowed the Berber cavalry to launch attack after attack on his beleaguered centre. Roderick perished in the fighting, but his body was never found and so escaped the final cuts of vengeance from Count Julian, though a bloodied golden slipper (washed up on a river bank) was later identified as his.

Tariq ibn Ziyad had lost a third of his men in the fighting, but was advised by Count Julian not to rest but to strike quickly. They rode straight to the capital of Toledo, which fell, complete with its royal administration, into their hands. The already divided Visigothic kingdom now toppled into further anarchy as each noble struggled to assert himself, allowing Musa ben Nasser to cross over and complete the Arab conquest of Spain. Musa sent an official written order that reprimanded his deputy, Tariq ibn Ziyad, for exceeding his orders, but it did no good. So astonishing a triumph must not go unpunished. They would both incur the envy of their master, the Umayyad caliph at Damascus, who found reasons to recall both of them for 'consultations'. Both of these two heroes, Musa and Tariq, were investigated, then stripped of their wealth and left to die in disgrace. The caliph's spies thought they had smelled a whiff of treason among all their astonishing victories and conquests, for they followed a line of reasoning that suggested that as well as avenging his daughter's disgrace, Count Julian might be working towards a Byzantine reconquest of Spain, by first destroying the power of the Visigoths.

The evil eye of Kubr-er-Rumia, the Christian Woman, had brought all to destruction, which is why it was believed she was buried in that great circular tomb atop a mountain, riveted by stone doors that would not open, each of them further barred with the sign of the cross that would only be released on the final day.

4

The Walls of Volubilis

I first visited the Roman ruins of Volubilis forty years ago as a teenager, and have kept on going back. So it has long since become as much a personal memory theatre as a monument.

My first visit was as a mere stop-off on a family camping trip to see the Saharan desert from our house in Gibraltar. My father had borrowed 'a vehicle' that had been personally adapted by its military owner, which left the door hinges projecting beyond the line of the car. It turned us into a lethal weapon, for my father, who normally affected an air of untroubled, shabby gentility as a naval officer, was transformed into an aggressive Toad of Toad Hall once he sat behind the wheel. All other cars had to be overtaken, and often sworn at, as he accelerated past them, 'Get off and milk it' was one of his habitual jeers.

In terms of accidental encounters, the trip began, as it was to continue, with the scrunch of metal, as my father put a six-inch gash into the brand-new car of his best friend in Gibraltar, who lived in a cottage perched near the top of the Rock. That had to be settled with a cheque, and a couple of stiff drinks to prove that all was fine between them, but on the way downhill he literally popped dozens of wing mirrors and brake lights as we swept through the alleys of Gibraltar. Normally I was alarmed by my father's driving, but that particular journey was the best, as I watched through the back window while a confetti of broken red, yellow and mirrored glass came bouncing through the streets behind us. 'But the pace was too good to inquire' (another of his favourite expressions, borrowed from Jorrocks), so all this damage was blithely ignored. We were booked onto the dawn ferry from Gibraltar to Tangier, which also allowed for an early escape from the potentially vast repair bill of the 'first test drive'. But he was slightly sobered by the experience, and made exaggerated manoeuvres once we were on Moroccan soil, especially if there was a risk of damaging an animal. For his animosity to other vehicles was coupled with a saintlike devotion to the welfare of animals.

So it was something of a relief when we reached the village above Volubilis. We slept in a tent, amongst a cacophony of chained dogs earning their keep by barking from the rooftops at the stars. Next morning we walked downhill through olive groves and paddocks of harvested wheat to this ruin of Roman power, with its crop of asphodel. My mother, not an early riser, was left guarding the campsite. Forty years later my younger brother still shakes his head slowly at the memory of that day, spent loyally trailing me around the stones, trying to see what I was seeing. It was the place where my own enthusiasm for shaking out a story from the past forever burnt out his own slight interest in ruins. I have an overexposed photograph of him from that day, looking dazed with boredom but trying not to show it, and trying to shelter his thatch of blonde hair from the midday glare of a Moroccan summer day, surrounded by dried-out thistles and eddies of dust.

In the late afternoon we stopped at a Moroccan tea-garden that in those days perched on the roof of a seventeenth-century royal arsenal, shaded by large trees that had been rooted into the brickwork for centuries – a living Piranesi, complete with long trails of capers cascading down the skylights set into the immense vaults. But as we sipped our sweet mint tea and wolfed down the almond cakes, my brother had already turned his back on Roman ruins for life. He has done well in the world, while I caught an obsession that has summoned me scores of times back to this place.

The visits have been enriched with picnics, often accompanied by dark local wine, in the hope that a siesta under the shade of an ancient olive tree will bring with it a rich dream of the past. I have also tried to open the doors of perception by taking dried magic mushrooms before an open-air concert here one summer evening. On another year I grated hashish resin over a bowl of fresh strawberries. We only left at dusk, for the woman who would later become my mother-in-law had grown totally entranced with Volubilis, its history shimmering with complex colours and vibrating with heat.

∴

Volubilis was wrapped in a protective circuit of walls during the reign of the Emperor Marcus Aurelius. We know the exact date, for a mason thoughtfully pushed a fresh-minted coin into his bed of mortar. There was good reason for these walls, as the Mauretanian tribes were once again on the warpath, albeit they were raiding Spain and the emperor was distracted from lending troops by a mass invasion of German tribes. If you have the stamina to fully explore every last Roman villa along the broad Decumanus Maximus avenue, you will cross over the line of these defence right at the end of your walk, as you pass under the keystone span of stones of the Tangier gate.

Out from the city, archaeologists have identified an outer perimeter formed from five Roman forts. In their heyday they housed garrisons of Hispanic, Belgic, Gallic, Syrian and Parthian cavalry. With a fair amount of persistence, and a local guide, you can track down the overgrown ditches of these forts. Tocolosida was the largest and has the most excavated stonework, and like every furthest southern frontier in North Africa, dates to the reign of Septimius Severus. On my way back from having led a group of elderly archaeologists there, I was shown a damaged but still extraordinarily beautiful statuette of Hercules that had literally been discovered that afternoon, freshly chipped by the ploughshare. When it was first unrolled from a piece of sacking, I had imagined it would be an obvious fake, but it was not. In the light of the setting sun, it was the most beautiful ancient thing that I have ever held.

Surrounded as I was by an exhausted but happy group of antiquarians, I can still hear myself pompously advising the young farmer to take his find to the antiquity department, while all the while wondering what I would have first offered him if I had not been escorted by such a fine group of principled British civil servants. Dusk was thickening, and we had yet to make our way back across the fields, so I asked to be allowed to take a quick photograph, but he rightly didn't want to be framed and incriminated. The locals had long memories, and recalled the time when some years ago someone stole the free-standing statue of Bacchus from the site, which got the tough old king of Morocco on the case. He never did find the culprits, but the police were kept busy for months, much to the inconvenience of the locals.

The evidence of these outlying cavalry forts and the extant traces of the city walls leave their emotional mark, especially for such a Roman frontier-inclined people as the British. For Volubilis was perched right on the outer edge of the empire. No Roman road stretches south, or anywhere eastward, from here.

It is the end of the empire, and so something of an emotional brood sister to Housesteads, on Hadrian's Wall, which is the finest, moodiest, Roman ruin in all of Britain. For at Housesteads and Volubilis everything that you can see comes with a burst of extra force. It can be imagined as the last gasp of Mediterranean civilisation, the last display of the finer arts of living before you cross the line and pass over into the lands of the barbarians. Out from the world of clean water, sharply dressed masonry, superbly engineered baths, latrines and drains, away from rectangular barracks, literacy, libraries and grain-storage silos, to the world of circular mud huts.

Volubilis is filled with architectural delights that one will struggle to find evidence of anywhere in Roman Britain. It has an imposing arch, standing in the centre of town (just like our arches back home in London, at Hyde Park Corner and Marble Arch), and it boasts a line of boutique-like shops (121 one of them have now been surveyed) shaded by an arcade that lined the broad processional avenue. It had a series of public fountains cascading water from a shaded apse, fresh fed by the town aqueduct; it has a meat-market courtyard; it has a modest forum set aside from the commercial traffic of the town and overlooked by the open arches of a wide and opulent public law court. It has an elegant Capitoline Temple courtyard, now much favoured by storks, which neatly frames the view of a sacred Muslim town on the hills above, a classic image of two cultures juxtaposed. It has dozens and dozens of opulent town houses, complete with easily imaginable dining rooms and bedrooms offset from internal garden courtyards. It was dressed by an imaginative school of local carvers, whose lively versions of the classical orders of capitals add an idiosyncratic provincial charm to the ruins. It has three vast ruinous public baths, a possible brothel and a visible local industry, for the city centre of Volubilis was filled with dozens of well-made olive presses. The millstones, the neatly incised drains set into the limestone floor (by which the oil flowed towards the triple-sealed storage tanks), the menhir-like stone lintels for the wooden beam of the press, never fail to impress with their purposeful engineered design. By chance or due to good surveying, the number of these olive presses (fifty-eight at the last count) dovetails rather nicely with the number of town houses and the villa–estates (fifty) that occupied the agricultural hinterland of Volubilis. So the first-time visitor is left with the agreeable sensation that this town flourished from that most estimable of all Mediterranean activities, which is the making of olive oil for our salad dressings, massage and oil lamps. Nor did these fifty landowners despise the sources of their wealth, for the oil presses can be found in close association with the most elegant of the town houses.

Then there are the mosaics – pictures from the past. So whether it is spotting the four seasons, working out the labours of Hercules, recognising Orpheus singing to the animals (so like our St Francis preaching to the birds) or Dionysus eyeing Ariadne on the Naxos shore, we are amongst artistic points of reference that we can aspire to recognise. The best of the mosaics are found in two ground-floor bedrooms, off a courtyard of the House of Venus. In one the naked goddess Diana, mistress of the wild things of the forest, is taking her bath in a spring fed by a fountain struck from the ground by the hoof of the winged horse Pegasus on the slopes of Mount Kithairon. Up in one (now rather damaged) corner of this mosaic she is observed by chance by Actaeon, her devoted follower. He will soon be punished by being transformed into a stag, and then torn apart, haunch from haunch, by his own hounds. It forms a punchy, almost modernist, short story by itself, that plays around with concepts of the untouchability of the divine, the safe limits of friendship, transgression, and a hunter learning what it is to be hunted. It is also a very, very ancient tale, which seems to lead straight back to Gilgamesh, and the capricious nature of the Great Goddess.

Next door there is a mosaic of the handsome, naked, blonde boyfriend of Hercules (his chosen companion for the Jason adventure), who has been sent ashore to fetch a pail of fresh water. Hylas is about to be abducted by nymphs and drowned in their pool, to remain their plaything. In the meanwhile some biting is going on. But it all remains in the best possible taste, ornamented with side panels that show little winged erotes being playfully whipped by their brethren. Here too there seems to be a direct, if not tangibly erotic, connection between our own times and the myths of the classical past. So the Western visitor immediately feels part of this classical world, especially in contrast to that of contemporary North Africa, with its Arabic calligraphy and non-representational art.

Close to this villa, in the bakery just across the road, is also where a series of exquisite bronzes was found buried beneath the floor in a secret cache of treasured art that includes a head of Cato and the pensive and reflective head of a Hellenistic prince, enthusiastically identified as the head of the young Juba II. It seems tragically clear that the owner had buried his household treasures but could never come back to reclaim them. A hundred yards to the north, an even bigger villa offers to tell us why this might have been so, for in this house (labelled the Gordian Palace) archaeologists uncovered a series of free-standing altar stones that commemorated the renewal of the frequent peace agreements made between the Roman provincial governor and the kings and princes of the Berber tribe of the Baquates (and the Macenites) whose territory began just beyond the frontier. They were barbarians, but obviously of some importance to get such polite wording in carved Latin. The Emperor Antoninus Pius was called upon to sort out the legitimate succession in AD 138, and a couple of years later a senator is dispatched to Volubilis to formally bestow the citizenship of Rome on this new king, Tuccuda. A similar investiture seems to confirm Canarta as the prince of the Baquates in AD 180. But these altars stop just before 'the end', in 280, just before the three Roman towns of north-western Morocco, Banassa, Thamusida and Volubilis, 'fall' as by a third-century domino theory to the enemy. It was another very tough time for the Roman empire, which seemed to be about to sink under the combined weight of its adversaries. The Alans had invaded Asia Minor with Franks and Vandals poised to invade Gaul and Hungary, Saxon pirates raiding Britain and Mauretanian Berber pirates once again plundering the coast of Spain.

As well as all these tribes besieging the frontier, there were other, arguably more vital things going wrong with the empire at this time, which was racked by agricultural revolts in such overtaxed provinces as Gaul and Spain. So in AD 285 the Emperor Diocletian abandoned the hinterland of the Roman province of Morocco. The provincial boundaries were redrawn to include just the port cities of Lixus, Tangier, Ceuta and their immediate hinterland. This decision would be backed by a first-hand inspection, for we know that in 296 Diocletian's co-emperor Maximian was based in Tangier, overseeing a campaign against the Mauretanian pirates and assembling a large army. He obviously thought better of using this army to repossess the old provincial boundaries and concentrated on pirates and rivals.

The empire clearly needed to husband its resources, for on the Rhine frontier in this period certain allied German tribes were now acting not as the enemy but as the imperial militia. A year later, Maximian had moved east and was based in the regional capital of Carthage. How much this was about suppressing Berber tribes on the Saharan frontier, how much about re-establishing the authority of the imperial tax collectors in the vital breadbasket corn lands, we do not know but can guess at. His propaganda speaks of driving the tribes beyond the Atlas mountains into the Sahara, but we also know that he dwelt in Carthage throughout the winter of 297 to 298. And that, though he campaigned that spring, he was already back in Carthage (celebrating a triumph over his enemies) by 10 March, which was pretty fast work for those of us who know the ground. A year later he would land in Italy and celebrate another round of triumphs that spring, before settling down to palace life in northern Italy.

So let us return to the vision of the smoking, abandoned frontier town of Roman Volubilis, waiting for the French archaeologists to lovingly excavate and restore it. It was a clear act of government policy for colonial regimes to restore Roman ruins, almost as if it justified the act of conquest. Work began at Volubilis in 1915, just three years after the French formally occupied Morocco, in the midst of the great testing crisis of the First World War. German prisoners of war were usefully employed to excavate the dirt. The desire for monuments was all-important, so that with a slowly sharpening eye for what is real and what is restored, I can now see that the Capitoline Temple that I have spent years admiring is nothing other than an imaginative rebuild. Indeed some historians argue that it was a hexastyle peripteral structure (which means that the shrine was wrapped in columns like a small Parthenon), while others disagree with the way the triumphal arch has been rebuilt.

But arches in particular have always been highly flexible things. To use London's Marble Arch as an example, it started off outside Buckingham Palace before being sent north to be turned into a roundabout, just as the arch at Hyde Park gets moved back from the traffic, before being turned into a peace memorial approach to the Palace, and just as Temple Bar and Euston Arch came down for impeding traffic flow, though the latter has recently remerged beside St Paul's Cathedral. The one at Volubilis was begun by the provincial governor (one Marcus Aurelius Sebastenus) to honour Emperor Caracalla and the queen-mother, Julia Domna. Just before it was dedicated news of Caracalla's death reached the town (he was murdered in AD 217 on the Parthian frontier at the temple of Luna), so the new ruler Macrinus was commemorated in the monument that capped the summit (a four-horse chariot) and through the nymphs in the four lower niches which poured fresh water into marble basins.

It was during the reign of this Emperor Macrinus that the handsome basilica and the Capitoline Temple were finished, so all three of the architectural glories of Volubilis actually date from just a three-year period, but there was good reason for this work to have been pushed ahead. Macrinus was a Roman-ised Berber from Mauretania, from a hard-working equestrian family of administrators from King Juba II's old city of Cae-sarea. Which is why Volubilis can look fairly imperial, rather than the humdrum trading town on the edge of the empire that it was. So in dozens of guidebooks and web pages it has been promoted to become a provincial capital, if not the site of the western palace of King Juba and Queen Cleopatra. The emotional power of an arch, a standing column or two, is astonishing, as is the vital importance of what you decide to reconstruct and show to the public. As we shall see, there are other moments in the thousand-year history of Volubilis that one might wish to dwell on.

As a young man first exploring these ruins, I followed the mythology of the union between the West and its classical past with a devoted passion. I found the city ruins inspiringly romantic, overwhelmed – as I liked to imagine it – by a vision of barbarian Berbers forcing their way over the walls. Like the tide obliterating one of the sandcastles of one's childhood, the barbarian tribes stormed this city of thirty-four towers, smashing their way through the eight fortified gatehouses. Then formally abandoned by their emperor, the faces of Juba and Cato and those sensual mosaics patiently waited 1,600 years before they were lovingly uncovered.

Instead, what seems to have happened is that during the long governorship of Clementinus Valerius Marcellinus, the procurator of Mauretania Tingitana from AD 277 to 282, the troops were withdrawn. Roman Morocco never had a permanent legion to hold its frontier, but instead depended on borrowing detachments of the legions from Spain, assisted by 9,000 resident auxiliaries (especially strong in cavalry). These were withdrawn for service elsewhere, in this case almost certainly to assist in the civil wars waged between rival Roman generals fighting for the throne. This was the ladder by which Diocletian assumed the imperial throne, as a popular commander of cavalry who had worked his way up the ranks.

So it seems that the classical city of Volubilis never fell. Freed of Roman soldiers and Roman tax collectors, it happily survived. Volubilis, which had existed as a market town for three hundred years before the Romans conquered northern Morocco, lived on for another thousand years, selecting its own priests and judges from its citizens and from the chiefs of the local Berber tribes. It was much smaller, for it occupied only about a third of the size of the old city in its second-century heyday, but it survived.* And sometime in the fifth century a new city wall was constructed by quarrying the old city, to defend and define the inhabited westernmost quarter of Volubilis, which hugged the riverbed. The ruins of the old city on the hill increasingly became a ghost town, literally so, for the ruins were used as a necropolis, a city of the dead. The area around the triumphal arch in particular was colonised by a Christian cemetery, and we know from inscriptions that there was also a synagogue here, though neither this nor a purpose-built church has yet been discovered. In the seventh century it must have fallen within the domains of the unknown Berber king who built the great round tomb of El Ghor that now sits, neglected and unvisited, in the flat agricultural plain between the cities of Meknes and Fez. El Ghor is consciously modelled on the circular royal tombs of the Numidian kings, proudly looking back to such monuments as Medracen and the Tomb of the Christian Woman that had been built a thousand years before. It is tempting to see this monarch as the prince of the Baquates or Macenite tribes remembered in the Latin inscriptions. I hold a candle out to the idea that the Maknassa (about whom we will soon hear) are the lineal successors of the Macenites.

Within a few decades of the completion of this royal Berber tomb, sometime around AD 680, Oqba ibn Nafi, an Arab cavalry commander, would have ridden this way, and accepted

---

* One specialist has argued that one of the finest mosaics in the House of Venus was actually created in the fourth century, though I am wary of that, for dating mosaics by style and identifying marble quarries from colour is an established graveyard of scholarship.

the submission of the walled town of Volubilis on behalf of his caliph in distant Damascus. Oqba ibn Nafi is an Arthurian figure, an historical character around whom the limpets of tradition have adhered. His story was written down two hundred years after the events of his life had passed, but there is surely no reason to doubt that this fearless conquering knight rode his horse into the surf of the Atlantic at the head of his marvelling army before raising his eyes to the heavens and declaring: 'Allah Akhbar, if my way were not stopped by this sea, I would still go on, into the unknown kingdoms of the furthest West, preaching the unity of thy holy name.'

His soldiers must have been greatly relieved to hear that their commander accepted that he had been stopped, for in another Oqba ibn Nafi tradition their commander enthusiastically compares his march to that of Alexander the Great, who planned never to halt his conquests. On his way back home, the old general was ambushed and killed, just outside the oasis of Biskra (Roman Vescera), by Koceila, an allied chieftain whom he had once humiliated. The battle is believed to have been fought on the wadi floor of the Oued El Abiod in the Aurès mountains, close to the old Roman military camp of Tahouda, where a mosque was built by the victorious Berbers. Oqba's tomb–mosque can still be found in a nearby settlement, the centrepiece of a village tucked into the palm groves east of Biskra. The mosque has been restored, with too lavish an allotment of state-funded marble, but the surrounding village, set amongst a dense forest of palm, remains charmingly quiet, peaceful and calm, in complete contrast to Oqba.

By 740 Oqba's heirs in business had severely antagonised North Africa. The Arab generals had achieved great things, such as the conquest of Spain, but only by using armies recruited from the Berber tribes, whom they foolishly began to treat as serf-like bondsmen rather than junior allies. These battle-hardened soldiers, especially those based at the old Roman provincial capital of Tingis (Tangier), mutinied under the command of one of their leaders, Maysara. The Berber rebels subsequently succeeded in defeating in battle two separate Arab armies that had been sent out to destroy them. Their first victory is called the Battle of the Nobles, where they defeated the Arab Jund, sent out from the provincial garrison city of Kairouan, followed two years later by the battle of the Sebou River. The Sebou flows through the coastal plateau a couple of days' ride north from Volubilis, and it was here that an Arab army that had marched all the way from Syria (and may have numbered 20,000 men) was defeated.

These Berber rebels kept faith in rejecting, not Islam, but the carpet-bagging Arab overlords who came with the first armies of conquest. To prove their point, the rebels adhered to a very early, very puritanical and democratic form of Islamism (known as Sufri Kharijite). They rejected any racial, ethnic or dynastic claims to leadership, or indeed to the membership of the Muslim community, which was henceforth to be defined, not by your Arab blood, but by how well you followed the teachings of the Prophet. They also insisted on electing their imam from among the most worthy believers, be he an ex-slave or a water carrier, though standing just a step behind this spiritual leader there was often the pragmatic reality of the backing of a Berber tribal chief. For example, the garrison in the far south (right on the edge of the Sahara desert at Sijilmassa, near to the famous sand dunes of Merzouga) chose a black African as its first imam, but he would be supported and then succeeded by Midrar, a Berber chieftain from the Meknassa tribe that was heavily represented in the first Muslim armies and among the leaders of the rebellion. (The other key tribes at this time seem to have been the Madyuna and the Ghayata.) On the Atlantic coast, Tarif, another of the victorious commanders of the Berber rebellion, presided as the first imam of a Kharijite state that would later become known as the Berghouata (or Barghawata) confederacy.

In western Algeria, another alliance of a hard-bitten Berber tribe, the Beni Ifran, in partnership with a charismatic Kharijite preacher would be the kernel around which a new state, the Rustamid Imamate, would form. The Beni Ifran were based on the city of Pomaria (modern Tlemcen), which provides us with another intriguing example of classical continuity to put beside Volubilis, for Pomaria was an old Roman marching camp (once again dating back to the energetic reign of the Emperor Septimius Severus) which after the collapse of imperial authority evolved into a self-governing Berber trading community, existing beyond the bounds of the empire but retaining both the Latin script and Christianity. Visually it also resembles Volubilis, for it was safely inland, miles from any seaborne raider, and sat below a handsome escarpment of limestone hills from which gush a series of freshwater springs.

This patchwork of Berber states, sitting on Roman foundations but embracing the new religion from the East, formed a uniquely hospitable region for any refugee escaping the civil wars of Arabia. For these Berber states were a safe haven: independent of the agents of the Arab caliphate, safely removed from the Byzantine empire (and any Christian pirate raids), yet respecting Islam. We know of a number of Muslim refugees who escaped the power struggles of the Middle East by travelling west into North Africa, but for the moment we are interested in just one, whose name is Idris. He travels incognito, with just one companion, his freed slave Rashid. They use the existing caravan trails that cross the arid steppeland by which the pilgrims of North Africa travel on haj to Mecca and later filter their way back to their homelands. They were political refugees, so they probably used some cover, posing as merchants or travelling scholars coming back from Mecca. There were many who used such disguises in this period. The intellectuals behind the Kharijite revolt (persecuted in the Arab homeland) communicated with the far-flung communities of the faithful, using the humble networks of trade that spread out from the Iraqi port city of Basra. It may be that Idris made use of this connection, for there were spies and agents everywhere and the truth, as we shall see, is elusive in this period.

Idris was on the run from the Abbasid caliphs of Baghdad. In 750 the Abbasids, kinsmen of the Prophet Muhammad through his uncle Abbas, had overthrown the previous ruling dynasty, and purged the ruling elite of corrupt and incompetent Umayyad princelings. The Umayyads had been hunted down, their desert palaces sacked, their tombs in Damascus opened and their bones thrown to the dogs. In public the Abbasids espoused the right of the family of the Prophet to lead the community, and as the senior male-descent clan they could argue that they had Arab tradition on their side. But there was also a secret purge going on, for the Abbasids were quietly removing all their cousins, especially those directly descended from the Prophet, to guarantee their hold on the throne. This lethal policy was never consistent, but there were enough attempted coups and revolutions being plotted for the Abbasids to remain ever watchful of their cousins.

Idris, directly descended from the Prophet Muhammad, would have been keenly aware of the toxic nature of his bloodline, which was pruned every generation. His family had been decimated at Kerbala (in AD 680) and then in the aftermath of Zayd ibn Ali's failed rebellion of 740. In 762 two of Idris's brothers had led an armed rebellion against the new Abbasid state. His brother Muhammad 'the Pure Soul' had managed to seize control of Medina, while his brother Ibrahim had led a rebellion in the East, but both had perished. In 786 one of Idris's cousins attempted another coup. At the head of 200 of his clansmen he had intended to win over the enormous haj caravan of pilgrims as they approached Mecca. Their force was intercepted and killed at the campsite of Fakh on 11 June. Idris had to escape or die.

It may be that Idris's sole companion on his travels, the ex-mawla (military slave) Rashid, was of Berber blood and knew exactly what he was doing when he escorted the refugee prince Idris to the ancient town of Volubilis. It was not part of any of the existing Kharijite Berber states, and the Abbasid forti-fied watchtower, or ribat, that stood beside the old city was now deserted. Idris was received by Ishaq ibn Muhammad, the commander of the Berber Awraba tribe that ruled Volubilis, as an extraordinary gift from heaven. Idris was the son of Abdul-lah, son of Abdullah, son of Hassan, son of Hassan, son of Ali (the cousin of the Prophet) and of Fatimah, the cherished, pious and modest daughter of the Prophet of God. To put it in a British perspective, it was as if the great-grandson of St James, the brother of Jesus, turned up at a hill fort on the Welsh borders and offered to build and bless a church. There can be little doubt of the sincerity of the welcome that Ishaq gave Idris, who would henceforth be called 'Moulay' – my Lord. To make him feel even more at home, he gave Idris his daughter Kanza in marriage.

And lest you should think that I have taken you off into an improbable storyline from *One Thousand and One Nights*, at the bottom of the city of Volubilis (in an area bizarrely not yet open to visitors) they have excavated the eighth-century bathhouse that was built for Idris and adjoined his house. Coins of the right date have been found. You need to be told this, because if you had just stumbled across this domed bathhouse you would almost certainly mistake it for a Roman structure, for the architect and builders continued to work within the classical idiom, and reused one of the carved stones from the town's triumphal arch to ornament one of the walls. It is extraordinary to think of the great-great-great-grandson of the Prophet leading the Friday prayers in this old Roman town with its mixed population of Jews and Christians. He had but a few years in Volubilis before the agents of the Abbasid caliph in Baghdad caught up with him and brought about his death. Fortunately his Berber wife Kanza gave birth to a boy two months after his burial. This child would be protected by his Berber grandfather and uncles, the chieftains of the Awraba tribe, and watched over by mawla Rashid, who it is said took the assassin's blade in his chest in 802 so that his young master would live.

Idris II proved to be an intellectually brilliant and dynamic young monarch, taking over the reins of authority, both tribal, urban and spiritual, in AD 805, aged just thirteen. He established the city of Fez as a brand-new centre for an entirely Islamic community, and welcomed other Arab refugees there. A flood of them arrived in 818, escaping from the unrest of Cordoba, and more in 824 when Kairouan was racked by civil strife. The two sets of refugees were given different banks, on either side of the central river.

Idris died quite young, and is buried in the centre of Fez. His shrine–mosque, with its great pyramid-like roof of green tiles, remains one of the spiritual poles of the city. Fez was still a city in the making, and so it seems that he actually died in Volubilis in 828. His son Muhammad ruled after him, though the Idrissid state was not fated to grow into a powerful kingdom. In part this was because Muhammad was a good and godly man, and divided his authority and inheritance among his twelve brothers. Nine of them (or in some accounts seven) took him up on this offer, and ruled over communities that were established in the hinterland of Morocco. Whether as an enriching historical fable, or as an absolute fact, such far-flung cities as Nakur (20 kilometres inland from the sea in the eastern Rif mountains), Basra (in the western Rif mountains) and Tamdoult (deep in the Anti-Atlas mountains of south-western Morocco) all claim to have been founded by one of these Idrissid missionary princes. It is a bloodline that has disseminated far and wide throughout the nation of Morocco and beyond into most of North Africa, so that I have met many a landless peasant who feels part of this spiritual dynasty. Even those of them who refused the distraction of political power and expedient marriages to Berber princesses have their followers. As a boy I remember the vast crowds that used to assemble around the beachside tomb of Sidi Kacem, just south of Tangier, who was a hermit Idrissid prince, one of the three, or five, brothers who refused wealth, the better to seek the face of God amongst the despised fishermen of the foreshore and beside a clutch of Neolithic tombs.

At that stage in my life, I imagined that the tomb of an Arab Muslim saint could have nothing in common with the romantic ruins of a Roman city. Surely they were like polar opposites. I now know that the two stories intimately connect, not just in the story cycle of legend but within the Roman walls of Volubilis.

5

Dougga

The ruins at Dougga cascade down an escarpment that over-looks an open valley carved through the Tell of central Tunisia. The rough ground above is dotted with ancient olives and tombs, and herds are still driven beside the walls of the Roman summer baths to make use of the spring that flows at the bottom of the settlement. The distant view over the vast cornfields of the Wadi Khaled, billowing in the evening light, provide the strongest impression of the old agricultural wealth ruled by this citadel of Numidia. Dougga was prosperous but never opulent, and so was built from local limestone, not imported marbles. This stone has weathered to create a patina, while the exca-vated sections glow with a cleaner, clearer hue, the colour of old butter set against rinds of Cheddar.

I once spent ten days in the nearby town of Téboursouk, whose centre is still enclosed by a Byzantine wall and hosts the only hotel in the region. I wanted to get to know Dougga street by street, house by house, but we also had time to walk out to discover the dozens of less famous ruins in the hinter-land. It was out of season, so my girlfriend and I had the whole place to ourselves, apart from the bar, which that winter was used as a warm clubhouse by one of the local landowners, who wore the healthy tan of a farmer and dressed in the uniform of an agricultural worker, a faded suit of blue cotton, which was imported from China and labelled 'L'Anti Cher'. He was fantastically generous with drinks and talk, and spoke in a marvellous babble of language that fused French, Berber, Italian and Arabic, empowered by a free-wheeling passion for history and recent politics that kept the bar staff chuckling with glee. It was interesting to watch their complete unaffected delight in his rhetoric, for this bar for foreigners was a place set apart from local life. His lack of political correctness in the one-party state of enlightened, progressive Arab socialism then dominant in Tunisia would have made him scandalous in the packed tables of the cafés, dominated by television, cigarettes, dominos and the state employees of the educational and agricultural ministries. I could but not think of him as representing something of the ancient spirit of the town: amused, highly cultured, agricultural, and entirely removed from the realities of political life.

Dougga has a beautiful, hill-hugging theatre, and an almost intact Capitoline Temple in which a broken face of Zeus lay on the floor. Beside the walls of the temple a dial has been carved into the paving-stones of the forum. When I first saw it, it took me some time to work out that these were not the names of the twelve hours, or the twelve signs of the zodiac. They were the names of the winds. It seemed a thing of pure poetic charm, which I remember sketching, for at that time of my life I was trying to balance the small income made from writing guidebooks with building follies and grottoes in England. I could see that this elegant bit of whimsical classicism might be just the sort of thing to adapt and work up into a project, set against a knapped flint-and-pebble floor.

It was while I was sitting still, working at a sketch, that I had the time to gradually sort out the different ages of the ruins. I was able to cut out the Byzantine fortifications (they had built a castle out of the ruins in the sixth century) and visualise the forum back in its original working order. It was only then that I began to understand that the wind-rose might have had a purpose. It stands in front of the temple of Mercury and beside the Capitoline Temple, dedicated to Jupiter the Best and the Greatest, Royal Juno and August Minerva. For here surely there was no better nor more prominent place in which to practise the lost art of taking the auspices, something that the British do all the time, for it literally means one who looks at birds.

I have found no surviving manuals, but a public augur was not looking for a specific oracular answer to a question (like an oracle), but checking that the decisions of mankind were in keeping with the wishes of heaven. So at the election of magistrates, which happened in the forum from the massed ranks of citizens in their tribes, at the passing of a new law (usually announced from the rostrum terrace of the Capitolium), or of a decree to honour a citizen, or the public reading of a will, it was customary to see if this pleased the gods. The flights of birds of prey, especially eagles and vultures, were useful signs of approval, as were the calls of the raven, crow and owl. At other occasions the number of birds, and the direction of their flight, were noted down and analysed for their meaning. I have high hopes that the simple chant about the number of magpies that you meet whilst out for a walk in the British countryside, 'One for sorrow, two for joy, three for a girl, four for a boy', is a sliver of augury science that has survived the millennia.

The Romans kept sacred flocks of chickens, and observed the way that they fed and moved to ensure that all was well. This seemed an especially suitable use for the Dougga wind-rose. I for one have never tired of the simple joy that can be found by scattering corn to chickens and watching who gets what and in what order. To do this clad in a formal toga, whilst a board of new magistrates fidgeted beside you, waiting to see whether or not this was the right time for them to offer up a public oath, could only have added further charm to the simple pleasure of feeding your birds.

The winds were linked to the points of the compass, and had moods of their own, some of them based on the practical experiences of sailors, fishermen and farmers as to which prevailing wind brought scorching heat, which wind brought rain and which meant summer storms. There was also an underlying mythic symbolism, so that alongside the cold winter winds from the north, the Boreas was also associated with fertility and sexual energy. Indeed one of the Latin titles for the north wind, *Septentrio*, links north with the seven oxen, that group of seven bright stars that like the Plough (Ursa Major) helps to locate the north star. Others read *Septentrio* as Commander of the Seven, giving the north that whiff of supremacy and primacy that it retains to this day, for all our maps are read as if the world aligns to the north. The east wind was ill-omened, and was so closely associated with death and plague that Homer (who loved the poetry of wind-adjectives) never gets around to naming it. Other cultures saw the east wind as good, and connected it with clarity and brightness. Its Latin name *Subsolanus* has a pleasing derivation of coming from under the rising sun. The Greeks loved the south wind, which they associated with warmth and moist loveliness, but Virgil describes it as 'black *Auster*', and links it with the shipwrecking storms of the midsummer and the autumnal equinox. The wind from the west was associated with the season of flowers, spring and gentle rain. It was literally the favourite wind, *Favonius* in Latin and *Zephyrus* in Greek, who takes physical form as a minor deity in his own right. Zephyrus, like all gods, could have his ethical off moments, like the time when he arranged for a wind to sweep up the discus thrown by the handsome Spartan athlete Hya-cinth, and then sent it straight back down again, like a boomer-ang, to kill him – but as this was a lovers' tiff, because Hyacinth was spending a lot more time with Apollo than with his old friend Zephyrus, this crime of passion could be forgiven. The south-west and south by south-west winds were connected with North Africa by both the Greeks and Romans. The former was known as the African wind, the latter as the Libyan, if not identified with the Garamantian homeland that was lodged deep south in the Libyan Sahara. It was subject to name change, and so can come out in the texts as either Libo-phoenix, Libo-Notos or Leucomotos.

Each province of the Roman empire had its own sensibility as to which wind was unfavourable, or favourable, in the four different seasons. The affect of the mistral, the north by north-west wind that chills France and Italy in the winter months by coming through the ice fields of the Alps, was not dreaded in the same way by the Greeks. They associated this wind with the Thracian hills and horse pastures.

Although we now think of lightning as the attribute of Jupiter alone, there was an older tradition that bestowed it on each of the twelve gods, or to the signs of the zodiac. So although the direction of wind might tell you one thing, light-ning added another layer of complexity. It was a good omen coming from the east, bad from the west, a matter of indiffer-ence from the south, especially unlucky from the north-west, but lucky from the north-east.

Despite all this weather and wind-watching science, there was also a delightful disorder in the actual number of winds. That fount of literary authority Homer speaks of six (but names only four), while Aristotle numbered twelve but then argued that only ten were important. The Etruscans divided the night sky into sixteen sections – which is odd, for otherwise they like to play around with twelve-strong slices like the rest of us – and famously formed themselves into twelve-strong leagues of confederate cities. The twelve-pointed compass has been traced back to Timosthenes of Rhodes in the third century BC, when that lovely Greek island was the headquarters of the largest merchant marine of the ancient world, and so ruled the science of map-making, nautical itineraries and marine insurance. Eratosthenes of Cyrene reduced it to eight, which is the number that the beautiful octagonal tower of winds (that still stands in Athens and was admired by Byron who lodged nearby) records. Vitruvius, the Roman architect and town planner, a stern voice on all manner of matters, multiplied, categorised and listed the direction of the winds up to twenty-four. He remains in charge.

Only at Dougga can you literally dance your way around the twelve winds, like a sacred chicken, beginning north, so that your face is brushed by the authoritative wind of Septentrio, allowing you to slowly spin around in a clockwise fashion, through Aquilo to Euraquilo, then Vulturnus, Eurus, Leuconotus, Auster, Libonotus, Africus, Favonius, Argestes and back to Circius. A comparable litany, blending poetic charm with threat, is the one that traces the possible storms circling around the British Isles: Biscay, Plymouth, Lundy, Fastnet, Shannon, Rockall, Bailey, Faeroes, Fair Isle, Viking, Forties, Fisher, Dogger Bank, German Bight.

There is a possible brothel downtown, a temple to Saturn on a hilltop, and a winter bath complex (with an intact subterranean service tunnel, so you can play out the role of slave) in the centre. Right at the bottom of the town there is the mausoleum of Arteban. This is one of only two extant buildings in the world with which one can try to reconstruct Punic Carthage. Its bilingual inscription is the acknowledged Rosetta Stone of

North Africa, for it brought us our first understanding of the native Libyan script of the Berbers. Hunger for this inscription led a British scholar to pull down the entire structure in the nineteenth century, though fortunately Arteban's tomb was beautifully reconstructed by a French archaeologist a generation later.

All these wonders are set amid a jumble of townhouses, markets, alleyways, mosaic floors and stone lintels. If there is a more charming ruined town in the Roman world than this, I have yet to find it. Even the local spring water tastes delicious, which I still feel gratitude for, as I first visited the place without adequate provisions, having hitched my way here as a student. And once you get your eye into the local landscape, you realise that this was not a lone outpost of urbanity, but surrounded by half a dozen towns, all within half a day's ride. I have taken picnics to them all, and never came across another person, unless they were shepherds.

I found my favourite place right at the end of my first day in the ruins, when butterflies were feeding on a fresh cowpat, and the light was softening. For just beyond the town centre of Dougga, abutting the old city of the dead, stands the temple of Juno Caelestis, its form partly obscured by ancient olive trees, so there was a wonderful sense of chance discovery. It is a place apart, then and now, for to reach it you had to pass out of the formal limits of the city of the living by walking beneath a finely preserved triumphal arch dedicated to the Emperor Alexander Severus. The temple space is defined by a semicircular colonnade, which once enclosed the sanctuary of the Queen of Heaven within a half-moon-shaped courtyard. Her temple was raised up on a shoulder-high platform and was surrounded by slender Corinthian columns, originally designed to echo the two sacred groves that stood on either side. Basins stand beside the two entrance ways, so that the worshippers of old could cleanse themselves before entering the courtyard of the holy place.

Its position is also very odd for a pagan sanctuary, for our ancestors always took care to keep the temples utterly removed from being defiled by the dead. And this shrine is no mausoleum in disguise, but a temple dedicated to the worship of Juno Caelestis, the Latin name for the all-powerful Carthaginian Mother Goddess, Tanit. To make this association doubly clear, a surviving inscription tells us that the temple sanctuary was originally furnished with a pair of silver statues of the goddess at a cost of 35,000 sesterces. Nor is this shrine the proud product of local particularism, such as might be offered to a patron deity of the city. Its universalism was signalled within the outer semicircular colonnade, where twenty-four columns framed a series of busts and inscriptions commemorating the cult of the Mother Goddess, under all her different titles and identities, in the various other cities and provinces of the Roman empire. It is a numinous place, and it is simply not possible to stand here and not feel that it was built with faith as well as a splendidly open purse. Indeed, it seems possible that Juno was in some way deliberately placed here so as to watch over, maybe even guide the dead on their way.

I remember the jolt of surprise when I learned (years later in the library of SOAS in London) that it was built in the third century AD. It means that this splendid temple, so full of confidence and belief, was being finished off, and ornamented with all its lavish statues, after such triumphant Christian writers as Tertullian (in nearby Carthage) were already dead. To read Tertullian, you might think that the last shreds of pagan belief were already blowing in the wind of change, and the future lay all with the Christians. Then you stand in the ruins of the temple of Juno Caelestis and you understand just how many things can be believed all at the same time. Nor must you allow the tranquil quiet of these ruins to entice you to look back towards a lost era of serenity and classical order. In its brief heyday, all the stonework would have been limed and painted in bright colours, and there would have been a bustle of gatekeepers, janitors and cleaners in and around the shrine, controlling access and no doubt soliciting donations to the temple treasury. Officials (*magistri*) ran the financial affairs of the shrine, and documented the landholdings, income and expenses of the temple, gifts and offerings, whilst a single priest ruled all public communication with the deity for the year of his election, once co-opted into the governing board of land-owners, the priestly college. On great festival days, musicians, singers and dancers would be employed, as would cooks and servants preparing and serving the sacred feasts. Professional sacrificers would handle the animals, lead them meekly to the altar, stun them with an expert blow of a hammer to the head, then cut their throats with a wide-shafted dagger, leaving the priest himself free to concentrate on a word-perfect address to the cult statue, and the physical offering, be it a pinch of incense onto the low flame of a small altar, or blood poured onto the main altar of the courtyard from a silver patera dish. Some have seen the two entrance ways and the two identi-cal cult statues as allowing for the semicircular shrine to have been divided, maybe between men and women, or citizens of Dougga and outsiders.

The cult of Royal Juno was certainly complex and multifac-eted. Her ancient role as the Queen of Heaven was proclaimed by her regular worship on the Kalends, the first day of every month, to coincide with the new moon, just as the first full week of the moon was celebrated every month with the Nones and the second full week of the moon with the Ides.* Her aspect as the incarnation of the fertile earth gave us the titles of the three productive months, with the month of April named after the earth's 'opening' to receive the seed, May as the time of her growing, while the name June and Juno is derived from Latin *iuventas*, youth.

The year-long celebration of the Goddess's fertility intensified on her special feast days. Juno's Night of the Wild Fig was on the Nones of July. It was a sensual, bawdy romp, celebrated with nocturnal picnics, deliberately dominated by ribald language (as an act of piety), with much sport made of the similarity of a ripe fig to a testicle and its sap to semen, and concluding with a sacrifice of goats and a midnight feast. September was punctuated by elaborate municipal processions that wound through the streets of the city and stressed the nature of the Goddess's royal power as the ruling Queen of the Capitoline trinity. The midwinter nocturnal festival of Juno Sospita, the Saviour, was the most awesome celebration of her cosmic reach. She would be appealed to as 'the merciful Lady' who would keep the forces of darkness at bay in the universe, discipline the ghosts, spirits and demons that were unleashed on the most unpropitious day of the year, the First of February, and help bridge the gap between the old year and the new. This was a night of sacrifices, of goats, splendid white sows and blemish-free cows and calves, when her altar was soaked in blood and offerings. At the back of her shrine, the gleaming bling of her solid silver statues would shimmer in the light of torches. We do not know the shape she was cast into, but suspect that at

---

* To add variety to this, the short months celebrated the first week of the moon on the 5th, long months on the 7th, while the Ides were celebrated on the 13th on short months and the 15th on long months.

least one of the two statues revealed her in the form the Greek sculptors embodied for her great temple at Samos: a strong and confident force of female power, capable of protecting the state, keeping the bonds of matrimony ever strong, and renewing the energy of the world. Her other form may have been based on the ancient cult statue of Tanit, which dominated the High Place of ancient Carthage, was taken to Rome after the utter destruction of that city, but which was piously returned to North Africa by Julius Caesar and Augustus.

The man who built the temple of Juno was Quintus Gabinius Rufus Felix. He was one of the Gabini clan, an old family of landowners. They built many of the finest public buildings in Dougga as a gift to their fellow citizens, to honour the emperor and the empire and their privileged position in it. Fifteen years before the temple of Juno was built, Hermiona Gabini had converted one of her town houses into a curious courtyard temple, ringed with statues of all the gods but specifically dedicated to honour the Emperor Caracalla's victory over the German tribes. In her will, she instructed the priests of this new shrine to offer up an annual dinner to the town's senate. A previous gift to the town had been one of her fields, up above the oldest of the city's half-dozen cemeteries, which was flat enough to be used as an occasional circus. These picnic races worked well for ten years, but the people had petitioned their magistrates to build them a permanent circus racetrack with wooden benches, which was achieved in 225.

Another of the Gabini-built monuments in Dougga is the temple of Concord. This worthy little chapel, dedicated to civil concord, is approached through a side door, down a side street. The modest street façade gave access to an extensive and complex building, for downhill from the Concord shrine the Gabini really went to town, creating a large temple courtyard to the god Liber Pater (the Free Father) which can only be accessed through an auditorium, looking like a theatre with its row of thirty seats, but in this instance a place in which sacred pageants were staged. From inscriptions we know that Neptune and Frugifer (a sort of North African identity for Dis Pater, father of the spirits, Lord of the Underworld) were also honoured in this complex. So like some mazy shadow dance of identities, three separate deities were worshipped here as an interlinked Trinity. Liber Pater, flanked by or merging into the Lord of the Underworld and his brother Neptune, master of the tectonic forces that separate the land which floats like a crust on the great Ocean, which is now and then punctured to release life-giving springs of fresh water. Liber Pater is an intriguing figure, for he is the North African version of Bacchus, one part ancient sacrificial fertility god, but two parts dangerous fun, for he, like Bacchus, is associated with wine, sensuality, divine madness and the transforming arts, such as the theatre. His worshippers in the old days were women, and the ecstatic frenzy of dance was the favourite subject of ancient sculptors. The power of these carved scenes is redoubled by the knowledge that these were otherwise normal women (mothers and matrons) who had been caught up in something that swept away all restraints. Lurking in shadow was the memory that these god-possessed female dancers could tear apart anything male they might happen upon that night, as an act of piety.

Dougga also has its hilltop shrine to the god whom the Romans addressed as Saturn, but who was known throughout North Africa as Baal Hammon. It is another place of power, built around an ancient cave. This hilltop area was riddled with deposits of sacred gifts, buried here for centuries and then encased within a conventional-looking temple pediment, though the working space of spiritual mystery always remained this ancient court, open to the great Lord of the Heavens. The classical exterior of this sanctuary was created in the reign of the Emperor Septimius Severus, a Roman-looking shell enclosing a very ancient Berber cult centre.

Over the years I have been able to stumble into other High Places, dedicated to Baal Hammon: on a mountaintop plateau above Petra of the Nabateans, on the summit of the hill that overlooks a mountain gorge behind the ruins of Tiddis, and in the unearthly calm of a coombe between the two peaks of Jebel Boukornine. All three take some resolve to ascend, and offer up magnificent views and the hill-walker's sense of achievement, but they are also marked by the absence of any building, save for the modest ruins of a small enclosure wall. The complete absence of sculpture, lettering or architecture makes them slightly disappointing, for there is nothing to work out or disentangle, but then if you wait long enough, this absence of distraction can cut alarmingly through the centuries to offer us the same essential vision, of a powerless man alone beneath the unblinking gaze of heaven. So this is where Abraham offered up Isaac to his god, not overlooked by the throngs of the city temple, but intensely alone, aside from the bundle of faggots for a burnt offering. Carrying hammer, knife and flame.

6

The Villa Selene

I have swum off Leptis Magna at the end of every visit, for life is too short to ever turn down the opportunity for a wild swim, which is like taking a free double espresso from nature. I have also found that a dip, be it in a Hampshire stream, a Highland loch or in the Syrtic Gulf of Libya, stamps a memory seal on the day. Never mind the odd ink drops of crude oil that you tread in on the sand, or the whistles of disapproval blown by the site guards: each British traveller should think of themselves as walking in the footsteps of Byron, lame on shore but a hero in the waters.

I have also always wanted to approach Leptis Magna the proper way, coming to this fabulous ruined Roman city on the Libyan shore from out of the sea. I have not yet managed this, but I have tried, by writing articles on Roman ruins for luxury yacht magazines, and even by taking a job as a lecturer on board a cruise ship in the hope of achieving this ambition, but it never quite worked out as planned. I always end up in the dusty car park by the old villas of the archaeological department, greeting the café owner and shopkeepers like long-lost friends, as well as an ancient Libyan archaeologist who sat in a wicker chair, like some protective deity in his white cap and cloak.

He deserved his tribute of respect, for he was the man who

discovered the Villa Selene sleeping among the sand dunes. This he did one summer by snorkelling his way around the rocks on the western edge of a long strip of sandy beach (20 kilometres west of Leptis Magna), where in trying to harpoon a fish he stumbled across blocks of stone covered in mosaic. They had fallen from the old marine terrace of a Roman seaside villa that the sea had taken a bite of during the winter storm of 1974. Fortunately most of the villa was buried under sand dunes, which just needed to be wheelbarrowed away.

It took me some time get inside the site, for there were local disputes about land ownership and access. I was also naive enough to go down the official route of requesting permission to visit, where I encountered hospitable enthusiasm, encrusted with last-minute avoidance. This obstruction with charm eventually unravelled itself into an everyday tale of bureaucratic caution. Libyan officials were proud to have identified and excavated the site by themselves, without the help of any neocolonial archaeological institute, but at the same time were anxious not to incur the scorn of the regime by being publicly criticised in the Western press. They were concerned that they might have restored it in an inappropriate way; that they had just cleared the site (not excavated it layer by layer like a proper technician); that they had never published their discoveries or revealed the small finds, and had in the end to call in the help of Italian specialists. So for years the site was fenced off with barbed wire, but postcards of its treasures were sold all over the country. The villa gates would be opened with a flourish for diplomatic delegations, but then slammed shut against foreign scholars.

There was also a second hurdle to cross, which was that the resident custodian was deaf, and proof against any amount of vigorous knocking on the gates once locked in his afternoon siesta. If you came in the morning, with a local he knew, and stayed well clear of any official Libyan channels, there was never a problem. I once took one of the world's greatest war photographers there, who was working on a book of the Roman ruins of North Africa. I had imagined Don McCullin would be enchanted by the place, but I noticed his cameras never left our jeep. Evidence of aristocratic ease was not a subject he cared to frame, but he loved the time-wrecked, half-pillaged ruins of Leptis.

I find the Villa Selene to be a perfect foil to Leptis Magna – an intimate domestic space set in contrast against the grand public monuments of that vast city of ruins. It is the seaside villa of a very wealthy individual from the Golden Age of the Roman empire in North Africa, but it is not grandiose in detail. There is a pleasing modesty in the proportion of the rooms, most of which interconnect. The villa is shaped like a broad U that looks north, directly out to the sea. All the rooms were designed to open out onto this marine-front open courtyard which was framed by a colonnaded walkway. It must have been a wonderful house to stay in, even for just one night, falling asleep and awakening to the sound of the surf on the rocks below.

Once again a modern visitor approaches the place from the wrong direction, by land, not from out of the sea. I have never come across any photograph that captures the essence of this magical place. This is especially true of the exterior, which looks drab, for the local ragstone walls were restored in the Seventies with mortar that looks wrong. But this can work its own magic on the visitor, for all the charm is reserved for the interior, especially the rooms of the north-west wing that cluster around a small light-well hall. Here the original frescoed walls stand intact, with the quick-drawn fluency of their coloured lines standing in contrast to the patient pebble-by-pebble detail of the floor mosaics. It is a stab of reality into our classical past, unfiltered by restoration, repair and textual debate, and reveals a time that looks, in this place, to have been totally gorgeous – playful, light, full of spiritual and sensual references, in need of no furniture apart from the voices of its old occupants, a few bronze stools and daybeds. This suite of rooms includes a small library, identified from the four deep corner cupboards.

The central room of the Villa Selene is the summer dining room that was furnished with the best-quality columns. On one side it is open to the sea and usefully flanked with alcoves for the days when you needed some shelter from the harsher winds. On the other side it backs onto a garden that may have filled this room with all the scents of the Mediterranean flora, protected from salt spray by high enclosing garden walls. A child's bedroom has been identified in the south-west wing, but the most memorable structure in this eastern half of the house is the bathhouse. It is set back from the sea terrace but entered through a splendid T-shaped hall, which I imagine to have been hung with family portrait-busts and scented with altars burning incense to the ancestral spirits and the guardian deities of the house. Here, one seems to be following in the wet footsteps of the ancient owners, following the shades of spectral hosts around this domestic labyrinth of hot and cold rooms, plunge pools and sweat lodges, all set around the domed room in the centre of the baths. Slivers of precious marble stand in pairs beside each other, like ossified Turkish end-papers riveted against the walls with bronze clamps.

Outside, a series of long flower-beds were planted beside a walkway paved in a simple but elegant red and yellow geometric mosaic. It seems that this was the formal entrance way to the villa, so that a gently sloping ramp, lined with plants, led up from the sandy beach to the east. This was the way guests would have arrived having been rowed in a skiff-like galley from the great city of Leptis Magna 20 kilometres to the east. Inland, it has been speculated that there may have been a home farm and a quarter of huts for the farmers, fishermen, servants and slaves that serviced the villa.

The biggest historical adjustment takes some time to register, for we look at such a house and think what a lovely place to live, amongst fresh fruit and mellow wine with summer sea breezes scented by the maquis, a place in which tomorrow you are free to bathe, to read or fish. But this attitude itself is the greatest luxury of this extraordinary villa, looking out to the waters of the Middle Sea, not with fear but with a trusting open-hearted contentment. For over most of the last four thousand years the people of the Mediterranean could not afford to build like this. Instead they needed to protect themselves from whatever might emerge from the sea, building city walls, watchtowers and hilltop sanctuaries against pirates and flotillas of pillaging sea-peoples. Only the late nineteenth and twentieth centuries and the Roman empire in the first and second centuries could have built the Villa Selene. It is this one fact that unites our era so dramatically with the occupants of this Roman house on the Libyan shore.

We know nothing of the occupants, when or by whom this haven was built, or how long it was lived in. We have no dates and no names. It is tempting to dream up some historical fiction for this magical place, as a literary retreat from the bustling city of Leptis Magna. It is harmless but foolish, for I think that an archaeological survey will one day turn up other buildings. Villa Selene is exactly a day's row west of Leptis Magna, and its fine beach would have been a known stopping place on the thousand-year-old maritime itinerary that skirted the North African shore.

The lack of hard archaeological facts did encourage me (on my third visit) to look ever more intently at the mosaics and fluently painted frescoes on the walls. Most especially because we know from three other villas also discovered on this coast (but which didn't survive so well) that the imagery selected was remarkably similar. So the chosen subject matters of the various mosaic floors can be read, not as a key to the owners' identity, but as mapping the mindset of their day.

If you return to the central room of the baths you notice that the wall mosaic offers fit, tough, strong men beating the crap out of each other. I didn't pick up anything camp or homoerotic here, despite the full-frontal nudity. Instead they seem to be of the same mood as the photographs from the sport pages of our newspapers, depicting muscular role models of the good citizen, more than capable of defending himself and winning respect from the expert application of physical force. On the floor, literally trampled underfoot by every user of the bath, is the head of the great lord of the oceans, his marine supporters looking ever bright and fresh from the splashed water of the baths. I thought at first this showed a surprising disrespect for Neptune, but learned that this mournful, watery-eyed deity represents fish-tailed Oceanus, an elemental giant of the old order of dethroned deities, relegated like Atlas to a geological role as a terrestrial supporter.

In the centre of one of the rooms in the north-west wing is an extraordinarily detailed depiction of a chariot race, laid out as a central panel so that it can be admired from whichever side of the room you are in. This has been used to illustrate history books, for everything is here like a scale model, and like a series of time-lapse photographs, we have a whole day at the races. The blank row of starter gates (either side of a central victory arch) stands at one end, waiting to be thrown open, then we see the four teams of four-horse chariots in a swirl of legs, colours and shadows. Then the slow victory circuit of the winner in the opposite direction (escorted by a mounted judge). In the centre of the track stands the architectural playground of the *spina* (a raised platform), complete with obelisks, memorials and fountains. It was a feature of the circus that each lap would be marked off by the sound of trumpets while some elaborate counter would be raised: a flag, a gilded spear, or something really lavish, like a series of fountains in the shape of dolphins, with eggs balanced on their beaks. Here if you look closely enough you can see both a row of dolphin fountains and an assistant moving about to set up a thyrsus-like club to mark the completion of the fifth lap. The cartoon-like vivacity of the scene breathes especial life into the ruins of the circus track beside the coast of Leptis, though it is safer to take this as a generic vista rather than an architectural plan. And with this exuberant floor, the villa-owner is surely trying to catch some moment on the wing, like the memory of the day when his team of horses won and his family was applauded by tens of thousands of their neighbours.

The room next door boasts a more complex image, a fully developed slice of mythic symbolism, looking like our equivalent of a gilt-framed masterpiece in a drawing room. For even if you don't know what on earth is happening here, the image reeks of urban literary culture from the great cities of empire, be it Rome or Antioch, Carthage or Alexandria, all cities equidistant from this villa as the boat crosses the waters. And no doubt the host would have been delighted to explain the symbolism of this piece to his guests. A seated deity holds a circular band through which must pass four well-wrapped but slightly reluctant matrons, each one clasping a bonny child. Off centre, the Lord Apollo and Lady Venus observe the scene. Apollo can be decoded as the sun, and hence the solar year, Venus as the moon that gives us our lunar cycle, whilst the circular band is chiselled with the signs of the zodiac, which subdivide our sky into twelve destinies akin to the twelve months of the solar year. The four matrons are identifiable as the four seasons, but can also be read as the four ages of mankind drawn through time by the lure of Venus and Cupid, who beguile off centre to the right with the power of love. Like so much of the art of the ancient world, it is empowered by the need to seize the hour, to live most fully now. And when your time comes, to die without regret.

This is emphatically repeated by the image of Lycurgus, two rooms to the north. Here a handsome, writhing male is caught in the grasp of a vine, having dropped his axe. This heroic nude is Lycurgus, king of Thrace, but here snared like a rabbit. His crime was to have foolishly attempted to resist the Lord Dionysus and his handmaiden Ambrosia, but he could stand in for any bearded puritan who takes an axe to a vine or attempts to place a prohibition on the transforming powers of wine and dance.

Less open to moral exhortation is the scene in one corner of the summer dining room, which lovingly records the tossing of prisoners into an amphitheatre, managed by a kilted gladiator and overseen by a togaed Roman magistrate. It looks chillingly like a specific event, some proud memory of orchestrated state savagery, a spectacle of ritual humiliation of the enemy for the delight of the home front – a hate session of the feared, objectified other. The victims wear trousers, which can be read as a label that these are the enemies of Rome from the Eastern front, though there is also a whiff of a sacrificial uniform about their gear, which chimes in with the mysterious inscription 'FiloSerapis Comp' – made by a lover of the Lord Serapis. This streak of violent propaganda enhanced the prestige of the house. The syncretic cult of Serapis was popular in the great cities of Alexandria and Athens, and strongly associated with the Ptolemaic heirs of Alexander the Great, as well as such recent heroes of empire as the emperors Vespasian and Caracalla, who both campaigned in the East. Once again the imagery of this villa allows us to fill the ruins of nearby Leptis Magna with colour. The amphitheatre in Leptis Magna remains in an astonishing state of preservation, for it was inserted into an old stone quarry down by the shore, and so is as much carved into the living rock as built from masonry. A visitor can explore the internal tunnels that allowed prisoners, wild animals and gladiators to make their sudden entrance into the bowl surrounded by thousands of seats.

The most important entertainments staged in the amphitheatres were the gladiatorial games. The city magistrate or electoral candidate paying for the show arranged matters through the *lanistae*, professional managers who ran stables of gladiators, provided wild beasts and arena attendants, as well as acting as judges on the day. The night before a show, a symbolic gladiatorial duel with muffled weapons was followed by a lavish public banquet. In the morning, as a warm-up, those sentenced by the magistrates to *damnatio ad bestias* were killed in the arena. First they would all be exhibited in chains, before being led out to their individual deaths; normally there was some form of torture, before they were mauled by wild beasts and finished off by a gladiator. As the villa mosaic makes clear.

Then it was time for the *venatio*, the wild-beast hunt. A troupe of dancing acrobats might entertain the crowd while the amphitheatre was transformed into a more suitable setting. Another popular interlude was for miniature catapults to fling tokens, which could be exchanged for prizes, up into the poorest seats. The *bestiarii*, gladiators specialising in wild-beast hunts, were a professional group, fighting and working with animals in a way not far removed from a professional English huntsman or keeper working today. They might slaughter antelope, wild ass and ostriches with arrows, spear wild boar, fight wildcats or face enraged bulls. In addition, they managed fights between animals, arranging for predatory cats to kill in the arena, or forcing pairs of chained animals, such as bears and bulls, to fight one another.

In the lunch hour it was the turn of robbers, arsonists and murderers to kill each other. The first pair were brought forth, one armed, one just dressed in a tunic. The business of the first was to kill the latter, which he seldom failed to do. After this feat he was disarmed and led out to confront a newcomer armed to the teeth, and so the butchery continued until all lay dead.

In the afternoon a fanfare of lutes, trumpets and horns announced the chief event of the day, the gladiatorial duels. First, the gladiators paraded in fine embroidered cloaks, their weapons carried by valets, before giving the famous collective greeting to the presiding magistrate: *Ave, morituri te salutant* ('Hail, we who are about to die salute you'). The duels were accompanied by music, the orchestra celebrating each success- ful parry and blow with a fanfare, by frantic betting and by roars of applause from the crowd. Gladiators, when disabled, could usually appeal to the crowd, who would wave handkerchiefs or gesticulate with their thumbs upright crying *Mitte* ('Let him go') or reversing their thumbs in a downward-jabbing motion and screaming *Iugula* ('Slay him'). The passions aroused were intense. Hawkers sold food and drink to quench thirsts and appetites along the benches, while prostitutes did a thriving trade in the dark vaults.

The courtyard of the Villa Selene was laid out with a grid

of geometric designs placed beneath the shaded walkway. This may have playfully suggested the knotwork of a woollen carpet, set in stone, or played a mirror-game of diversity with the painted woodwork struts of the ceiling. This severity has been broken on the south-east and north-west by a bit of pure whimsy that depicts a series of bearded white miniature men doing defensive battle with storks and crocodiles, using shards of broken pottery as shields, set about with sprigs of olive, lotus flowers and indifferent ducks. I found it impossible not to be charmed by scenes whose humour is largely based on mocking the grandeur of the staged set pieces in the rest of the house, yet they too contain dark references to the entertainments staged in the amphitheatre.

So what profile emerges from the owner of this house, who commissioned these mosaics? A family man, physically confident, a well-established member of a local landowning class, educated in the great cities and living towards the end of the Antonine Golden Age.

The house was never built over or quarried by later ages, for its end came suddenly – on the dawn of 21 July AD 365. The Cretan earthquake launched a tsunami of devastation to overwhelm its halls, maybe even buried it in the sand that covered and protected its walls and floors for the next 1,600 years. Light has already dulled the frescoes, rain has leached the walls, and shoes will gradually erode the mosaic floors. The fluently painted scenes will crack and crumble, and blow away as powder in the wind.

7

The New Forum of Leptis Magna

Leptis Magna was always an important link in Mediterranean trade, but it exploded into opulence in the third century when the Emperor Septimius Severus transformed his native city into the third-largest port in the Mediterranean. The haphazard scattering of offshore islands that had hitherto sheltered this wadi-mouth anchorage was united by vast masonry walls. These were then extended northwards to send two arms reaching straight out into the sea, their extremities capped by a lighthouse and a string of temple–shrines. A system of walkways led down from these ocean-defying ramparts to a broad pavement lined with warehouses and customs houses, from which another flight of stairways led down to the actual waterfront quays. Even in decay, with the harbour basin now filled in by wind-blown sand which is seasonally transformed into a boggy reed bed, the scale of the works is magnificent. This is no Potemkin backdrop for an imperial tour of inspection, for every detail of the workmanship, such as the stone mooring rings set into the walls, remains solid, and enduringly impressive. Having watched the completely exposed lighthouse being assailed by a winter storm, with great breakers smashing against the ancient walls like so many timed detonations, I felt like taking my hat off to the skill of these ancient masons. Nature did that for me, for a gale ripped the black sailor's cap off my head and flung it as an offering into the roaring sea. I was about to feel sorry for myself when my companion that day gave out a dry laugh: it reminded him of a journalist who had been scalped by a sharpshooter for having poked his head over the top of a bomb shelter.

This harbour was equipped with its own bathhouse, which stands just to the east, right above the shore. The excavated baths are impressive now only in their scale, but were a useful gift to sailors wishing to sluice away weeks of grimy life on deck before they promenaded up into the city, on a sailors' run ashore towards the delights of the circus track and amphitheatre.

On the southern edge of the docks, where the shallower draught of the harbour basin was used by smaller fishing boats, a pair of massive temples flanked the Wadi Labdah riverbed and overlooked the docks from raised terraces of stone. They are both now in total ruin, and can only exist in the imagination, though you can push through the undergrowth to stomp around among their vaults and raised podium. Or leastways I have always made sure to stomp here, ever since coming across a large black snake that seemed to own the place, and that deserved advance warning of trespassers in the precinct. The western temple was designed as a pair of shrines, united by a shared inscription and a colonnade of white Corinthian marble columns. It was raised to the glory of the deified Flavian emperors Vespasian and his son Titus, the conqueror of Jerusalem.

On the eastern bank stood the colossal temple of the Zeus of eastern Syria, Jupiter Dolichenus. You reach its raised podium by way of a vast monumental staircase which indicates that this must have been one of the largest such cult centres in the entire empire. It was raised by the Emperor Septimius Severus, as part of his grand transformation. What was this temple to Jupiter doing right down by the harbour front, instead of standing

right in the heart of a classical city, in the way that Rome's
Capitol overlooks the Forum? Fish harbours are places of animation, but they have always been stronger on scent than high
rent. Yet here at Leptis, rather than being hidden away behind
courtyards and porticoes the temple stairway leads straight
down to the harbour front, which on most days would have
been crammed with nets, baskets, guts, and the hubbub of a fish
market. Fish were never offered to the gods in sacrifice. What
on earth could explain this most unlikely of juxtapositions?

The cult of Jupiter Dolichenus was a mystery, and still
remains so. It was physically centred on the city–shrine of
Doliche (modern Dülük in eastern Turkey, near the Syrian
frontier), which stood, then as now, on a cultural frontier.
Recent archaeological work has confirmed what the ancients
knew all along, which is that the shrine of Doliche is immeasurably old – part of a settlement with 40,000 years of continuous
history behind it. The sky and storm god of Doliche was known
as all-father Teshub by the Hittites, as Adad by the Akkadians,
as Baal by the Canaanites, and by the Semites of Arabia as
Hadad. He was customarily depicted with thunderbolts, with a
double-headed war hammer, and, in the very recognisable style
of the ancient Middle East, was often portrayed as standing on
the back of a bull, just as Juno Dolichenus rode on the back
of a deer and Ishtar on a lion. He can sometimes be depicted
wearing a Phrygian cap, haloed with a sunburst or a helmet of
bull's horns. From Latin inscriptions we hear that Jupiter Dolichenus' titles had remained unchanged over the centuries, for
there he was 'preserver of the firmament', 'invincible provider'
and 'paramount deity'.

The intensely secret element of his cult slips in and out of
the margins of the most ancient of texts, for it appears that, like
Tammuz and Osiris, he was fated to be killed in battle by his

divine brother but then redeemed and reborn. However, these matters were too important, too fearsome and ill-omened, ever to be committed to a text. The sacrifice of a bull in a subterranean cave – akin to what little we know about the cult of Mithras – was wrapped up in this inner mystery of his rebirth. Once again, recent work in Doliche (by a German–Turkish archaeological team) has unearthed an ancient underground cult cavern. These beliefs were not alien to the Hellenised classical world, for in a comparable manner the Cretans knew Zeus as the great all-father but also were aware that the birthplace of the great god was in the cave of Mount Ida in Crete. This was also whispered to be the place of his death, bound up with the archaic veneration of 'the Boy' – the island's secretive cult of the beardless boy Zeus Welkhanos, with a cockerel on his knee. Cocks in the ancient world were the gift of choice from an older man to his young male lover.

Behind the greatest, most powerful deity of the universe lurks something so dark that it cannot be named. We know that the cult of Jupiter Dolichenus was very popular in the Roman army, especially in the middle of the second century AD. The first Latin inscription about his cult has been found in North Africa, in southern Algeria, at the legionary headquarters of Lambaesis, and has been dated to AD 150. Nineteen other shrines, altars and temples to Jupiter Dolichenus have been located, and no doubt more will turn up. So far, the most significant fact is that all of them are associated with a soldier emperor or an active military frontier, such as along the Rhine, the Danube or Hadrian's Wall.

The patronage of the Emperor Septimius Severus took the cult to its zenith of popularity. There were various reasons for this. First, we know that as a middle-aged, middle-ranking careerist he had consulted the oracle of Syrian Zeus at the city of Apamea, on the Orontes River in central Syria. There for the first time he had been saluted as a future ruler. The second connection was that the emperor's Syrian wife (and mother of his two male heirs) was descended from a line of priest–kings of the ancient city of Emesa (present-day Homs). The city of Emesa was just like Doliche in that it stood on the frontiers of Syria and was dominated by a cult temple to the all-father sky god Baal El-Gebal (the Lord of the Mountains). Third, I believe that the emperor was determined to complete the transformation of the Roman empire from an ethnic imperium based on the city of Rome to one that embraced all the provinces as equal partners in a Mediterranean commonwealth. Syncretic cults that took elements of Syrian, Egyptian, Hellenistic and Anatolian cultures and blended these into Latin forms were a central part of this policy, the more so if they also pleased the army and helped elevate his own family into a divinely sanctioned monarchy.

This is why I believe that he ordered the construction of a magnificent temple to the Syrian Jupiter at his home city of Leptis Magna. It looked out of the harbour, greeting every person who arrived by sea, reminding them that the rule of the emperor (and his sons) had been ordained by Zeus. We know little about the workings of the second-century cult of Zeus Doliche, though it seems that only those who had been admitted into the mystery were permitted worship at the shrine. The shrines of Zeus Doliche were equipped with side aisles, which may have been used for the sharing of a sacred meal by the initiates, in a similar style to the way that we think Mithraic chapels were used. We also know that the temples were equipped with colleges of priests (one inscription lists fifteen names) that included a rank of worshippers whose task was to carry the bier of the god. This office of bier-bearer is an intriguing detail, for we know that in Syria the gods were honoured with annual processions that made use of the monumental avenues that are such outstanding architectural features of the ancient Syrian cities that have survived to our own times, such as Apamea, Damascus, Jerash and Palmyra. The cult statues were carried in procession from one temple to another, in a form of sacred marriage that included a complex and ornate ritual vocabulary of solemn ablutions, adornments, visits to cult caves, springs, mountains and holy gardens. If this is what Septimius Severus had in mind for his native city of Leptis Magna, all sorts of things begin to make sense about his radical reworking of the city centre.

The harbour he built was primarily designed for the export of olive oil and the safe housing of the fleet that carried the imperial court. It would also have been a magnificent theatre in which to enact the annual opening of the trade routes of the Mediterranean with the arrival of the mother goddess in the spring. This ritual happened all over the Mediterranean in countless different forms, and to an extent continues in some form to this day. But Septimius' embellished city of Leptis Magna now boasted a temple where the all-father Zeus could entertain his consort, borne straight off the boat up the slowly ascending temple stairs.

This was just the beginning, for Emperor Septimius also constructed a vast processional way on the eastern edge of his old city. He did this by hiding the old wadi riverbed within an embankment and placing his new avenue over the land thus cunningly reclaimed. This processional way now lies in ruins, but every now and then the visitor to Leptis Magna catches a glimpse of the colossal scale, the unbridled magnificence of this project. It is still staggering. On either side of the processional carriageway stood a towering arcade, made of gorgeous, slender, pale-green cipollino marble columns, given an additional boost of height and elegance by being perched on altar-like marble plinths. Some of the arches of this arcade have been reconstructed by the patient hand of the archaeologist, and though designed to be seen at a distance, lose nothing from a close inspection. Nor do the gorgeous Corinthian capitals, carved from white marble, which midway through the processional route transform themselves into the lotus-and-acanthus form of a Pergamene capital. At the crossing place of a side street with the processional avenue, this arcade throws out a wider and a higher arch, as if the emperor and his architect had looked long and hard at the examples offered up in Syria (including the one that used to stand at Palmyra) and here strove for a final stab at perfection.

We don't know whether this central way was paved, or whether the said aisles were intended to be lined with rentable shops. In Palmyra the central avenue remained camel-friendly, and so was left covered with the welcoming crunch of desert sand, while in Euesperides (an ancient harbour in eastern Libya) the streets were covered with an exotic gravel made from the recycled detritus of crushed murex seashells.

One of the oddities of Leptis Magna is that this spectacular avenue doesn't seem to lead anywhere, but instead to terminate at the back wall of one of the city's major bathhouses. But once again, if one perceives this thoroughfare as primarily designed for the processional cart of a god, or gods, then there is indeed a destination. It is the vast, three-storey apsidal fountain, looking like the back wall of a theatre mated with a temple interior, that the emperor placed at the top of his new processional avenue. Although this offered water in glorious abundance to the citizens, it could also briefly become, at the proper season, the ablution shrine for deities. It is set at a slight angle to the avenue, to allow a piazza to emerge before this extraordinarily lavish water-fountain. Even in Rome it would have looked opulent; in water-scarce North Africa, in a city only 50 miles from the Sahara desert, the effect of this profusion of columns, statues, basins and fountains must have been multiplied tenfold. It would have been dazzlingly magnificent.

When architectural historians look for references, for precedents to explain this nymphaeum at Leptis Magna, they add to the confusion by referring back to the Septizodium of Rome. This is one of the most tantalising lost buildings of Rome. It was an enormous, mysterious façade, believed to have been imbued with spiritual and mystical references, and which was also constructed to the explicit orders of the Emperor Septimius Severus. With this building in Rome he also created a plaza, which became a popular meeting place for the people, where the Via Appia ends before reaching up towards the Palatine Palace of the Caesars. So the Septizodium gets lots of literary references but no single description. There is one etching that shows a fragment of this building before it was quarried for medieval building stone. This conveys a three-storey arrangement of columns, like the back of a Roman theatre, but there are dozens of variant reconstructions of the rest of this lost monument, some of which favour a half-dome, whilst other versions rise to seven storeys. Some contend that it portrayed the emperor's favourable nativity horoscope, others that it was a monument to the seven planets, which also played on the emperor's given name of Septimius. Whatever it was, one can be certain that it was designed to display the emperor's rule as celestially ordained, inevitable, and set in solid stone – just like the nymphaeum he created for his home town of Leptis Magna.

Then there is the little matter of the New Forum that he bequeathed to the city. It stands just beside his processional avenue. The shock of first walking into this space, twenty years ago, has never left me. We were totally alone – Libya had been put into diplomatic and trade isolation, by the USA – and the place was raked into vivid colour by the sunset. None of us could speak, as we tried to sort out our emotions and reference points and then quietly unfolded maps to orient ourselves. For even in its quarter-restored state, heaped with half-sorted piles of stones and a low stretch of the arcade, like a stonemason's yard, it is the single most magnificent remnant of the Roman empire left to us. Then we were joined by a chorus, a group of beautifully turned out Filipina maids with sun-umbrellas from the hotels and embassies of Tripoli, on their day off, who were singing hymns as they were led around the ruins by an enormous and voluble American missionary, determined to tick off all the places where early Christian martyrs might have been enslaved, abused or put on trial. It was evangelical, self-centred, unhistorical, but heartfelt. It also broke the ice on our restraint, and we began to see that this place was bigger, bolder and more magnificent than anything anyone of us had seen, or had imagined.

Over the years this splendour has grown, for as with a favourite jigsaw puzzle I can now sort the random pieces strewn over this great piazza into their proper places. The magnificent outer walls, with their Egyptianised gateways, which still totally enclose this rectangular piazza (100 by 60 metres) and dominated my memories for years with their height and strength, would have been near-invisible from here. They are the bones that shaped the city's flesh. Shops lined the southern and eastern faces of this square, but even these would have been out of direct sight, for the whole square was enclosed by an arcade that marched the magnificence of the great processional avenue into this square and then festooned it around this forum. The same superb slender columns of pale green cipollino marble were also here, standing on matching white marble bases. But the Pergamene capitals were given one final touch of sophistication, for like a pendant jewel, between each arch of the arcade was set an individually sculpted medallion of Medusa-like heads alternating with Nereids from the oceans.

These were to be overshadowed by the great free-standing temple that rose in the south-east corner. A slow ascent of stairs rippled upwards to reach the high podium, once dominated by a forest of pink granite columns hewn from the quarries of Aswan, in the furthest southern reaches of Egypt. On the lower faces of the temple, deep reliefs were carved into the marble, staging the popular theme of the gigantomachy, the battle between fish-tailed giants and the Olympian gods. On one level, this chosen image is a foundation document of mankind's experience, when the anarchic masters of Ice and Volcano were at last subdued; on another it is a potent metaphor for the harmony of an ordered society, and for the triumph of agriculture over the unruly passions of the hunter–gatherer. The temple has been comprehensively looted for building stone, and also mined by Byzantine lime-burners racing to piece together a defensible fortress wall, so the full inscription has never been found, and probably never will be. And yet it is unthinkable that such an obsessively pious emperor as Septimius Severus could have committed the hubris of raising a shrine to himself in his own lifetime.

But this is what guides and guidebooks continue to tell us. The temple must have been dedicated to the twin gods of Leptis Magna, Phoenician Shadrap and Malik–Ashtart (Liber Pater and Melkarth), better known as Bacchus and Hercules. Cassius Dio, not normally hard on his old boss Septimius Severus, records in his history that the emperor 'built an excessively large temple to Bacchus and Hercules'. And though he doesn't locate it, this must surely be it. Any possibility of a doubt is removed when you leave the forum–piazza and pass into the Basilica, the monumental ruins of the law courts, which has the size and feel of a cathedral (it became one 400 years later). For in the two apses of this double-ended law court, some richly carved pilasters that flank these monumental niches have somehow survived centuries of marble theft, iconoclasm and lime-burners. They are artistic largesse from the past, gorgeous in their deeply undercut details, and are believed to have been the work of the skilled marble carvers of Aphrodisias – the city of Venus in Anatolia (modern Turkey). One set is dedicated to the adventures of Hercules, while at the other end we can still admire the attributes and associates of Bacchus intertwined with his grapevine. So the pairing achieved in the great temple shrine is also articulated in these law courts, which from their surviving inscription (whose monumental, chiselled Latin script dominates the centre of the ruin) was begun by Septimius Severus, and completed in AD 216 by his son Caracalla.

The Basilica is the peak of their gifts to their home town, which began with the vast new harbour and dockyard, overlooked by the vast new temple to Jupiter Doliche, then continued with the construction of a brand-new grand processional avenue worthy of an ancient city of Syria and culminating in one of the world's most opulent nymphaeum water fountains, to lead through the spectacular New Forum, complete with a sensational temple to the two patron deities of Leptis Magna, and then finally on to a magnificently imperial law court.

It is an extraordinary bequest, but I have always been convinced that more was intended. For I have long believed that the Severan New Forum complex was built in loving reference to the Trajanic New Forum, which for centuries remained the most admired structure of ancient Rome, the central goal of all visitors and pilgrims to the city. So it gave me a rush of pleasure to discover that the New Forum of Leptis Magna was designed on exactly half of the scale of Trajan's Forum in Rome, so that the Leptis piazza is 60 by 100 metres, to Rome's 120 by 200 metres. Trajan had placed his basilica to the north of his forum, just as it appears at Leptis. On the other side of this open-doored basilica he had constructed a smaller piazza, which housed the famous Trajan's Column in its centre and was fronted by a pair of libraries and a temple. Just such a space also exists in Leptis, already walled off from the rest of the city, but never developed. This would also help explain the blocks of masonry found by puzzled archaeologists to the north of the Basilica, already shaped but clearly never used in any of the structures. Somewhere in the imperial palace there must have been plans drawn up for the column of the Emperor Septimius, who had indeed restored the imperial frontiers in the Middle East to those that Trajan had established. As we will see, in other corners of the empire he planned to match and exceed what any of his great predecessors had achieved.

8

Septimius Severus

It was not just his home town of Leptis Magna that prospered, for there is hardly a Roman city in North Africa that did not grow more beautiful, more useful and more holy during the reign of the Emperor Septimius Severus. His influence is everywhere proclaimed: the view through an imperial triumphal archway designed to frame the prospect of rolling acres of farmland; the construction of an elegant new marketplace flanked with colonnaded walkways, lined with shop stalls and kiosks and overlooked by a fountain and a public weighing scale; a new piazza built as another element of the good life, halfway between the forum and the theatre; a delicate line of three interconnected temple–shrines overlooking an ancient spring-fed sanctuary; or a vast new bathhouse ornamented with statues and marbles like some royal palace but used every day by the people. If you have walked in wonder among the haunting ruins of Volubilis in Morocco, Timgad in southern Algeria, Dougga in Tunisia, Djemila in northern Algeria and Leptis in Libya, you will identify these places.

On the southern edge of Leptis Magna, astride the coast road to Carthage and the roadstead south into the Sahara, stands one of the most distinctive monuments to this man, the triumphal arch of Septimius Severus. It is a cube of white marble scooped through by four arches, a bold, imposing and innovative experiment in architecture, a first essay in baroque, for the pediments have literally been turned on their heads. So instead of supporting the projecting edges of a temple roof, they stand upright like four guardian horns, perched on the free-standing corner columns. Those who have travelled deeper south into the desert will be able to recognise how this radical architectural innovation also dances a reference to the acroteria that embellished Saharan tomb–altars.

The whole edifice of the arch was also mounted on a traffic island, so that it looked down on the swirl of provincial traffic that once flowed around it. If you advance out of the African sun to take shelter in the shade, you will find that the four archways support a hexagon of massive stone beams that carry the dome. It is a pregnant model, an experiment pointing the way to all the domed churches of Byzantium and Ottoman Istanbul built over the next thirteen hundred years. The walls have everywhere been lined with carved marble, a triumphal profusion of winged victories, trophies and imperial eagles. Those on the attic, the uppermost portion of the arch, are exact portraits of the imperial family, engaged in the solemn business of offering up sacrifices to the gods on each face of the arch.

Emperor Septimius Severus was born in Leptis Magna, so he is a fascinating individual for anyone interested in Roman North Africa. But it was not just his own city and home province that benefited from his rule, for under him the whole Roman empire reached its dazzling apogee. He is arguably one of the greatest lawmakers, statesmen and architects in the history of Rome, a man worthy to stand in line, and clasp the hands of both Augustus and Justinian. He was also a conqueror, who expanded the empire in the east, the south and the furthest north-west, so his personal battle honours (after he had won three rounds of civil war) included Iraq, the Sahara and Scotland, places that tested the logistics of organised warfare to the utmost degree, yet he triumphed in all these very different zones. He was also a family man, endlessly depicted as a contented middle-aged father, full beard framing a round face, beside his companion-wife and two healthy sons. He was also pious, both as man and as emperor, paying lavish respect to all the gods whilst taking a personal interest in mystical cults, so that he came to develop a syncretic intellectual philosophy that might encompass everything together. He was also the last really convincing pagan ruler of the empire, creating not reacting, so not concerned with prosecuting schisms or minorities, but rather with slowly combining all traditions into a common culture, seemingly on the point of creating something both ancient and modern, much in the way that Buddhism formed itself out of Hinduism, but cherished its heritage and did not destroy it – unlike the way the Christians would behave with the shrines of the classical world. As we look closer at this extraordinary man, we may find these qualities all of a piece with the paranoid, psychotic traits of a ruthless autocrat.

Septimius was born into one of the leading mercantile families of Leptis Magna, a city-port of Libya. It traded both ways: out into the Mediterranean and the slipstream of shipping connections that led east towards Alexandria, westward to Carthage, and northward to Sicily. Its other trading valve ran south, to the vast olive groves of the agricultural hinterland, as well as the filament of trade routes that led into and across the Sahara. Leptis was not alone in this, for it was part of an ancient confederacy of three cities, the Tri-Polis, that dominated this most southern section of the North African coast. Tripolitania worked well against any exterior threat, but within this league the three cities were furious competitors. Each of them was linked to a rival web of alliances with the tribes of the Berber hinterland, so the whole region could explode into internal turmoil based on nothing more substantial than these long-standing civic rivalries.

To the east of Leptis stretched nothing but the Syrtic desert, for the Sahara dominates most of the Libyan shore. The Syrtic desert discourages amateurs. It was, and remains, a bleak expanse, flat, saline, dusty and desiccated, patrolled by sand-charged desert winds from the south and humid briny sea mists from the north. You would have thought the shore might at least have been enriched by the most wonderful series of sand-scapes, where the charm of the desert crescents mingles with the coastal dunes. But this is not so, for the wind has not deposited its load of sand here, but instead has sculpted the sandstone shore into a sharp-edged series of shelves, some submerged, to rip out the keel from your boat, while those on the tideline will rasp the face and hands off any sailor flung onto them by the waves. Only deep inland does this desert grow more attractive, with the awesome reach of the red and then the black deserts. Once again this is not a zone of sand but of rock, so aside from a thin line of cleared tracks, the wind-etched rocks and pebbles of this volcanic landscape make for arduous going. This whole region was the territory of the Nasamones, a Berber tribal confederation, hewn into a nation of lean, tough warrior-herdsmen by the Darwinian forces of their environment. To their south, holding the deep Sahara from a handful of isolated oasis–valleys, was the land of the Garamantes.

Westward of Leptis, the landscape could be taken for anywhere in the Mediterranean, especially in the spring and autumn months, though the long summer is unmistakably

Saharan. There was also useful grazing land in the limestone hills of the interior, intolerably arid by any European standards, but in the hands of the right farmers, with the right livestock and the back-breaking work required for dry-farming, it was viable country. The shore anchorages of this western region were in the hands of an allied confederacy of Phoenician–Berber merchants, who knew their way around the salt flats and the complex web of sandbanks and tidal straths that encircled the island of Jerba. They formed the Emporia, the sprinkle of trading places turned towns beside the cities of the Tripolis.

To what extent the populations of all these ports were Berber (which is to say indigenous natives of North Africa) and to what extent Phoenician (natives of half a dozen port cities along the Syrian coast) is a moot point. I would guess that a DNA test would find that 80 per cent of the bloodline was Berber, flavoured with Mediterranean and Saharan strands. In terms of language and culture you would have turned these proportions on their head. The ports were proud daughters of Tyre, Sidon and Byblos.

The Phoenician port cities along the North African shore had emerged gradually. They grew up from a ready interbreeding of peoples and practices, and not through sudden settler colonisation – osmosis rather than conquest. The cities slowly emerged from out of a string of anchorages astride a trade route that had been in use for many thousands of years. They were certainly used by the Canaanite merchants of Bronze Age Syria, and they passed as a birthright to the half-dozen Phoenician cities that somehow survived the shipwreck of Canaanite civilisation caused by the Iron Age. So from about 1000 BC Phoenician merchants were consistently working their way along this North Africa shore, usually as part of their eastward-bound run home, as the prevailing tides and winds dictated.

These journeys were tough, and as about as romantic as driving a caravan of container lorries full of scrap metal across the USA. It was the commercial spur of this ancient trade route: the export of ingots of tin, copper and smaller quantities of gold and silver to the great manufacturing cities of the Middle East. The Phoenicians tried to buy at the best rates by going direct to the mines, but more often than not were forced to deal with cabals of merchants and local monarchs, who all added their cut to the price. Take Cyprus as an example, where copper had been mined in the foothills of the central Troodos mountains for thousands of years. This export trade was controlled by a dozen monarchical city-states that fringed the coast, all riven by ancient feuds with their neighbours while trying to become the export hub for the inland towns that sat beside the mines. For the tin trade to Cornwall, or the trade in gold dust from West Africa, there was no choice but to stand at the end of a long chain of intermediaries.

These were not family excursions, indeed the crews (on the evidence of a few chance shipwrecks) were quite small, often no more than half a dozen. From these wrecks we can see that each sailor seems to have travelled with his own mess kit and in one case a bag of weed, to while away the boredom of long crossings. Worms and woodrot, even in the salt-pickled Mediterranean waters, progressively weakened a boat, which might be careened on beaches by careful owners, though too thorough a drying of the timbers by a desert wind could also shrink and warp them and cripple a craft. Unless repaired, a wooden boat tended to have a useful life of between twenty and twenty-five years, which fostered a tendency to anchor ships as storage boats towards the end of their working life. So the first communities were probably formed from a few sampan-like boats that were too old to go to sea and had been anchored around an offshore islet. A good local supply of spring water, which would attract all the passing merchants in order to refresh their water supply, was an essential feature. Then over the years huts were built, and these gradually converted into ragstone houses, which for all their modesty proclaimed their loyalty to the Near East in their rectangular, courtyard-framing layout.

In such a context, the brides, housekeepers and mothers for these Phoenician traders would all have been local women, which brought the added advantage of connecting the isolated merchants on the shore to the local tribes through a marriage alliance. So within a few centuries a network of cousins and in-laws allowed for trade goods to flow inland. Craft techniques would also spread like this, for the Phoenicians introduced better ways of weaving and building, as well as dyeing and working cloth, leather and wood. There was never any sense of racial pride, and even the great nobles of Carthage married 'out', taking Greek, Sicilian, Sardinian, Spanish and Berber brides, be they labelled Libyan, Numidian or Mauretanian.

Surprisingly, for a nation of urban-based seafarers, the most useful Phoenician innovation in North Africa flourished in the gardens and orchards. They understood the mysterious techniques behind the transplanting and grafting of fruit and nut trees, as well as the exact science of pruning: when to cut a tree back so savagely that it looked half dead, but would treble the fruit yield the following year. Even so, this same act, performed at the wrong season or too often, would kill a tree, which might represent an investment of generations of toil. The saplings must be watered but not drowned, their roots encouraged to spread, not blighted by over-irrigation. The years must be counted off in threes: one modest, one bad, one bumper, as is still the way with olives. The arid land had to be ploughed twice a year, but despite all this intensive labour, it should not be planted up, even with fodder crops. In a well-watered oasis, however, the reverse could be applied, as a hierarchy of palms, then olives, then pomegranates allowed more delicate plants to be grown in the protective cover of their shade. Some trees pollinate themselves, others – like the palm – need assistance. In the arid lands of the far south, it took intensive labour to terrace the bleak-looking mountains, not only to hold enough soil for a tree to root itself, but to channel, divert and control the occasional desert rainstorms, for the rains make up for their rarity by the violence of their nature. A Saharan farmer had not only to catch this sudden surplus, but also to tame it, less its torrents should rip apart his terraces. I have seen a dry dusty gravel bed turn into a raging Nile before my eyes, which bowled vast boulders along its course like skittles, and then watched it drain away in three days. Any traveller in desert lands will also have shared the experience of walking up a dry mountain gorge and looking up astonished to see vast tree trunks wedged into rocks a hundred feet up the cliff-face, evidence of the scale of these periodic desert floods.

Orchards require years of investment before they offer a return, but all the while have to be protected against local livestock, wild herds, and the even wilder herds of nomads. We don't know quite when or how this all happened, but happen it did, and as any traveller in the lands of Libya can tell you, one of the most bizarre and impressive sights to stumble across is the ruins of an ancient olive mill. The first time I saw one, it looked like a classical version of Stonehenge, a series of dolmens formed from clean-cut masonry. Time had swept away all traces other than these massive blocks of stone, whose weight was a counterbalance to the force of the timber-presses. Once excavated, I learned to pick out such telltale details as the circular drain cut into the floor stones to pool the oil. Scent, animation, pulp and the harmonious stacks of reed mats would be learned later.

One Christmas about twenty-five years ago, my wife and I took a picnic out to a hill fort on the edge of the Sahara, a simple affair of fresh bread, a tin of tuna and some olive oil. I found a flint tool which was accepted as a pendant, though we had promised not to ruin the purity of the day with presents. We have it still, for it turned out that we were not looting the desert of prehistoric artefacts, but recycling the rejected plate from a nineteenth-century flintlock rifle. We were joined by a family who had come to harvest their grove of olive trees, which we were sitting under. They insisted that we stay, and enlivened our picnic with gifts. We watched entranced as the ground was swept, then reed mats placed under the trees to catch the olives. I noticed that only the women picked the fruit, using clawlike gloves fashioned with goat's-horn fingers. These horn gloves looked just the sort of thing that a chorus of Bacchic women might use to rip a young musician apart if he had trespassed onto their holy mountain. They were also terribly efficient at raking the olives off the tree onto the mats, which were then scooped up and carried to a threshing ground, where the fruit was rapidly graded and sorted into piles, and separated from leaves and bad or unripe fruit. Cones of glistening green, black and purple grew ever taller. The men did the carrying and mat-laying, the children and old women did the sorting, and the young mothers harvested the trees. We were told that there was always plenty of work at the harvest season, though clearly this particular family was proudly self-sufficient in labour. In the old days, nomads would come with their flocks and graze the orchards after the harvest, whilst their women helped pick the trees, and would be paid in olive oil at the end of the season, but now I was told the hired hands only wanted coin.

A chartered lorry turned up later to take the crop straight to the mill, which we were taken to see, in the half-light of dusk. It was like an ants' nest, for everyone was working flat out at their tasks but no one was shouting. Batches of fruit were publicly weighed on great scales, then signed for, as they were poured into collective silos. In the background, a series of presses were being worked. Cascading ripples of oil oozed out and then ran off together in a golden stream as another turn of the winch would tighten the mast-like timber and increase the flow again. As one press flowed, another would ebb. Elsewhere in the mill other presses were being prepared. Shovelfuls of crushed olives were being taken from the trench upon which the upright millstone turned, and were then packed into raffia 'scourtins' (which look like giant tea-cosies) that were strung together like a necklace on the upright pole of the press. At other stations, the press had finished, and the tightly packed olive husks were extracted from the scourtins, washed for the next session, and the husks added to the vast reeking mountain at the back of the mill. In a corner, a team of young men, their clothes uniformly greased and blackened with oil, were being given a break and sat in a companionable circle dipping bread into a common stewpot (of peppers, onions and eggs) while a teapot brewed on top of a blue gas bottle cunningly fitted with a terracotta ceramic hob.

All this had to be done at breakneck speed, to catch the olives before they spoiled. The mill had been at work since the end of September, and would be run flat out for about three months, after which the men could rest. We had caught them right at the end of their annual campaign.

It gave me an idea of how things might have happened, or at least smelt, in the ancient economy, for I was fascinated to see how a tiny patch of family-owned olive trees had been integrated, but not subsumed, into a complicated process. Local patterns of landowning did not have to be altered to enable this agricultural industry to thrive. Family plots can coexist with orchard estates, and the oil once pressed was divisible into any number of fractions, allowing the mill-owner, the merchant and the tribal lord to all take their percentage, their tithe, their rent, as well as the grower. But once you had an olive press at work, other things naturally fed into the cycle. You needed amphorae to store the oil, so you required local potteries. You also required some security over the tracks that led down to a local port. And you needed surplus labour at harvest time.

∴

And this is how Leptis enters our historical narrative, as a Phoenician port rich from the export of olive oil, and one highly integrated into the Berber hinterland. Historians have looked at the historical names of the three cities of Tripolitania: Leptis, Oea (modern Tripoli) and Sabratha, and seen how they clearly evolved out of their Punic inscriptions: Lpqy, Wy't and Sbrt'n, but it is only recently that linguists have realised that these words are ultimately Berber in origin, not Phoenician. We also know that it was a Berber tribal confederation, the Macae, who allied themselves with the three coastal cities, to drive out the Greek colony that had been suddenly established in their midst, at the Wadi el-Caam. This is clearly not the action of a repressed people, groaning under the yoke of the colonial traders of the coast. Indeed the whole nature of this regional economy suggests a deep integration between the cities on the coast and the agricultural interior.

The region was allied to the Carthaginian empire but remained self-governing. It is believed that Masinissa took refuge here, somewhere between the Emporia and the Saharan Garamantes, before he became an ally of Rome. Later he tried to extend his direct rule over the zone, and managed to briefly levy a tribute of a talent a day. This is testimony to the region's extraordinary wealth, for a talent could pay a skilled workman for nine years or keep a galley crew paid for a month. The death of the old king and the fall of Carthage freed Tripolitania and the Emporia from paying this supertax.

Instead the city of Leptis was free to pursue its own foreign policy, weaving a careful path between the power blocks, bending with the wind, whichever way it blew. For instance the city opted out of the destruction of the Jugurthine wars by formally becoming an ally of Rome during the consulship of Bestia. It was a wise but callous policy that met with local opposition. A local leader named Hamilcar orchestrated support for the embattled Berber prince so successfully that the pro-Roman party in the city had to invite four Ligurian cohorts (second-rate militia from the northern Italian coast) to stiffen the loyalty of the city. But Leptis weathered its way through this factional split, and also negotiated its way through the intricate, murderous faction fights of the Roman civil wars. This was a dangerous period, when the eastern half of Libya (Cyrenaica) was first subdivided from the Ptolemaic kingdom of Egypt, then annexed by Rome in 70 BC. It was also the opportune moment when the city fathers who governed Leptis, having chosen well, could afford to build themselves a formal new city centre, embellished with twin temples.

The choice of the two presiding deities of the city speaks volumes about the nature of the community at Leptis. Not for them the fickle storm gods of war and the gloomy blood sacrifices of children required by the ancient deities. Instead Leptis decided to look out towards the universal through two spiritual heroes, Shadrap and Melkarth, who offer us a totally different perspective on the Phoenician belief system.

Melkarth was the Phoenician original for Greek Heracles (Roman Hercules). He was a god but not a god, as his whole legend cycle stresses his origins as a doomed mortal. He was a hero, a deified man, whose achievements and suffering (including an agonising death) led him to be elevated among the Olympians. His adventures were drawn partly from a Phoenician take on the story of Gilgamesh and partly from an idealised hero-king of a city. That made Melkarth a very humanistic choice for a spiritual hero, like elevating Lenin, Gandhi or King Alfred to stand on the national podium. Leptis was not alone in this choice. His most famous sanctuary in the Phoenician world was in the furthest west of all their cities, at Gades (now Cadiz), where blood sacrifices were forbidden and the priests were clad in simple linen, like a group of resident philosophers.

Shadrap was freely equated with Greek Dionysus and Roman Bacchus, the most fun-loving and least austere of all the divinities. He is a beardless god, cast forever as a carefree young man who brought the gifts of wine, ecstatic dance, mystery plays and sensual pleasure to the world. Though a god, he was also, once again, almost a demigod, for his cult has been traced back to the cult of the sacrificial young king, the representative of the burst of vegetable growth in the spring, who is doomed to be sacrificed with the harvest and reborn. So there are trails of a Prometheus-like hero mortal at the root of the Dionysus cult, a doomed Orpheus figure, who has to die for us to prosper, just as the vine has to be cut and pressed to create that magical liquid called wine. This god was also forever associated with somewhere not quite home, coming from outside, from the East, somewhere not quite decent, appealing to women, youths and an underclass, not the proud ruling patriarchs. The combination of these two figures, Melkarth and Shadrap, as the ruling deities of Leptis reveals an inclination towards honouring the achievements of mankind rather than bowing to the diktats of heaven.

The city fathers needed all of their mortal skills about them if they were to succeed in maintaining their prosperity and independence. They had from their own traditions created a balanced constitution, neither democratic nor aristocratic nor monarchical. The city of Leptis was governed by a pair of elected magistrates (the suffetes we have seen in Carthage) whose power was balanced by a council of the great and an assembly of the people. From the telltale evidence of inscriptions we know that there was also a prefect of sacred affairs, who oversaw the college of priests that ran each shrine. There was also a curator of public money and a pair of junior officials, the Mahazin, that watched over the markets.

We have already heard that King Juba I of Numidia was a close ally of the aristocratic senatorial faction in Rome. He used these connections in an attempt to annex Tripolitania during the Roman civil wars, reviving a traditional dream of the Numidian kings, but it made the political situation even more tense when Cato marched an army across the Syrtic desert to join forces with Juba and rested his column of men at Leptis.

So the city (whatever its actual freewheeling inclinations) looked as if it had been an ally of the Roman senatorial party when Julius Caesar finally triumphed. He fined Leptis a million litres of olive oil, to be shipped annually to Rome and distributed to the people as part of their dole. It is astonishing that the city could not only manage to bear this colossal burden, but could draw on resources enough to embark on a series of building projects in this era.

The construction of the towering city-centre theatre, complete with a piazza to distract the audience during the intervals, was achieved by AD I, whilst the magnificent marketplace

had already been erected eight years before by the same generous hand, one Annobal Tapapius Rufus, son of Himilcho. It is
impossible not to be charmed by this place, where all the imposing ornaments used to furnish a temple or a court of justice
with dignity are here combined to make a supremely elegant
place for the daily shopping, a formal square made pleasingly
complex by two central pavilions, all wrapped up in colon-
nades that offer welcome shade. Though it is the details carved
into the marble counter tops, supported by legs in the shape of
dolphins, or by heraldic griffins and handsome haunches, that
most impress the visitor. This place was formally policed by
the city authorities, who maintained public weights, scales and
ideal units of measurement so that the public could trust what
was purchased here. As a symbol of the diverse multicultural
loyalties of this city, the public units of measurement displayed
at the Leptis market naturally included the Alexandrine cubit
as well as the Punic and the Roman foot. Annobal most certainly earned the proud title of 'adorner of his country' that was
voted him by his fellow citizens.

In this same period the Forum of Leptis was upgraded, as too
was the town hall, which stood on a site that had already been
occupied for 600 years. There was also some delicate spiritual
footwork. The role of Melkarth as the idealised city king led
his temple to be associated with the contemporary role model
of such a figure, who was the Emperor Octavian–Augustus. To
amplify the image, the interior of this shrine would be packed
full of statue portraits of every conceivable member of the
newly minted Julio-Claudian imperial family. Many of these
have miraculously survived. Another temple was built and
dedicated to Hercules, so that the north face of the forum was
now fronted by an elegant interlinked terrace of three shrines,
each with its own stairway. Even in near-total ruin, it remains

an impressive and commanding urban vista, with the waves pounding out their music on a beach just behind this trinity. It clearly impressed itself on many visitors throughout the centuries, for a hundred years later it would be used as a role model for another city centre dominated by a terrace of three temples, which still stands magnificently intact in central Tunisia, at Sbeitla. To complete this picture of absolute loyalty, the name of the ruling Roman proconsul, Piso, was lovingly picked out in bronze lettering across the breadth of the forum – an idea that was once again borrowed by another city, Hippo, in western Algeria, which did the same. But in coping with the Roman ego, in bending with the wind, Leptis led the way.

All of this was for a very good cause, for under Octavian– Augustus' rule the city remained to all practical purposes free. Its legal title was In Provine, a free ally of the city and people of Rome, hence free to elect its own rulers, to mint its own coinage, to keep the titles of its own magistrates and to continue to use its own language and nomenclature. Indeed, the first Latin inscription has not been dated before 8 BC, which is doubly surprising because we know that for the previous two generations the city had been home to a Levantine influx of bankers, commission agents and Italian traders. We know a little about this motley mercantile crowd, as they are occasionally cited in the Roman law courts, implicated in corruption charges. While many of the powerful families of Leptis were proving their worth, and their great wealth, by building and dedicating an exquisite architectural heritage for their home town, there were other pathways to fame.

One wealthy family from Leptis Magna, as well as adorning their city with colonnaded markets and shrines, had also started to invest in Roman real estate. By the end of the first century, the Septimii had acquired three separate farms in central Italy, which gave them the opportunity to mix with the imperial ruling class. Italian landholdings were a vital first requisite, for Roman senators had to derive all their wealth from this stable source, and were forbidden to be directly involved in either trade or finance. So no merchants and bankers sat in the Senate, though brick-making and brewing were permitted activities of a gentleman. It was believed by the Romans that only the solid, reliable income produced from farming gave a man the right sense of independence to join this ruling council of ex-magistrates. It was also vital not to be seen to be too pushy, or else you were riding for a fall. The proper Roman pathway was to rise by gradual, well-measured steps, which slowly extended the family's web of connections and friendships, and spread the vital filaments of patronage and clientage.

The first social breakthrough for the Septimii came when one of their number, a leading magistrate in his home town of Leptis Magna, realised that the Latin he spoke in North Africa made him sound like an ignorant provincial in Rome. This was especially true in the public law courts that overtook the Senate and Forum as the vital theatre of intellectual ambition in the empire. He knew it was too late for him to remedy this on his own behalf, but he made it his business to have his brightest son reared in the household of Marcus Fabius Quintilianus, known in English as Quintilian. Such a placement probably cost a fortune in gifts and fees, but as the holder of the imperial chair of rhetoric, Quintilian was simply the best. In this household the young man from Leptis met some of the brightest sparks in the whole Roman empire, for we know that Pliny the Younger, the historian Tacitus, the poets Martial and Juvenal and two grandsons of a reigning emperor all passed under the influence, if not the personal tuition, of Quintilian. He was also an inspiring role model, for although a provincial born in northern Spain (he came from the red wine-producing region of Rioja) he had yet achieved eminence in the cockpit of Rome. Quintilian also championed the pure forms of Cicero's Latin against the affected rhetoric of Seneca. He had passed through some dangerous periods, when he was swept into the murderous politics of the court of the Emperor Domitian, but he yet managed to keep his soul. The same could not be said for Quintilian's own patron and teacher, Domitius Afer, whose eloquent tongue evolved into a murderous tool. He was used as the palace hatchet man, publicly denouncing individuals for treason in the courts. Domitius Afer literally grew monstrous from his ill-gotten gains, and ate himself to death, like some bizarre sketch from a Monty Python film.

It may have been these sorts of experience, that encouraged the young man from Leptis educated in the household of Quintilian to keep his head safely below the parapet. But he fulfilled his duty, trained himself in Latin speech and Roman law, and served as a juryman in a professional panel of barristers that gave cases their first hearing, in order to decide which court they should be held at. He became a member of the equestrian order, with the right to wear a silver ring, but made no attempt to get himself elected as a magistrate or serve in the legions. This was the only way up towards a seat in the Senate. He would undoubtedly have heard of, if not attended, the famous prosecution of Marius Priscus in Rome. Marius was from the top flight, the son of a senator who had risen to become one of the two consuls of Rome, but was prosecuted in the courts for corruption, for taking bribes while judging cases as the proconsul governor of North Africa. To make it even more fascinating to the young man from Leptis, the case was conducted by two of his old classmates, Pliny and Tacitus, when the latter delivered a celebrated five-hour prosecution speech before the

Emperor Trajan himself. It was the talk of the town, especially once the ex-governor was found guilty, though the sentence confirmed the innate privilege of the ruling class. Priscus was merely ordered to return the bribes and remove himself from the Senate and the city of Rome and retire to his estate – a bit like the punishment meted out to the British traitor Anthony Blunt, who was stripped of his knighthood.

Juvenal was provoked to turn the incident into verse, but then very few escaped the mirth of the poets. Martial also famously bit the hand that had fed him. He mocked his old master Quintilian's social ambition, calling him 'the man who longs to surpass his father's census rating'. But the social and political reticence of the young man from Leptis was noted. He may also have been a generous host to his old classmates, with the revenue of three Italian estates to draw upon. So instead of a jab of envy, what has survived is a couplet of praise, offered up to him by his friend, the poet Statius:

Your speech is not Punic, nor your dress
Your mind not foreign, you are Italian, Italian.

This young man from Leptis was the Emperor Septimius Severus' grandfather.

He had achieved the acclimatisation of the Septimii into the Roman ruling class. He may have also achieved much more, through such useful old school friends as Pliny, who was close to the Emperor Trajan. For it was Trajan who raised the city of Leptis to the status of a *colonia*, a high-grade city, and the city subsequently bent over backwards to show its gratitude and loyalty to this attention. For they had effectively been co-opted as fellow citizens of Rome. So a triumphal arch was raised in honour of the emperor, and all the city's wards respectfully named after members of the Emperor Trajan's family, while the old Punic titles of the urban magistrates were hurriedly dropped in favour of Latin ones. To help push through these measures of total assimilation, there was a Septimii cousin, one Lucius Septimius Severus, ruling as one of the two chief magistrates of the time. He would be the first to be listed as one of the Latinised town consuls, *duoviri*.

A generation later, the Septimii had succeeded in embedding themselves even more deeply in the Roman hierarchy. One made it right up the ranks of the Roman magistracy to become a praetor (judge), after which he was given the command of the XVI Legion at Samosata (on the Parthian frontier beside the river Euphrates). Another Septimii cousin made it to the consulship itself, out of which the governors of provinces were recruited.

At about the time of these heady promotions, our Septimius Severus was born, on 11 April 145 at Leptis Magna. He was the grandson of that youth who had been sent to school under Quintilian at Rome. His own father, Publius Septimius Geta, was not one of the talented, literate careerist members of the clan. He remained a home boy who had stayed contentedly at Leptis Magna, maybe helping manage the olive-oil orchards and the shipping business. His household spoke Punic just as readily as Latin, and probably understood Berber. Septimius' father had married a local girl, Fulvia Pia, who claimed to be Italian, though the family had lived in Leptis for generations as merchant traders, and had become accepted members of the local elite. Septimius spent all the formative years of childhood in Leptis and the hinterland of Libya. The city was large enough to have filled his youthful horizon, for it had a population of 40,000 and was the proud home of a theatre with 150 years of tradition behind it, aside from the spectacular amphitheatre, sunk in a magnificent old quarry, which directly connected to the shoreside circus track for chariot races. It must have seemed a world complete in itself, and full of mystery and local tales, that sucked in some of the intrigue that swirled around the palace of the Caesars, though every political adventure would become embroiled in the age-old rivalry of Leptis Magna with its two sister cities, Sabratha in the west and Oea in the middle.

The rebellion of Tacfarinas was still whispered about in the rural markets, as a time when the whole of Berber North Africa seemed on the point of expelling the Roman soldiers out of their continent. The wise old merchants of Leptis knew that had never been possible, but they also suffered at the time. It was they who had pushed for the construction of a road that cut like a knife due south from Leptis for nearly 50 miles. Resentment of the new Roman roads, hacking their sinister swathe through old tribal grazing grounds, had been one of the reasons that many of the tribes had backed Tacfarinas. It had taken years of litigation for the lands lost during that war to be finally returned to Leptis Magna, which had celebrated this with a gesture typical of their obsessive love for their city, paving all the streets with stone in AD 36.

Much more dangerous to talk about, especially in the company of soldiers, were the bizarre events that shook all of Roman North Africa in AD 68, though just now and then a coin stamped with the head of Clodius Macer would fall into your hands, and you were forcibly reminded of one of the darker passages of provincial life. The whole world might know otherwise, but you must always pretend in public that soldiers were obedient and loyal servants of their emperor. Even so, in the year that the Emperor Nero had toppled into madness, a lot happened that was no longer safe to talk about in public. Such as the fact that the legate (the commanding officer) of III

Augusta Legion was nearly propelled into the imperial purple by the resident garrison of Roman North Africa. He may have been in secret correspondence with Galba, the leathery-tough old aristocratic hunchback who at the time commanded the soldiers in Spain. But once he made his move, it was clear that Clodius Macer must have been contemplating his own ascent for some time, for overnight coins appeared with his head in which to pay the soldiers and his fleet of ships. His agents were in place to close all the ports and hold back the export of corn that Rome depended on. In the meantime his centurions marshalled a fresh legion out of thin air, or rather from auxiliaries, city police and allied tribes within Roman North Africa, all pressed into the brand-new uniform of the 1st Legion, Macriana Liberatrix. It all looked a very promising, very well planned ascent towards the imperial purple, but Clodius Macer was literally stabbed in the back by an agent working in the imperial financial department.

An incident like that exposed all sorts of cracks in the pavement. The city fathers of Oea were caught in the act, having stitched up an alliance with a dissident Garamantian clan to pillage all the farms owned by Leptis Magna in the south, and move the boundary stones that marked off the agricultural estates in their favour. That scandal took years to die down, largely because the circus of Roman politics once again intervened. For the newly appointed legate of the III Augusta was one Valerius Festus, who was caught between loyalty to a distant kinsman of his, Vitellius, who had also thrown his hat into the imperial ring, and his old military colleague, Vespasian. No one has ever quite sorted out who was betraying who at that time, especially as Vespasian had many friends in Carthage, from the days when he had served as proconsul. But the end result was that the legate Valerius Festus had the official governor in Carthage, Proconsul Lucius Calpurnius Piso, executed for treason, and then declared for Vespasian. It was a lucky call, for Vespasian triumphed.

The special imperial commission of AD 73 led by Rutilius Gallicus was meant to tidy up all these affairs, as well as finally sort out the boundary between Oea and Leptis, but the net beneficiary of all this bureaucratic attention was the imperial financial department. Yet it was not all bad. The number of men from North Africa entering the confines of the palace was everywhere noted, be it scholars like Marcus Cornelius Fronto (tutor to Marcus Aurelius), or men of action like Quintus Lollius Urbicus, who as prefect to Antoninus Pius stood literally just a heartbeat away from the emperor as his prime minister. There were also other local heroes to take one's mind briefly off politics, like the North African writer Apuleius, leaving behind him a smoking trail of intellectual glamour, seduction and witchcraft, as revealed by the sensational details of his court case, held in nearby Sabratha when Septimius was an impressionable thirteen-year-old.

Four years later, as a seventeen-year-old, Septimius Severus made his maiden speech in Leptis Magna, a rite-of-passage ordeal for a young noble, marking the end of his days as a schoolboy. This was the occasion when his bulla was removed, the secret amulet that had been hung around his neck nine days after his birth. Every boy had a bulla. The poor had one of leather, the child of the rich one of gold, strung from his neck, but none looked on the holy contents of this good-luck pouch, the sacred object often sealed up with an inscribed lead envelope. We know that it was a phallus, a natural piece of red coral, a carved root or a bronze casting, a totem against the power of the evil eye. The discarded bulla was placed under the protection of the house altar, for it might be needed again, if the owner rose to high military rank, or took the lead in a civic procession. The walls of Leptis Magna are still ornamented with phallic evil-eye carvings that reflect the widespread fear of the power of the evil, the envious or jealous eye. So at street corners you come across monstrous phalluses, sometimes supported by snakes and scorpions which do battle against the eye, which often morphs into the shape of a vulva. The casting of the evil eye could not be avoided, for it was an almost innate manifestation from a poor old woman observing anyone conspicuously in the public eye, most especially a proud young man. It was a belief wrapped up in widely feared power of the Fates, of hubris, of pride before a fall, of the gods laughing when they hear a man making plans for the future. It was also universal. Bullae are found not just along the Mediterranean shore, but from ancient Iran to Bronze Age Ireland. As are their modern manifestations: an eye painted on a boat, blue glass amulets attached to the rear-view mirror of a car, or gilt coins tied with red ribbons to a cot.

Septimius, unlike his hometown father, was bright and ambitious enough to be sent to Rome to study and improve his Latin and his rhetorical skills. But he was not under undue pressure to succeed, for his elder brother, Publius Septimius Geta, was the acknowledged hope, the rising star of the Septimii clan. Geta had been hand-picked as a member of the Vigintivirate, the board of twenty, which comprised all the really active young magistrates of his age. Their powers and responsibilities were enormous: judging lawsuits about who was a slave and who a freedman, running the Roman police force, including the prisons and execution squad, minting the coinage and maintaining the roads in and out of Rome. Geta did well at his first posting, so the next career door was then opened to him, serving as one of the senatorial tribunes in the II Augusta

Legion. As luck would have it, this gave him some experience of action, fighting the hill tribes in the wild western frontier based on the Welsh frontier fortress of Caerleon. This would be followed by a job on the staff of the governor of Eastern Libya (Cyrenaica), who also governed the island of Crete.

Septimius, in contrast with his elder brother, looked lame and third-rate. He had to wait five years before he was offered the chance of serving as quaestor, the most junior rank of the magistracy. Unlike his brother he didn't make it into the list of 'the twenty', and his subsequent military appointment, to serve with the tiny garrison in Sardinia, must have appeared almost an insult. Islands were places of exile on the Roman political map, most especially as in this period there was hard fighting: in Greece the Danube frontier had been breached, and the Berber free tribes of Mauretania were raiding southern Spain. Sitting in Sardinia was not the way to get noticed as a young man of ambition.

Septimius' one useful career appointment, serving as one of the legates for the proconsul of North Africa, was a blatant piece of nepotism. One of his elderly cousins had been appointed governor, and as the frontier wars had siphoned off every young man of talent, he had slim pickings for his staff, so he gave the post to Septimius, who at least knew the region as a native.

Septimius, devoid of achievements and lacking an active service record, comes across as a reticent young man. This is remembered in an odd but revelatory anecdote, for he stood pompously on the dignity of his new office, ordering an old acquaintance from Leptis Magna to be flogged for treating the legate with excessive familiarity. Something of his social isolation from the great and the good of Roman high society can also be concluded from the fact that whilst serving as legate at Leptis Magna he fell in love with a local girl from his home town, one Paccia Marciana, and married her. Again this was not the act of a young man of promise and ambition.

Brother Geta's star was meanwhile climbing ever higher, for after Cyrene he served in Britain, where he became a friend of Helvius Pertinax, a brilliant young Roman (from a humble Italian background) who was rising rapidly in the service of Emperor Marcus Aurelius. Pertinax could do anything – teach grammar, command a cavalry regiment on a distant frontier (which he did at Housesteads on Hadrian's Wall), rebuild the Roman navy on the Rhine, or expel an invasion of barbarians from out of the Balkans. It was undoubtedly the friendship of Pertinax that enabled Geta to be given a key appointment, the legate of the I Italica Legion stationed on the vital Danube frontier.

On the back of this vital patronage alliance with Pertinax, Geta's younger brother Septimius at last gets a leg up, a job as one of the eighteen praetors (judges) chosen to serve in the Roman courts in 176, after which he gets a judicial appointment in Spain. Septimius is still in the backwaters, but his very obscurity probably helped him win the approval of the new emperor, Commodus, who didn't want anything to do with the men that his father had employed and promoted. So, as a bolt out of the blue, Septimius is picked for one of the really key jobs in the empire, and given command of a legion in Syria, the IV Scythica. It was the making of him. The legion was based on the Zeugma bridge crossing of the Euphrates, on the road out from the great teeming city of Antioch, then half a million strong. Maybe his Phoenician blood, the Punic speech of his childhood and boyhood helped, but the region spoke to him, and so did the complexity of the diplomatic landscape. For just beyond the Roman military frontier stood cities like Edessa and Palmyra, which had remained independent states, speaking the Semitic lingua franca of Aramaic (and Greek of course) but remaining under the capable rule of their own princely dynasties, who at vital times assisted Rome with allied Arab cavalry armies and Armenian highlanders.

Once his command was over, Septimius used the opportunity to travel and learn from the Near East. He studied in Athens, and was befriended by Apollonius of Tyana, the formidably intellectual hierophant of Demeter the Mother Goddess at the cult centre of the Eleusinian mysteries. Nor did he neglect the temple–shrines of ancient Syria, indeed at the oracle of Zeus Belos at Apamea something very odd happened to him. It addressed him with a well-known quotation from Homer, which describes King Agamemnon 'with eyes and head like Zeus who delights in thunder, slender his waist like Ares, his chest like Poseidon'. This was a surprising, if not awe-inspiring event, but also a treasonably dangerous thing to have happen to him, to be likened to a monarch, especially in the reign of an emperor like Commodus. But he had important local protection, for in this period he fell in love with an intellectual Syrian, Julia Domna, daughter of the high priest of the sun god in the city of Emesa – which was how the old royal dynasty of Emesa had survived within the Roman empire. She and her sister were Bassianus, from the priestly title of Basus worn by their father. Her sister Maesa had married a cavalry officer.

Septimius' confidence and abilities had grown, and this had also been recognised. He, not just his elder brother, was now seen to be an integral part of the team of bright and principled men who gathered around the able Pertinax. So when Pertinax was given the governorship of Britain (a tricky appointment at the time, for the legions there were all on the point of mutiny) Septimius was also promoted beside him and helped to cover his patron's back by taking on the governorship of a third of

France, the region called Gallia Lugdunensis, which bordered the English Channel. His young Libyan wife had died, after ten years of marriage, which left Septimius, now aged forty, free to marry Julia Domna. She stood way off-centre from the Roman networks of political influence and wealth, but she had 'the attractions of beauty, united to a lively imagination, a firmness of mind and strength of judgement'. She gave birth to their first son in Lyon, the provincial capital of Gallia Lugdunensis. The second son was born in Sicily, for Septimius' subsequent appointment was as governor of that fascinating island.

Pertinax, due to his modest birth – he was the son of a freedman (an ex-slave) from northern Italy – never fell under the paranoid suspicion of Emperor Commodus. The Senate and the emperor's own family were however purged of anyone who might be imagined as a threat. Aside from Pertinax, the other most important official at Rome was Quintus Aemilius Laetus, prefect of the Praetorian Guard, and likewise from North Africa. He was born at Thaenae (near modern Sfax) in southern Tunisia, and was ready to go out of his way to help the careers of other North Africans such as Septimius and Geta. In AD 191 Pertinax was made both consul and prefect of the city of Rome. You could rise no higher in public administration.

It was this combination of two very influential patrons that enabled the two brothers to receive their own promotions. Geta was given the command of the two legions in Upper Moesia (the lower Danube) and Septimius the command of the three legions in Upper Pannonia, on the Danube frontier closest to Italy and Rome. It was a staggeringly powerful position for one family to have achieved, and a personal vote of confidence in their loyalty. It looked to be the apogee of their public careers, and one in which Septimius had overtaken his eldest brother.

The Emperor Commodus' paranoia had taken a further twist, though to the outer world his fame still shone. The young emperor had proved himself a star in the Plebeian games, hunting with javelin and bow in the morning, and in the late afternoon took his turn amongst the gladiators fighting with his left hand. The populace of Rome adored him. They had known him as the much-loved crown prince (son of the philosopher–emperor Marcus Aurelius), and he was now a sporting superstar. Think Prince William proving himself a David Beckham on the field and ruling over both palace and stadium.

But something went haywire one night in the palace, which left the young emperor dead. The event had clearly not been planned, for Pertinax, after some hesitation, assumed the throne. For all his previous administrative brilliance his reign was fated to last just eighty-seven days before he was murdered, killed by a squad of Praetorian Guards three hundred strong, who stuck his head up on a pike on 28 March AD 193.

The throne was once again empty, which led to two senators (from old Italian families) bidding for the opportunity to sit on it. They competed with each other with the size of the donative they intended to present to the Praetorian Guards, once they ascended the throne. They were well-respected individuals, one a virtual stepbrother to Marcus Aurelius (the consul Didius Julianus), the other an emperor's father-in-law (Sulpicianus). Didius Julianus won the throne with his offer of 25,000 sesterces (the equivalent of twenty years' pay for a normal legionnaire), but the rest of the army was disgusted, for these soldiers had already been awarded 18,000 sesterces by Pertinax which had failed to win their loyalty.

So over the following month, various armies in the provinces backed their own commanders for the purple. Six legions in the Near East acclaimed Pescennius Niger, the three legions in Britain saluted Clodius Albinus as their Caesar, while Septimius Severus was acclaimed by all six legions along the Danube frontier.

Of the three candidates, Septimius was by far the weakest in battlefield service, and lacked those vital links of loyalty and comradeship within the upper ranks of the Roman army, for apart from his year as the commander of a legion in Syria he had no previous military experience. But his half-baked career was behind him: he now emerged as a leader of dazzling efficiency and confidence. He also stood forth with courage as the official heir and avenger of Pertinax.

Septimius led his entire army to within 50 miles of Rome in under eight weeks, stopping only to sacrifice to the gods. He listened in ominous silence to delegations from the Senate, formally dissolved all four legions of the Praetorian Guard and banished them a hundred miles from Rome. The regimental standards of the Guard were formally dragged in shame through the streets of Rome by his men, marching fully armed through the streets of the capital.

The symbolism, for those who could read it, was clear. A man from the provinces, leading a provincial army, had militarily occupied the capital city. It was usual for soldiers celebrating a triumph to march through Rome unarmed, not in full battle-dress. Septimius' first acts were sternly pious: to make a sacrifice at the Capitoline Temple and to organise a public funeral for Pertinax. Only then did he permit the Senate to do his bidding: Julianus was condemned, Pertinax deified, and Septimius was proclaimed Imperator. He then gave the eternal city just thirty days of his attention whilst he raised three new legions, named Parthica I, II and III, and then formally marched out to subdue his rivals in the East. But even before this public exit, Septimius had ordered some of his junior officers to lead an attack. They landed and Pescennius was defeated at two battles in Bithynia (northern Turkey) and then at Ipsus (southern Turkey).

These victories (achieved by his subordinates) allowed Septimius to focus his attention on the defence of the imperial frontier, rather than squabbling with rivals in a civil war. His previous knowledge of the region was put to good use as he and his wife Julia made a triumphal tour of Syria. He raised the status of the ancient city of Tyre (the motherland of all those of Phoenician descent along the coast of North Africa) while reducing the importance of Hellenistic Antioch. He led a series of marches in strength against the border fortresses of Parthia, which enabled him to annex the province of Mesopotamia (the flat lands of Iraq east of the Euphrates), but he allowed Edessa to keep its status as an independent ally.

He did not pursue the war into Parthian home territory. For a man with strategic ambitions on other frontiers of the empire this was a sound decision, even if the Parthian empire at this period must have looked invitingly weak, racked by internal rebellions of the Medes and Persians. There was also an intractable knot of stubborn resistance yet to subdue, for the city of Byzantion (the future Constantinople) refused to submit to his rule and was only stormed after a laborious two-year siege. It was sacked and thoroughly destroyed.

Once Byzantion had fallen, Septimius was free to attack his last rival. He had recognised Clodius Albinus as a co-Caesar for the first four years of power, and left him in command of Britain whilst he was on campaign in the East, conquering Iraq and destroying his rival Pescennius Niger. This alliance was no longer necessary, and so in 195 Clodius Albinus was declared a public enemy. At the same time Septimius set up his sinister cousin from Leptis Magna, Gaius Fulvius Plautianus, as his agent in Rome. Having served as Septimius' spymaster general, in charge of the imperial postal service, Plautianus now ruled and watched over Rome as prefect of the police, with seven cohorts of the Watch at his command.

Two years later, the vast army of Septimius clashed with Clodius' British legions outside the city of Lyon. It was a hard-fought battle, for Roman legions were pitched against legions, so there was no tactical difference between either army and absolutely no doubt that, as in every civil war, the losing side would suffer badly. After the defeat of his army, Clodius was beheaded, then his body trampled under the horse of the triumphant Septimius, before it was butchered into pieces and thrown into the waters of the Rhône. To add interest to this savagery was the fact that Clodius Albinus came out of a very similar background to Septimius. His family were from North Africa, from the Phoenician–Berber city of Hadrumetum, and Clodius had served as a loyal ally of Septimius in the first round of the succession struggle. Nor was the city of Lyon spared, which Septimius had once governed and where his wife had given birth to their second son. For the crime of having obeyed the orders of Clodius it was subjected to a ruthless sack. Septimius' soldiers would reap a proper reward for their victory, even if the capital city of an imperial province was to be treated worse than a foreign enemy.

Much worse indeed. For in the absence of the legions that usually served in Britain, the Maeatae led a successful rebellion (better called a struggle for independence). They were a confederation of the Pictish clans from the southern Highlands of Scotland, who had never been conquered by Rome. They had however watched the progressive advance of the Roman frontier, first to Hadrian's Wall, then further north to the line of the Antonine Wall, which abutted their lands. So they chose the expedient hour of a Roman civil war to launch their own counter-attack on the empire. In the absence of the three legions that Clodius Albinus had taken with him to fight at Lyon, they brushed through the walls and plundered northern Britain. The Roman governor of Britain was ill-equipped to resist, so he was forced to pay the rebels to return home and was later permitted to use public money to buy back the prisoners of war from the Maeatae. It was a public humiliation of imperial authority that had been directly caused by a civil war distracting the legions from their duty on the frontier. Septimius' policy may have looked timid, but he was merely buying time, biding his moment to reassert authority in the British Isles.

For now was the hour in which to discipline the Roman Senate. He had not struck at this august body whilst any of his rivals lived, but Septimius' ruthless cousin had the opportunity to work his way through the captured correspondence of Clodius and identify some enemies. To add a further touch of theatre to the occasion, Septimius first berated the cowed Senate. His speech paid ominous tribute to the severity of Sulla, Marius and Augustus, who had all purged the Roman ruling class of their enemies. Then sixty-four of Rome's 600 senators were named, denounced for their treason and arrested. Their estates were confiscated, half would be pardoned, but twenty-nine suffered execution. The wits on the city streets called it the revenge of Hannibal, for many of the victims came from the oldest families of the Roman aristocracy. Much was made of this purge, but in his day the divine Octavian–Augustus had been much harsher. He had worn body armour in the Senate, and had ordered the execution of three hundred senators and knights on the fourth anniversary of the Ides of March. Their blood was literally splashed over the newly consecrated altar to the hero Julius Caesar.

But now once again the eternal city of Rome was abandoned

and the Emperor Septimius led his army away to the East. He would rule the empire from a mobile army camp for the next five years. This campaign had been meticulously planned, and once again started with the capture of a key fortress on the Parthian frontier. Then the Roman army, assisted by a fleet of river boats, occupied the Euphrates valley, seizing control of the ruins of Babylon and Seleucia before they stormed the Parthian capital city of Ctesiphon. Septimius, alone of all the Roman emperors, could now be seen to be an equal of the great Trajan in this second conquest of Parthia. And lest anyone be in doubt, exactly a hundred years after Trajan's accession Septimius awarded himself the same proud title that his great predecessor had won, Parthicus Maximus. This he had earned by adding a new province to the empire: Mesopotamia, the old heartland of all the great empires of the Near East.

Septimius was consciously measuring his own achievements against the magnificent shadows of the past. He would personally inspect the trunk road that Trajan had created on the frontier of Arabia, down the spine of modern Jordan. But things were never just repaired under Septimius, they were always advanced. So for the first time a line of Roman forts now guarded the Wadi Sirhan route to the Persian Gulf, and new strongpoints were occupied just south of the brooding mass of the great walled fortress city of Dura-Europos – the Verdun of the Parthian frontier. The oasis city of Palmyra was also now formally placed within the empire, not balanced right on the edge of it. Whilst he was there, Septimius commissioned the city's Triumphal Arch, one of the old wonders of Palmyra, which united the colonnaded avenue of the city centre with the approach avenue to the great temple of Bel, making a virtue of the 30 per cent slant between the two avenues.

The realities of the Eastern front never allowed for

megalomania, not when a single city such as Hatra could successfully resist two Roman sieges, with all the strength the emperor disposed of. He recognised this fact and made a peace of the brave with its citizens, just as his understanding of history allowed him to arbitrate a truce to halt the ancient vendetta between Jews and Samaritans.

He also made time to revisit Apamea, that beautiful city in central Syria that sits astride the Orontes valley. Even in ruins it is a magnificent place. It had a theatre to rival Rome in its capacity, and is still dominated by a dazzlingly wide and glorious central avenue that seems to march on for ever, girt by a vast colonnade. Stout city walls armoured the citadel, as mountains guard the fertile surrounding valley. The Seleucids stored their treasure here, both stamped coin and their magnificent stud of Arab horses, while the incident of the oracle further confirmed its importance in Septimius Severus' eyes. (Here we recall that while he was a legionary commander the oracle had greeted him with lines addressed to Argive kings in the *Iliad*.) Latin writers label the oracle at Apamea that of Zeus Belos, which brings to mind the oracle oak grove of Greek Dodona, but that is the wrong mental image with which to reconstruct this place. The temple of Bel at Apamea has been imagined as rivalling the god's vast sanctuaries at Palmyra and at Baalbek, for as well as the shrine and the oracle, it housed a sacred library and a scholastic tradition that attracted many of the leading Neoplatonist scholars of the late empire to work here, such as Amelius and Iamblichus. Julian the Theurgist had created an edition of the shrine's oracular pronouncements stretching all the way back to ancient Chaldea. Zeus Belos, the Bel of Apamea, was also addressed as 'Adad', which the priests interpreted to the scholars as 'One–One', just as they drew diagrams to the peasant cultivators of Adad as the sun whose rays allowed for the fertility of the earth goddess. Unlike the theatre, which is still under excavation, the temple was utterly destroyed by jealous fundamentalists, literally flattened by the envy of a Christian mob led by Bishop Marcellus in AD 380. But it is useful to bear in mind that at Apamea, Septimius had been greeted, not by some hole-in-the wall fortune-teller, dabbling in the occult, but by one of the principal intellectual sanctuaries of the ancient world, a sister to Delphi, Siwa, Didyma, Olympia and Dodona.

This striking incident would become the hinge for the subtle rewriting of his own life, so that instead of dwelling on the small humiliations of his early career, his autobiographical memoir was written as a chain of divine revelations that display how he had always been marked out by the gods. So immaculately fortunate was his horoscope considered to be, that the exact conjunction of the stars and planets at his birth was marked out in the design of a domed reception room of the palace in Rome. It was propaganda, sheer imperial spin, which towards the end of his life he may have started to believe in himself.

If so, it did not stop him from also taking a ruthlessly hard line about actual political realities. He never forgot that all power rested with the soldiers, that their loyalty was to their paymaster, and that the men most dangerous to him were not foreign enemies but his own generals. He knew he had risen to the throne purely from the chance conjunction of being made commanding general of the Danube legions just before the political anarchy of 193. A year before, or later, and he would have been rendered just another powerless office holder, another fearful senator hoping to nod his head towards the right man in power. So he made certain that his most brilliant young commanders, such as generals Julius Laetus (who had won the decisive battle of Lugdunum for him) and Claudius Candidus (who had won that first string of military victories against Pescennius Niger for him), were carefully watched. Then when they least expected it they were struck down by the agents of his Roman police chief cousin Plautianus. The Castra Peregrina was one of the headquarters of the dark, secretive and powerful forces at the centre of the Roman state. It had started off as the headquarters of the Frumentarii, literally wheat collectors, who had started as skilled assessors of provincial harvests. Their remit had grown as they collected together all sorts of strategic information on port capacity and road conditions, from where they progressed to the mood of the provinces and thence to identifying potential traitors.

At the same time as these acts of ruthless tyranny, killing without trial the very men he should have most rewarded and honoured, there was also an extraordinary freedom to his actions, as if the chaotic, accidental turn of events by which the Roman empire had been formed was being critically examined for the first time, and was now being expanded.

One of the early signals of this policy was that grim speech he had made to the Senate when he praised both Marius and Sulla. They were the first 'dictatorial strongmen' within the fabric of the old republic who had reformed the Senate with murderous rounds of proscriptions. They were very rarely coupled together, as they had been political rivals who had stood on the extreme right and left of Roman society, twin incubi of that long series of civil wars. It is a bit like a ruler aligning Cromwell with Charles I in the same breath, or Robespierre with Napoleon. For Marius had been the Populist commander whose political position had been inherited by Julius Caesar, just as Sulla's position had been inherited by Pompey. But the one vital element that united them was that they had been successful generals. They had ruled with the backing of a victorious army, and had used this reality to push through much-needed reforms. They were also exemplars for the rise of meritocratic men of talent, as opposed to aristocratic placemen – climbers such as the murdered Emperor Pertinax, not to mention his avenger and political heir, the Emperor Septimius Severus.

The concept of a new political role model for the new empire would be further expanded by Septimius' journey through Egypt. His first act was highly symbolic, for he restored the tomb of Pompey at Pelusium and made public sacrifice to his spirit. This was a bold gesture, for Pompey had been the chief enemy of Julius Caesar, whose very name had become a title of power for the emperors. But Septimius had his reasons. It remembered the time when Egypt was the ally, not the subject, of Rome. For this was to be but the first act in the liberation of Egypt, which ever since the victory of Augustus over Mark Antony and Cleopatra had been treated as the personal estate of the emperor, and a zone closed to all other Romans. Septimius Severus single-handedly reversed this, and proclaimed Egypt to be the equal of all other provinces within the empire. He started promoting its leading citizens to the Roman Senate for the first time, and for the first time allowed the city of Alexandria its own governing councils.

Of almost equal importance was his journey down the Nile, treating Egypt not as a conquered territory but as a devout place worthy of pilgrimage. He paid public respect to its ancient learning and spiritual traditions, helping Egypt escape from centuries of Roman prejudice and fear. He worshipped at all the great shrines of Egypt, the forty-two sacred sanctuaries that stretched a thousand miles up the Nile from the Mediterranean shore until he reached the great island shrine of Isis at Philae, which stood just upstream of the cataract at Luxor. This is where the Great Goddess had reunited the portions of the murdered god Osiris. It was both his tomb and their wedding bed, where his avenger son Horus would be conceived. For thousands of years it was known as The Unapproachable, a sanctuary of the utmost mystery and power. Here in May AD 200 Septimius was able to perform the sacrifices himself. You can still follow his route today, and if you consult the dates of the Roman-era constructions that further embellished the ancient Egyptian sites of temple worship, you will find just how many of these great works date from his reign.

The Egyptians, with their extraordinary sense of historical depth, were vastly more experienced than the Romans in the traditions of mythical inclusion. Which is not to deny that the Romans had always been piously respectful of all the gods: they just lacked the intellectual tools and the passion to weave all these threads together into a coherent form. Septimius spent time at the two great holy cities of ancient Egypt on this trip, both at Thebes (modern Luxor), which was the spiritual epicentre of Upper Egypt, as well as at Memphis, the holy city of Lower Egypt.

At Memphis the Ptolemaic dynasty had already done much useful work in this area, fostering the cult of Serapis, which was but a new manifestation (a face sculpted to the Greek artistic traditions) of the ancient sacrificial story of Osiris wrapped up in the local traditions of Apis, the sacred bull. The two titles of Osiris–Apis elide together to form Serapis. To make this comparatively recent tradition even more potent, it was known that Alexander the Great had sacrificed to the Apis Bull of his own time, who was a physical incarnation of divine-sanctioned royal power and virile fecundity that stretched back into the mists of time.

Subterranean necropolises still exist at Saqqara (near the stepped pyramid outside Cairo), where generations upon generations of these sacred bulls were mummified for eternity.

Somewhat in the manner with which we select our modern Dalai Lama, the new incarnation of Apis was identified after the death of the old, not just from the body of his descendants, but from a black calf with white markings that had been born at the right astral moment and who bore the distinctive marks of the deity: which included a white triangle on his forehead, the shape of a vulture wing on his back, the sign of a scarab under his tongue, a white crescent moon on his right flank and double hairs in his tail. The mother of the newly identified Apis was also suddenly propelled into the royal purple, and treated as a mother of the god. It was believed that each Apis was born of a virgin, conceived in a Zeus-like flash of lightning, or incarnated by a moonbeam. Septimius' autobiographical memoir was clearly fashioned to set his emergence to supreme power within this tradition.

Next year the emperor ruled from Antioch. His family travelled with this highly mobile court, which included the best letter-writer of the day, Aelius Antipater (from Hierapolis in western Turkey), who had been appointed tutor to his two boys. Septimius' intellectual Syrian wife was meanwhile encouraging a young scholar, Philostratus, to write a biography of Apollonius. This conjunction of subject and writer speaks volumes about the interests of the imperial family, as Apollonius was a revered if mysterious figure. He was a Pythagorean philosopher who had lived the simple life of a wandering scholar, like some medieval dervish. Born in Tyana, an ancient Hittite city on the borderlands of modern Turkey and Syria, he managed to travel all over the ancient world – not only Spain, Italy and Sudan, but he crossed into Iraq and travelled through Parthia into India, learning and teaching, and according to some, working miracles. He was a Christlike figure from the pagan world, clearly in touch with the Buddhist and Hindu belief systems of India, who led a simple, vegetarian existence. He lived a long and full life (probably from AD 40 to 120), but already the myth was on the point of overwhelming the simple facts, as pious disciples and followers embroidered their cherished memories.

While it took Philostratus years to finish this task (by which time his patron, the Empress Julia, was dead), his earlier works reveal the impressive range of his other interests. A collection of erotic love letters, a life of the sophist teachers, and *Heroikos* (*On Heroes*), a mock-heroic conversation between a Phoenician trader and a vine-worker. If Photius is right in claiming that he was a Phoenician, originally from Tyre (where he would retire at the end of his life), having spent time in Athens, Lemnos and Rome, we have further evidence of the cultural leanings of the imperial family. They were disposed to favour Syrians and Phoenicians, they were interested in things that came out of the East, but above all in uniting the different currencies of religious tradition into one overarching philosophy.

On his journey north through Turkey, the emperor visited and ordered the restoration of the tomb of Hannibal, another instance of integrating the different historical traditions within the empire into one overarching system. It was also during this period that he commissioned the rebuilding of the city of Byzantion, which he had flattened at the end of the civil war. His most enduring monument there is the circus, a superbly positioned racetrack which overlooked this strategic strait. The vaults and terraces that compose it have an opulence way beyond the size of the town, and to my mind make sense only as a contrite offering to Poseidon, visually combining the domain of the lord of the horse with the lord of the ocean and master of earthquakes. The massive arcades have survived, to serve as the physical power centre of both the capital cities of the Byzantine empire (for the palace sat beside the Hippodrome of Constantinople) and the

Ottoman empire (where palaces and royal mosques overlooked what was to become the At Meydani square).

By September he had left behind these building projects and had crossed over the Bosphorus strait, to journey on through northern Thrace into Bulgaria. He then made a tour of inspection of the defence systems of the Danube frontier, his old command, and springboard for his ascent to the throne.

When at last he returned to Rome, he made certain that it would not be forgotten. A treasury of coin was emptied to reward the loyalty of the guard, as well as the citizens of Rome, with the gift of ten gold pieces a head. Having bought their love, he modestly refused a triumph, even that celebrating his victory over Parthia and the conquest of the new province of Mesopotamia. His son was married off to the daughter of his devious cousin, who had watched over Rome in his absence, assisted by the police and his network of spies. The mythic importance of seven – the seven circuits of the racetrack, the seven planets – all neatly chimed in with his given name, and was reinforced by a festival in which 100 unblemished animals were slain each day over a seven-day celebration.

Rome would not markedly delay him, for he had long been planning to inspect and reform the defences of North Africa along the natural frontier of the Sahara. It may have helped that, among all the emperors, only Hadrian had been there before him. Once again he would measure himself against a potent shadow from the past, and then exceed their achievements. He crossed to Carthage and then journeyed south-east down the great Roman trunk road of North Africa, which led directly from the provincial capital across the corn-growing plateau of the Tell mountains. Then the imperial court continued on that long journey towards the legionary base, perched at the edge of the Sahara desert at Lambaesis.

The emperor's deep knowledge of North African history and its grievances was to be quickly demonstrated as, one by one, all the ancient citadel-cities with a Berber and Phoenician identity were freed from metropolitan rule from Carthage and given their own self-governing identity. It was as if the collar of Roman control that had been tightened around the old Numidian towns such as Dougga, Thignicia and Thibursicum Bure was at last loosened, and the door closed on the era of compulsory Roman colonisation imposed in the days of Julius Caesar and Octavian–Augustus. Septimius would have known the names and careers, if not the faces, of most of the dominant clans in these cities. Indeed, during his recent tour the governor of Thrace came from Oea, just as the governor of Upper Moesia came from the family of the Anicii, from the little Numidian hill town of Uzappa, who bred a dynasty of tough officers that served for centuries on every frontier of the empire. I have tried to sketch one of the ancestral altars of the Anicii, which is held in the storeroom to the right of the stage in the restored Roman theatre at Guelma. The spirit of the ancestors is depicted as a serpent coiled around the altar and seemingly about to eat from the offerings placed there.

Lambaesis was the garrison town of the III Augusta Legion. The neat rectangle of barracks arranged around the command-ing officer's quarters, complete with its shrine to the genius of the emperor and the eagle of the legion, would not have inter-ested the emperor for very long. What would have held his atten-tion were the half-dozen cities that existed as satellites in this far southern province, right on the edge of the forested Aurès mountains. Discharged veterans had been fed into the citizenry of these settlements for the last hundred years. In a number of sites one can feel the hand of the emperor himself, or rather the staff of architect–engineers who worked to his dictation, especially the ornamentation of fountains and springs, made more practical with basins and well designed drains, but given a twist of grandeur with a colonnade and an apsidal frame for the statue of a nymph.

Then he was off again, conveyed by the immaculate logistics of his staff officers to inspect some of the new frontier fortresses that he had ordered built in AD 198. At sites such as Castellum Dimmidi the empire had been pushed to its very furthest geographical limits. These fortified outposts didn't hold any useful land. Instead they watched over the wells. They were the bases from which the vast grazing grounds of the nomadic Berber tribes could be observed by sending out patrols to attend the seasonal tribal markets and to police the timing of the great annual migrations and festivals. This was not just a matter of security, of intelligence in depth, of collecting customs tolls, it was also about recruitment. Many of the toughest, most competent soldiers in the Roman army were not citizens, they were auxiliaries, exclusively recruited from the tough tribal badlands on the edge of the empire. This was especially true of the cavalry. At the end of their period of service, these second-class soldiers but first-rate fighters were given Roman citizenship. Their children often rose to the very highest military ranks of the army. They were a potent force, and so it was one of the most basic rules of imperial policy to keep these detachments of the auxiliary army small, have them under the control of Roman officers, move them about, and place them in garrisons very far removed from any affiliation with the local tribes. These Saharan frontier forts had not even been built by the III Augusta, but were the work of a detachment of the Syrian-recruited III Gallica Legion.

Whilst on this personal tour of inspection the Emperor Septimius was the first ruler for several hundred years to have taken a long hard look at the reality of Roman North Africa, especially the ragged western end. He realised that, some 160 years after Claudius' abandonment of Caligula's ill-planned annexation of Mauretania, nothing had been done to sort out the problem. Most of the vast extent of the Mauretanian shore between Tetouan and Cherchell was effectively in the hands of Berber tribes, who when the empire was troubled by invasions of barbarians on the frontier, such as the one that occurred under the reign of Marcus Aurelius, were free to launch pirate raids all over the Western Mediterranean. Roman Morocco was not connected with the rest of North Africa by any road.

The emperor seems to have been paving the way for a possible campaign to sort this out, whether by himself or by some future ruler. He pushed the frontier some 55 miles east of the forts that ringed Volubilis, and was probably the author of the Roman structure that was discovered at Bou Hellou, in present-day Morocco, as well as creating Pomaria as a base from which to rule westernmost Mauretania Caesariensis. He also appointed a succession of governors, who for the very first time exercised authority over both provinces of Mauretania, all the better to achieve some joined-up tactical planning.

But then the focus of his attention shifted eastwards. The imperial court marched from Lambaesis back to the city of Theveste (modern Tébessa), now on the Algerian–Tunisian frontier. It was an old Carthaginian military headquarters that had also briefly served as a base of the III Augusta. In this period Theveste was adorned by the lovely extant temple of Minerva, which the emperor may have consecrated. Ten years later his personal presence here would be loyally recalled by the construction of a triumphal arch raised by the prefect of the XIV Legion, Gaius Cornelius Egrilianus, who was a native of the town. Then the court was away across the forested mountains to

Thelepte, then followed the line of the Sahara as Septimius rode east to the oasis-city of Capsa (modern Gafsa, in Tunisia) with its spring-fed water basin, before riding east through the steppe-lands to approach the vast olive orchards that stretched outside Tacapae. The court was now back on the Mediterranean shore. This route must have also allowed his home province sufficient last-minute warning to ensure that nothing was left undone, seeing that the emperor now processed through his homeland of Tripolitania (western Libya) and was able to personally inspect the vast number of votive statues that had been raised in honour of himself, his wife and his sons – not forgetting his cousin, the ever-watchful chief of police and spymaster in Rome.

To top all the other arches of welcome, the processions, speeches, inspections and feasts, Septimius' own city of Leptis Magna had erected that fantastically inventive triumphal arch that sat astride the coast road between Alexandria and Carthage and the road that led due south into the Sahara. On its triumphal summit, the imperial family were immortalised piously offering up a sacrifice, while the gods clustered around in approval.

To the south of the city, the distant Saharan frontier was watched by forts that can still be found in the dry valleys of the Jebel Nafusa range, such as Gheria El Garbia and Gheria Esh-Shergia, which stand a day's ride apart. Though they are now rather confusingly covered in medieval overbuildings (and embraced by Italian colonial military camps), these are not just fortified manor houses, but have the regular playing-card-shape plan (181 by 137 metres) of a military garrison post, pierced by four gateways guarded by two-storey towers. We also think that a Roman military garrison was planted in the strategic but iso-lated oasis of Ghadames, though no archaeological find has yet confirmed an independent military post.

One of the best-preserved links in this broken southern chain of forts can however be very precisely dated to the reign of the Emperor Septimius Severus. The first garrison to occupy the walls of this fort rode in on 24 January AD 201. The engineer–architect in charge also clearly emerged from the same Phoenician culture of the province of Tripolitania and Leptis Magna as his emperor, for the unit of measurement was the Punic cubit, not the Roman foot. This Roman fort, again with its familiar playing-card plan (of blunted corners), measures exactly 270 by 180 Punic cubits (138 by 93 metres) and was designed to hold a garrison of five hundred men. This is also the standard size of an *ala* (Latin 'wing') at this period of the empire, the auxiliary cavalry regiments recruited from non-Roman citizens. I have twice been fortunate enough to wander around the sand-filled streets of Bou Njem (variously spelled in Roman inscriptions as Golas, Gholaia or Golaia).

Any Roman soldier familiar with any frontier post would at once have been able to find his way around this fort, even in a sandstorm. Entering by the main north-east gatehouse, you pass beneath two watchtowers and find yourself on the central avenue approaching the regimental headquarters building. To your left and right stand two of the four barrack blocks that occupy the four corners of the camp. These blocks were usually subdivided into eight (or ten) rooms, with eight men to a room. The headquarters (known as the *principia*) occupied the centre and consisted of a colonnaded courtyard, bordered by small offices and a tribunal meeting room. The most important room, the chapel of the standards, was always placed in the largest room in the centre, straight across from the entrance way. Here stood the eagle, flanked by the high pikes that bore the silk standards, literally guarding the pay-chests of the soldiers, which were placed in a strongroom cellar beneath the chapel.

One of the little row of offices on the south face of the head-quarters courtyard at Bou Njem has been identified as the scriptorium. This is a unique find, for the central stone writing desk, surrounded by benches and pots of ink for the military clerks, has somehow survived, buried by sand, along with hundreds and hundreds of files for the years 253–9 thrown out from the storeroom onto the rubbish heap. For like Vindolanda on Hadrian's Wall, Bou Njem is one of those miraculous places where the sounds of the past come alive. At Vindolanda, the literate soldier clerks used folded slivers of birch, oak and alder to write on, but out in the treeless Sahara they made their notes on broken pieces of pottery . They also made use of the white-washed walls, painting notices on them that could be reused after another wash of lime. So we can hear all the humdrum details of garrison life: the constant roll-calls that gave the active strength of the various units, which squadron was to be sent out on patrol, who was in the sick bay, which unit was being transferred to another fort, as well as receipts from the granary storehouse and sundry other supplies brought in by camel caravan. The coast is 100 kilometres due north. There is even a flicker of routine intelligence work, as we can eavesdrop on the arrival of a party of Garamantian tribesmen from the deep Sahara introduced by letter to the commanding officer. They were escorting two Egyptians, four donkeys and a runaway slave that they had captured and were returning. No doubt a bounty was paid on the return of runaways, or was this a quid pro quo? The Garamantian tribal elder may have brought along some nephews who he was hoping to get signed on as new recruits to the Roman auxiliary. He may also have brought in news from the oases to the south, to keep up good terms with the camp commandant – some gossip about the jostling of clans for dominance within his tribe, the safe arrival of a trade caravan from West Africa ...

Some of these conversations might have been held in the formal tribunal or the private quarters of the commanding officer, which stood just to the south of the headquarters building with its own small dining room. The commander was the *praefectus* and his quarters the *praetorium*. Attached to the Bou Njem *praetorium* is a small two-room chapel dedicated to the Spirit of the Place; a pair of inscribed altars were discovered here in the name of the Genius of Gholaia, later addressed as *numen praesens*. It feels a very private space, a place for the formal witnessing of an oath, and for propitiating the guardian spirit against all the digging and construction which had disturbed the peace. In the sprawl of huts that grew beyond the walls, which housed local concubine wives, soup kitchens, kebab houses and bars, some modest temple–chapels have also been found. They once again testify to the very specific local loyalties of the soldiers here, for one is dedicated to Jupiter Ammon, after the famous oracular temple at the Libyan oasis at Siwa (deep within the Sahara), while the other is to Mars Canapphar, another specific Libyan Berber deity, whose only other inscription has been found in Leptis Magna. They are modest, hut-like temples, but they also testify to an intimate relationship with the divine, for the Mars shrine is lined with benches (not unlike a Mithraic temple) designed for a shared sacred meal.

What manner of man served as commander in this isolated fortress? He would have been a Roman citizen, and almost certainly of equestrian rank, if not from a senatorial family, who already had some training in law, rhetoric and basic administration. He would have already served a first appointment as a military tribune, one of the half-dozen young men attached to a legion as officer cadets – sometimes known as thin stripes. And once he had built up enough experience, he might have been given this chance of his own independent command, though it must always have been a tough posting. In the mid-third century, this network of frontier forts, the *limes* (border zone) of Tripolitania, was given its own *praepositus* commanding officer. It seems likely that this officer would have been based at the Gheria El Garbia fort, which was twice the size of Bou Njem. During the reign of Septimius Severus, I imagine that some of the *praefecti* of the fortress of Gholaia would have been ex-centurions, promoted from out of the ranks of the sergeants of the III Augusta Legion and bumped up to become a tribune. In this period of the empire this was likely to be as high a rank as they could rise to, but on retirement they might be rewarded with equestrian rank, and so the sky would have been the limit for their sons.

By another happy chance, we can hear the voice of one of these centurions echoing out from the walls of the frigidarium in the bathhouse. He was remarkably well educated, for he composed a verse inscription that was then cut into a tablet of grey limestone (118 by 45 cm) and mounted on the walls. It could be that he was the second in command, left in control of the fort whilst the bulk of the regiment went out on a long and arduous patrol deep into the Sahara desert, and that the baths were built at his order to keep the depleted garrison busy, and as a welcome home to the returning column. But more than these idle speculations, the inscription provides a fascinating insight into the mind of a humanist who can think of no better temple to construct than a bathhouse dedicated to the health of his brother soldiers, and no deity more important than Salus – good health. Here he speaks:

> I have much sought what to hand down to memory, while acting in command of all the soldiers in this camp, what vow

to be shared by all and on behalf of the safe return of the army, to be discharged among earlier and future vows. While seeking in my mind for worthy names of deities I at last discovered the name and power of a never-failing goddess to whom to consecrate with everlasting vows this place: and for so long as there are worshippers of Health here, in so far as I could I have sanctified her name and have given to all the genuine waters of Health amid such great fiery temperatures, in the midst of those endless sand-dunes given by the south wind that intensifies the burning flames of the sun, so that they might soothe their bodies by bathing in tranquillity. So you who feel sincere gratitude for what I have done, that the spirit of your seething soul is being revived, do not be slow to speak genuine praise with your voice for one who wanted you to be healthy for your own good, but to testify ever for the sake of Health.

The poem is also designed as an acrostic, so the bathers can indeed speak out genuine praise to his memory, for his name is spelled out from the initial letters of each line, Q. Avidius Quintianus. We also know the name of another centurion from this fort, one M. Porcius Iasucthan, whose Latin inscription was not nearly so polished, and who was clearly a Berber, for once his tour of duty was over he was returned to his regimental base camp, the III Augusta Legion at Lambaesis, where an altar dedicated to the 'Di Mauri' (gods of the Mauretanians) has been found which bears his name.

When I first visited Bou Njem I asked a Libyan how I would be able to spot it, in the hundreds of miles of bleak desert. He told me to keep an eye out for the first clump of palm trees south from the Mediterranean shore. It seemed a vague enough direction at the time, but it works. The palms follow the dry wadi bed, the oued el Kebir, just below the fort and prove that a well can easily be sunk to reach the water table. The fort was clearly sited by someone who intimately understood this landscape, so much so that when a crisis meant that the regiment had to abandon Bou Njem in the years between 259 and 263, civilians moved in straight away. It stands astride a geographical frontier, and only a hundred years ago was still used as a caravanserai, where the camel caravans from the deep Sahara would break up their loads and transfer them onto mules for the shorter 100-kilometre journey to the coast.

I like to imagine the emperor making use of the triumphal arch at Leptis Magna, then setting out on a personal tour of these works on the far southern edge of the desert. Perhaps the baths were even built for his use after a lightning inspection of the Saharan frontier. But there were other calls on his time whilst he was at Leptis. Aside from these new frontier forts, he was deep into the plans and schedules of work that would transform his home city with a monumental New Forum and the Syrian-like processional way from the harbour, incorporating the never-ending theatre of a three-storey water shrine. Then there was also the massive expansion of the harbour itself, not to mention the new temples, their reliefs and their dedicatory statues. All this would have just been the background stuff, for all the affairs of the empire were funnelled to this mobile court, which had briefly halted in Leptis Magna in the spring of AD 203.

By May, the court was back in Rome. Not to be outdone by Leptis Magna, the city of Rome had commissioned a massive, but also supremely graceful, triumphal arch, ornamented with all the emperor's victories and tours of inspection. It still stands. The forum of Rome was packed so full of monuments that there had not been room to add anything to commemorate any of the emperors over the last eighty years. For the Emperor Septimius an exception had been made, set up by the Senate and People of Rome and inscribed with letters of gilded bronze. Another stroke of ingratiating servility had been the decision of the board of fifteen, in charge of sacrifices in the eternal city, to celebrate the birth of the Seventh Era (based on Etruscan units of 110 years) and to ask Septimius to take charge of the celebrations. They knew their man. I can imagine no task that would have given him greater pleasure.

The city was first purified with incense and offerings, to allow the first fruits to be offered up three days later to the three presiding deities: Jupiter Optimus Maximus, the Best and Greatest, August Juno the Queen of Heaven, and Apollo, the Beautiful and the Good. At the kalends of May the city was once again purified with formal rites through to midnight, so that on the second hour of the morning the Empress Julia and 109 other married women processed to celebrate a solemn banquet in honour of Juno and Diana. This was followed by three days and two nights in which the Emperor Septimius and his sons invoked the protection of all the known gods, using exactly the same ritual and formula used by Augustus. The final dedicatory hymn (composed by Horace to mark the occasion) was sung by twenty-seven boys and twenty-seven girls to close these three days of spiritual dedication. This was then followed by a seven-day festival of games, theatrical shows, circus races and feasts. The heralds summoned the people of Rome to see what had never yet been seen by any mortal, nor would ever be seen again. The city was at its apogee, for Septimius had restored the Pantheon temple and fitted the temple of Peace with a new library that bore on its lower wall the *Forma urbis*, an exact map of Rome, carved in marble, with every building named and identified in red. I have seen a portion of this. It is the most elegant, precise and ambitious map that was ever made of any city, just as the Septizodium – probably a monument to the seven planets, 100 feet high and 300 feet long – may well have been the most ambitious and spectacular water fountain ever constructed. The ceiling of the law courts had also been redesigned so that the arrangement of the planets at the emperor's nativity now filled the vaulted ceiling.

The law courts also witnessed the emperor's most lasting gift to Western civilisation. Septimius had always been aware that the full genius of Rome was expressed in the transparency of its law courts and in the dignity of public justice. He always gave litigants plenty of time to articulate their arguments, and his advisers full freedom to speak their minds, even when there was a backlog of 3,000 cases awaiting his attention. And though Roman law always supported the power of the state, he coined a perfect expression of how the autocratic power of the emperors yet dovetailed with their respect for the processes of the courts: 'Although we are not bound by the laws, nevertheless we live in accordance with them.' So he had set the jurist Aemilius Papinianus – Papinian – the task of distilling centuries of law-making and case-making, boiling down the inconsistencies, removing the irrelevances in order to complete a single code of Roman law. It had never been done before.

Papinian was connected to Septimius through a distant cousinship with his Syrian wife, the Empress Julia Domna, but he had risen to eminence years before the emergence of the emperor's rule. His exceptional talents had been first spotted in the reign of Marcus Aurelius, when he had served as the legal adviser to the prefect of Rome. He was to be assisted in his new task by two brilliant young jurists, who by coincidence also came from Syrian families – Domitius Ulpianus (known as Ulpian, who came from Tyre) and Julius Paulus. The project, though energetically continued by Septimius' son, was never completed, though it did provide most of the groundwork when two hundred years later the Emperor Justinian returned to and completed this visionary project, a classical inheritance that still actively flows through the Roman law of Europe and Scotland.

There had however been a heavy price paid for all these magnificent intellectual, judicial, military, spiritual and architectural achievements. Septimius had permitted Plautianus, his baleful young cousin from Leptis Magna, to assume enormous powers whilst he concentrated on these great public works. Plautianus became the dark face of Septimius' rule, the ever-watchful chief of police, master of spies, all-powerful prefect of Rome. It was probably a conscious decision by Septimius to allow the person of the emperor to bathe in cultured light, while all the darker elements of state power seemed to be directed by a hated other. Septimius certainly had total trust in Plautianus. They were cousins and close childhood friends, who may even have been lovers in their adolescence.

The strength of these old bonds in their relationship may also have benefited from Septimius' knowledge that Plautianus could not easily occupy the throne. An early disgrace (discovered by Pertinax) had left a black mark on Plautianus' official career and denied him any experience of military command. He was also said to be physically unprepossessing and awkward, pale and trembling in public – though one gets a whiff of the classic lurking bad man in these descriptions, which may well have accreted to his memory once he had fallen from power. The historian Herodian seems a little more honest when he describes the effect of his power, not his looks: 'When he went out in public he was an object of fear. No one would approach him, and even those who came upon him by chance turned aside. The guards who preceded him did not allow anyone to stand near him or even look at him. They ordered people to step out of his path and keep their eyes fixed on the ground.'

Septimius had rewarded Plautianus with vast powers, enormous wealth and the prospect of a golden future for his descendants, since his daughter was married to the emperor's eldest son. So it looked very possible that their shared offspring might one day reign, if the dynasty lasted for three generations. A similar bond had cemented the long political alliance of Augustus with his tough, loyal henchman, Agrippa.

But in 204, Septimius' elder brother Geta, who had never been permitted to share in his younger brother's imperial glory, took the opportunity to privately denounce Plautianus. He captured his younger brother's full attention, for he was on his deathbed, and with the old sibling envy discounted he had nothing to gain. I doubt that Septimius was surprised by any important disclosures his brother could have made against Plautianus, as Septimius himself was the true instigator of most of his infamous actions. But brother Geta may have provided Septimius with important family gossip such as no one else would have dared to confide. For the emperor's son and the chief minister's daughter loathed each other, despite the public harmony of their state marriage. Geta was able to point out that after years of sharing the same marital bed, no grandchildren had been born, and that the two young people locked into this loveless and sexless marriage now feared, and not just hated, each other. In the streets they spoke of Plautianus as the fourth Caesar, who would never tolerate the disgrace of his daughter being divorced by the heir apparent. Which would also remove the dream of a grandchild descended from both Septimius and Plautianus sitting on the throne. In this sort of situation, with the honour of his daughter at stake, and suddenly bereft of the fruit of a lifetime's career, anything might happen. Septimius listened carefully.

On the night of 22 January 205 a message was sent to Plautianus asking him to the palace for dinner, but on this occasion the palace guards had been instructed to bar Plautianus' staff from entering the great imperial dining room with their master. A number of centurions were produced who swore that the prefect had given them orders to kill the emperor and presented a sealed letter to this effect. It was almost certainly fabricated, but as Plautianus protested his innocence, his sword was deftly taken from him. The emperor's son then rose from his couch to attack his father-in-law Plautianus with his fists, after which the guards joined in and stabbed him to death. His body was dragged into the streets to be kicked and abused, while his supporters were rounded up and executed. His vast wealth was confiscated and efficiently siphoned off into the imperial purse.

Septimius would later explain to the Senate that only he was to blame, for he had loved and honoured Plautianus too much, before lamenting at the weakness of human nature. What had convinced him of the need to act was a dream in which his old rival Albinus was alive and plotting against him. It all sounds pretty deranged, but the Senate had long since learned to interpret the emperor's dreams as a matter of life or death. It may be that Septimius' autobiography (which only survives in references) was designed for public presentation, in which case the whole population of Rome would have known about the succession of portents, dreams and revelations that led Septimius to the throne and damned his rivals as traitors. Technically it had been an efficient palace coup: sudden, savage and decisive.

Septimius had at his personal direction two regiments of bodyguards (*Corporis Custodes*) who stood outside the army and could execute any order of his without question. They were mounted horse guards (a bit like the Blues and Royals who guard the English monarch), but were recruited from non-citizen tribes outside of the empire. Known as the *Equites Singulares Augusti*, or Scorpions, from the device on their regimental badge, they were a force created by Augustus and improved by Hadrian, but reached their organisational peak under the Emperor Septimius Severus, who brought their numbers up to two thousand men and fostered a healthy rivalry between the two regiments, the *Cohors Germanorum* and the *Numerus Batavorum*, Germans and Batavians. Each cohort could field 720 mounted men, subdivided into twenty-four squadrons of thirty riders. One of their barracks, the two-storey Castra Nova, has been identified beneath the foundations of the basilica of San Giovanni Laterano. From out of this gateway, ornamented with Ionic capitals, would gallop the dark enforcers of the emperor's will, speaking German amongst each other and loyal to no other Roman.

By this stage of his reign Septimius had little further need for Plautianus' dark arts. He was the unquestioned hero of the entire empire, as well as its autocrat through his command of the legions. His sons were the greatest beneficiaries of the murder of Plautianus, for their private lives were no longer under the scrutiny of their powerful North African father-in-law, and they were at last free to do what, and with whom, they wished. Like all Roman princes born into the purple, they were fawned upon and so flattered that they were made into little monsters of entitlement, who 'treated women shamefully, abused boys, embezzled money' and hobnobbed with the popular sporting heroes of their day, the gladiators and charioteers, who alone seemed to win their respect. Their father, the emperor, had at last settled down to an established daily routine in Rome. He attended to state papers before dawn, after which he would go

for a walk with his staff, discussing affairs and making decisions. Then he would ride or take exercise in the gymnasium
before taking a bath. He would have a meal with his family,
then take a siesta, then set off for another walk whilst discussing affairs of state with different secretaries in three or four
different languages, mostly Latin and Greek. This would be followed by another session in the baths, followed by dinner with
his intimate friends and trusted agents. One night this might
admit so great a scholar from Syria as Ulpian, collating Roman
law into one great free-standing document; on others it would
have included Oclatinus Adventus. This imperial procurator
had started his career as a military policeman and then rose to
become centurion, then commander of the Frumentarii, the
secret service.

Oclatinus Adventus had been sent to Britain by Septimius,
with powers that included the supervision of the governor, but
also to start mapping out the structure of a new campaign. The
emperor had never travelled to this most north-westerly edge of
the empire, though both his brother Geta and his patron Pertinax had served in this archipelago, bathed in mist and swept by
implausibly deep tides. He would also have been aware that it
was Lollius Urbicus, a Roman general born in a small Berber hill
town in North Africa (Tiddis, outside Constantine in central
Algeria), who had pushed the frontier north to take control
of southern Scotland. Lollius Urbicus had constructed the so-
called Antonine wall, which stretched between the Clyde and
the Forth (modern Glasgow and Edinburgh).

Septimius knew that Roman authority was at a low ebb
on the island, for Urbicus' line had only been held for twenty
years, and by AD 160 the Roman army had been forced back to
the previous defence line, known as Hadrian's Wall. But even
this position had been rocked by large-scale rebellions, which

caused the death of the governor (in AD 183) and which were apparently repeated fifteen years later. Earlier in his reign, Septimius had been content to reinforce the line of Hadrian's Wall, for which we have the architectural evidence of the strengthening of such forts as Birdoswald and Vindolanda. Later (probably after Oclatinus Adventus had completed his fact-finding mission) we find him giving orders for structures to be built that would enable a massive increase in the military presence. Such previously small cavalry forts as Coria (modern Corbridge) and Arbeia (South Shields) were transformed into supply bases, packed full of twenty-two state granaries that could feed an army of 40,000 on a three-month campaign.

The emperor next turned his attention to the commander of the Roman navy that guarded the British shores, the *classis Britannica*. He was promoted so that he could start selecting the best units from the German fleet, as well as recruiting volunteers to join his force from the river squadrons that worked the Rhine and Danube rivers and deltas. It was intended that this Roman navy would not only supply the army, working its way up along the eastern shore of Scotland, but maybe complete the conquest of Britain by annexing the many islands scattered in the western ocean.

The core of the mobile field army would be provided by just one legion, II Parthica, massively increased in strength by being lent units (*vexillationes*) seconded from other legions and auxiliary cavalry regiments. This not only enabled all the frontier legions to remain at their posts (so that the borders still looked firmly guarded), but it also brought all the most capable, ambitious young officers together in one army. The emperor clearly wished to use the campaign in Britain to provide his two sons with battle experience, and with it the chance to bond with the most vital element of the Roman state, the army. They had already been sent in 207 to gain combat experience on the Danube frontier, while the emperor nipped over to inspect the state of his many building projects in North Africa. We think he toured the works of Leptis Magna, but he may also have had time to inspect the building projects that he had commissioned in such cities as Djemila and Timgad. The army would be guided by two *comites*, military counts, who were a safe if undistinguished pair of hands, and Syrian cousins of the young imperial princes through their mother's bloodline.

There was also a grand strategic logic to the whole affair, for if Britain could be decisively conquered and subdued, the empire would no longer have to provide such a large garrison (four legions) to hold the place down. The imperial frontier would be shortened, leaving forces enough for other problem corners of the empire, such as Germany or maybe unconquered Mauretania, to be finally subdued. For as we have seen, ever since Claudius' invasion of Britain, this frontier had been depleted of the four legions that had been sent to try and subdue the country we now know as Morocco.

In AD 208, travelling (as was his custom) with dazzling speed, the emperor rushed north to take personal command of the invasion army. He was aged sixty-three, and now travelled as much by litter as in the saddle. The legion of VI Victrix, based in York, had been given orders to expand its base camp, which was made spaciously imperial by a grand line of high towers and elaborate gatehouses. This town now became the centre of the empire, the residence of the secretariat served by the imperial postal system. Here Septimius' youngest son, Geta, equipped with a council of senior advisers, administered justice and answered all the petitions of advice. So on 12 September, for instance, we know that the delegation from the town council of the free city of Aenus, on the coast of Thrace, received a favourable answer to its petition.

In the spring of AD 209 the emperor and his eldest son, Antoninus, had ridden north into the unconquered land of the Caledonians. By measuring the lumps and bumps that have been left in the ground you can follow their course like a game of join the dots. Three giant 165-acre camps must have contained the whole army as it advanced across the Southern Uplands towards the old Forth–Clyde line, and then the army split, one column pushing due north towards Inverness, while the bulk of the army headed north-east to occupy the good farmland of Angus and Aberdeen and remain in close contact with the Roman navy. The garrisoning of this long line of fortress camps took its toll, and the army became ever leaner. The tribes meekly made their submission, seemingly awed by the size and efficiency of the Roman army – but really just biding their time.

The Romans for their part began to realise that they were dealing with a very elusive army that had no cities or fortresses to capture, no citadels to flatten or treasuries to seize. The campaign became an exercise in extreme logistics, filling up swamps and bridging rivers, 'running into immense difficulties because of the terrain and failing to get the enemy into battle'. The historian Dio recorded that 'the tribes [of Scotland] inhabit wild mountains and deserted marshy plains, they have no walls, no cities and no agriculture, but live off their flocks, from hunting and from certain fruits – but they do not touch fish, of which there are vast and inexhaustible quantities.' He reported that their war leaders were chosen from 'the boldest, because of their love of plunder, live naked and barefoot in tents, have their women in common, have iron belts and necklaces and tattoos all over their bodies ... the atmosphere in that country is always gloomy, because of the thick mist arising from the marshes formed as most of the country is flooded by the continual ocean tides'.

It might sound like stock rhetoric about the horrible life of the barbarian savages beyond the frontier, but many of the details have been proved true by subsequent archaeology, including that detail about the Celtic taboo against eating fish. The Emperor Septimius, ever the traveller and scholar, as well as the master of preliminary staff work, observed most accurately the variation of the sun's motion and the length of days and nights in summer and winter respectively, which includes the astonishing fact that the sun never quite sets in midsummer. His wife, doing her own anthropological researches, was much struck by the Caledonians' apparently shameless habit of public sex, to be told that 'we fulfil the demands of nature in a better way than the Roman women, for we have intercourse openly with the best men, while you allow yourselves to be seduced in secret by the worst.'

In the winter the rebellion began, led by the Pictish Maeatae tribe. We have heard of them before, when they led the rebellion once Clodius Albinus had stripped legions from the island of Britain to fight at Lyon. They may have held some position of primacy within the tribes due to their proximity to the cult centre of Abernethy. The easy smiles of the summer submission were now replaced by guerrilla warfare. Bands of young warriors swooped out of the mist to hit at the vulnerable supply line that fed the Roman camps. When pursued by the Roman cavalry, they had the habit of literally disappearing, by submerging themselves in impenetrable marshlands. On other occasions the prized sheep, ponies and cattle of the tribes were left as tempting bait for the Romans to seize, luring them towards ambushes in the mountain glens and hidden bogs. It was also noted that the 'barbarian' enemy preferred to kill off their own wounded rather than let them fall into Roman hands.

In the spring of 210 a second invasion of Scotland was

launched. No submissions were accepted. This was to be a war of attrition summarised by a pitiless quotation from out of the mouth of King Agamemnon from Homer's *Iliad*. 'Let no one escape utter destruction, let no one escape our hands, not even the babe in its mother's womb, lest it be male – so let not even this escape our utter destruction.' In the process the hitherto neutral tribes of northern Scotland now joined in the resistance. The Roman marching camp at Carpow, where the resistance probably first triumphed, was now rebuilt as a castle of stone with walls 3 feet thick. It defended a keep of 24 acres. The emperor may have inspected these defences, which guarded a bridge of boats that now spanned the waters of the Tay. It was held by two *vexillationes*, units seconded from the VI Victrix and II Augusta legions to serve on the north-western front.

Septimius could also read the land, as he had on the Eastern frontier when the Roman army had met similar patterns of determined resistance (when they twice failed to storm Hatra), and it seems that over the winter of 209, whilst publicly preparing for the bloody second invasion of Scotland, he was also strengthening the defences of Hadrian's Wall. His troops clearly knew his enthusiasm for expressions of syncretic faith that would link all the cults of the empire together, for a detachment of Syrian troops set up a shrine to their great goddess Ashtoreth, specifically linking her with Carthaginian Tanit, as well as with Juno and Ceres. At Coria they raised a shrine both to Ashtoreth and to Melkarth of Tyre and Leptis Magna.

Over the winter of 210 and 211 the old emperor was once again based in York, catching up with his correspondence, and raising his second son, Geta, to the rank of Augustus. Even on his deathbed, on 4 February 211, he was said to have said to a secretary: 'Come give it to me, if we have anything to do.' Privately he advised his two sons with a bleak slice of realpolitik:

'Give money to the soldiers and despise everyone else.' He had already commissioned an urn carved from purple granite to hold his ashes after his cremation. He advised his sons to stick together and not to disagree, but this was an impossible request. A peace of sorts was imposed on the Caledonians, who were to be watched by a line of forts that snaked north out from Hadrian's Wall to the fortress of Carpow.

Then the imperial court took the road back to Rome. The two sons of Septimius Severus ruled jointly for almost an entire year, but their rivalry was tangible, and held at bay only by their love for their mother Julia. On 26 December one of her attempts at reconciliation in the palace went horribly wrong. Her youngest son Geta was stabbed by her first-born, Caracalla, whilst trying to seek refuge in her arms. It was a critical season, for the annual oath of loyalty given by the army was due to be renewed on 3 January. Caracalla was the clear favourite of the Roman army. He was a man who could dig a trench as fast as any soldier, and was strong enough to carry the eagle of the legion whilst on the march. He could grind his own corn to make flour and then make a fire to bake his bread. Even his nickname, Caracalla, was a badge of affection: it was the Celtic nickname for the distinctive thick woollen cloak with a hood that was worn by the Numidian soldiers of North Africa, and that can still be found used all over North Africa as a defence against the cold. Geta was the more cultivated and intellectual of the two sons, but even his father had delayed giving him the title of Augustus for twelve years. Even Caracalla's enemies commented on his sharp intelligence, how he could sum up the principles of a case and reach a quick verdict.

Caracalla now ordered that all inscriptions mentioning his younger brother's name be defaced, and the space of the missing letters filled by a new title for his mother, who was now not just Mother of the Camp but 'of the Senate and Fatherland' as well. She remained one of his chief advisers, a fixed element in his mobile court. He showed every sign of fulfilling his father's example. He was merciless to all the friends of his brother Geta, who were hunted down, but once that had been achieved he left Rome to campaign on the upper Danube frontier, then headed east on a tour of the eastern frontier that took him to Antioch, which effectively became the administrative centre of the empire, whilst the young emperor led a number of armed probes to understand and strengthen the Parthian frontier. He was also watching his back, and made a useful adjustment to the provincial frontiers, effectively to see that no governor have command of more than two legions (to reduce the chance of rebellion) even in distant Britannia, which was divided into a pair of equal north-eastern and south-western provinces.

The most spectacular fulfilment of his father's policies was the momentous decision to make all the people in the empire equal citizens. Rome had at last evolved from a predator city into the common fatherland. It was a potential commonwealth of nations united by a shared framework of laws – for he continued his father's work on the codification of Roman law by Ulpian and Paulus – and an empire that would delight in a syncretic, interlinked structure of religious belief that married Egyptian, Syrian, Greek, Celtic and Roman spiritual identities into one form that was ultimately unified by platonic philosophy. This was all finally achieved not by a Greek philosopher or a Roman lawyer but by a young man with a Libyan father and a Syrian mother ruling from Antioch.

The tragedy was that young Caracalla lacked the savage stealth of his father, who used to mask his actions until the very last moment, then move decisively. Caracalla had inherited three very tough operators from his father's inner court whom he had appointed to the utterly vital posts, those of the prefects. We have met one of them before, the ex-military policeman, ex-head of the intelligence service who had helped design Septimius' invasion of Scotland: Oclatinus Adventus. Another was the emperor's own cousin, Sextus Varius Marcellus, who was prefect of the military treasury, with the key task of paying the soldiers on time in solid silver coin. Marcellus managed to increase the soldiers' salary as well as providing better bounties for veterans.

The third of the key prefects was Macrinus, the praetorian prefect, the commander of the palace guard. He had been one of the very few members of Plautianus' inner circle to survive his fall from power. Marcus Opellius Macrinus was a man of talent. He shared the same sort of family background as Plautianus and Septimius Severus, for he was a Moor (an indigenous native of Mauretania) of Punic–Berber ethnic background from a provincial North African city. He was born in AD 165 into the parochial elite of the port city of Caesarea, Juba II's old capital in eastern Mauretania. That province, despite its royal past, was not a player in Roman imperial politics at this period, for only seven senators have been identified from it, and most of the men who had risen to high rank (such as Lusius Quietus earlier in the century) did it through a military career. Macrinus' family hadn't been in the political theatre as long as the Severans, but he was nevertheless an equestrian, and his family had been wealthy enough to provide him with a top-notch legal education in Rome. He had been hand-picked by Plautianus to be a legal secretary, and had survived his patron's fall only by the direct intervention of Lucius Fabius Cilo, an old ally of the Emperor Septimius Severus, who had fought on his side in the civil wars and was trusted enough to have been made tutor of the young princes. Cilo not only saved Macrinus but got him his first job, as superintendent of the Flaminian Way, which allowed him the chance to show his paces as an efficient administrator. His lack of a senatorial background probably made him easier to trust, for here was surely someone who could not become emperor, especially as he had no experience of military command. He was a safe pair of hands, one of the pool of procurators who actually ran things, beneath the gilded edifice of senators, consuls and governors.

Problems only began when Macrinus got advance warning of his young master's mistrust, for the Emperor Caracalla started dismissing Macrinus' allies from the staff, and his suspicions were confirmed when he opened an imperial order to find that it was his own death warrant. It may not have been an isolated incident, but part of a pattern of creeping paranoia that was stifling the likelihood of the young emperor trusting any man of talent – an especially dangerous fault given that he was about to lead a Roman army into an invasion of Parthia. If this is all true, it explains why instead of falling on his sword, Macrinus took 'appropriate precautions'. Whilst out scouting with Caracalla, he arranged for an assassin to kill his master, only to be killed in his turn.

Macrinus had put his trust in the other prefect, the old spymaster Oclatinus Adventus, who agreed that he had faced a lethal dilemma and so agreed to cover his back. So four days after this mysterious double murder (on the Parthian frontier on the road between Edessa [modern Urfa in Turkey] and Carrhae) the troops seized the occasion of the old Emperor Septimius Severus' birthday (11 April) to hail Macrinus as their new commander. He promptly added the cognomen Severus to his own name, as if he were part of the dynasty, and later publicly named his own son as Caesar in the city of Apamea, where Severus had first learned that the gods had acclaimed him emperor. For a

time it worked: Macrinus did seem to rule as the lineal successor. Even the old dowager-empress Julia Domna was initially
won around, and agreed to recognise what fate had decreed.
Many of the projects that were clearly started during the previous reigns were to be finished by Macrinus. The triumphal
arch that punctuates the skyline at Roman Volubilis, which is
lovingly dedicated and inscribed to Caracalla and his mother,
and was once crowned by a chariot with six bronze horses, was
completed in his time.* It also saw the completion of the brand-
new forum and handsome basilica in the centre of Volubilis (a
scaled-down version of the complex at Leptis Magna), flanked
by a magnificent set of public baths – which alone were allowed
to be associated with the emperor's new name. But as ordered
by a Moor who still proudly wore the earring that was part of
the recognised identity of the Numidian cavalry of the Roman
empire, it is likely that a building project associated with the
new emperor's home province of Mauretania got an accelerated
budget and the highest priority. Even the handsome rebuilding of the Capitoline Temple, approached up a flight of thirteen stairs, in an enclosed courtyard behind the Basilica, has
been dated to 218, to Macrinus' reign. We simply know too

---

* The dedication reads:
  For the emperor Caesar, Marcus Aurelius Antoninus [Caracalla], the pious,
  fortunate Augustus, greatest victor in Parthia, greatest victor in Britain,
  greatest victor in Germany, Pontifex Maximus, holding tribunician power
  for the twentieth time, Consul for the fourth time, Father of the Country,
  Proconsul, and for Julia Augusta [his mother Julia Domna], the pious,
  fortunate mother of the camp and the Senate and the country, because of
  his exceptional and new kindness towards all, which is greater than that of
  the Princeps that came before, the Republic of the Volubilitans took care to
  have this arch made from the ground up, including a chariot drawn by six
  horses and all the ornaments, with Marcus Aurelius Sebastenus, procurator,
  who is most deeply devoted to the divinity of Augustus, initiating and
  dedicating it.

little about his background to guess if he had some family connection with this city that might justify this extensive building works. We hear from the *Augustan History* (not always the most reliable of sources) that his wife's name was Nonia Celsa, and that she gave birth to a son in September 208 named Diadumenianus because he had been born with a halo-like caul.

The empire had been administered from Antioch by Caracalla. Macrinus continued this regime, striking the donative coins for his soldiers at the city's mint. In the process he increased the purity and the weight of the denarius to strengthen the imperial currency. But the dowager-empress had grown furious with the way the death of her son was being celebrated, especially in the streets of Rome, and began to ask awkward questions. She was bidden to go into perpetual exile. Julia Domna was in the advanced stages of breast cancer and saw no more interest in life, so starved herself to an earlier death. Macrinus had probably always opposed the Parthian adventure, but Caracalla had made war virtually inevitable, for he had intrigued in a Parthian civil war, and then for some small gain betrayed the ally who later emerged victorious. Even the Roman historians considered that Artabanus IV had right on his side when they recorded Macrinus' speech to his soldiers:

> You see the barbarian with his whole Eastern horde already upon us, and Artabanus seems to have good reason for his enmity. We provoked him by breaking the treaty, and in a time of complete peace we started a war ... This is no quarrel about boundaries or river-beds; everything is at stake in this dispute in which we face a mighty king fighting for his children and kinsmen who, he believes, have been murdered in \
> violation of solemn oaths.

Artabanus invaded the Roman province of Mesopotamia (so recently conquered by Septimius Severus from the Parthians), and so Macrinus marched south to defend this territory.

The battle of Nisibis in AD 217 (modern Nusaybin on the Turkish side of the Syrian frontier) is often described as if it were fought in some sandy desert of Arabia, not the southern mountains of Armenia. It was an exceptionally bloody and confusing battle in which the neat block formation of the Roman legions faced the mounted archer-knights of Iran over three consecutive days. Nisibis broke the back of the Parthian cavalry (indeed the dynasty would be replaced by the Sassanids a few years later), but Macrinus was not to know this. It was his first experience of battle and he was alarmed at the decimation of what was the hand-picked elite of the Roman army. A peace was negotiated, which left the Romans in command of their province, but in exchange the Parthians negotiated an enormous pension-indemnity of 200 million sesterces. It did not look good to his army, especially as compared with their experience under a soldier-emperor like Caracalla and the seemingly endless series of victories achieved under Septimius Severus. The opinion of the army was the bedrock of imperial authority. If a revolt had any chance of working, it needed to incubate within a legion.

The Dowager-Empress Julia Domna was now dead, but her sister Maesa was now resident in the city of Emesa, where their family had once been kings and remained hereditary high priests. She had a grandson who was the spitting image of Caracalla. This fourteen-year-old boy, Varius Avitus Bassianus, was displayed at dawn on 16 May 218 to the assembled ranks of the III Gallica Legion based at Raphaneae (one of the twelve cities of the Decapolis in modern Jordan). He was acclaimed by the soldiers as Marcus Aurelius Antoninus but is better known to the world as Heliogabalus. Macrinus' new prefect of the guard rushed to quell this mutiny, but he was beaten off by the III Gallica, and his authority instantly started to dissolve. The other legions garrisoned at Apamea now failed to respond to his commands, so within a few weeks a battle had been fought and lost outside Antioch on 8 June 218, and the heads of Emperor Macrinus, his young son and his supporters now adorned a row of pikes.

It took the new boy emperor eighteen months to process to Rome. He was not just master of the Roman empire but the heir to an ancient tradition of sacred priestly authority, and he took the unification of the religious cults to new heights. The sacred betyl of Emesa (an uncarved conical black stone, probably a meteorite, that represented the deity) was processed through the empire as he advanced north. He paused at the provincial capital of Nicomedia (Izmit in north-western Turkey), where he purged his court and became ever more dependent on the advice of his mother, Julia Soaemias, who was the niece of Julia Domna. He summoned the sacred cult image of Tanit–Juno Caelestis, the mother-goddess of ancient Carthage, to be sent by ship so that she could be married to the sky god at Rome.

By the autumn of 219 the now sixteen-year-old boy emperor had installed himself at Rome. The sensual cycle of the Syrian fertility cult, with its open celebration of sacred marriage, the death and rebirth of young male gods, clearly came as something of a culture shock for the Romans. As did the silk vestments, and the very different traditions of sacred music, dance, ritual and face paint. Most historians depict the young high-priest emperor as sexually depraved, prowling the public bathhouse of Rome for the most physically attractive men. But he also took three wives, and in the words of a more sympathetic chronicler, Herodian, 'he had no wish to sin in secret. He

appeared in public with his eyes made up and rouged cheeks.'
I have heard the same sort of shocked comment by travellers
observing for the first time the warriors of Afghanistan and the
North-West Frontier, who are amazed to see that these men
apply kohl to their eyelids, dye their hair orange with henna,
wear skirt-like baggy trousers, smoke hashish, have multiple
wives, but also like watching boys dance. Perhaps Heliogabalus
was not an oversexed degenerate, just culturally different. He
was certainly visible, and much more interested in the cult
practices of temple worship than in the proper ordering of the
Roman army. He had appointed the last surviving male cousin
of the Severan family as his heir by naming him Caesar. When
this young man reached the age of fourteen, the unsatisfactory
Heliogabalus was murdered by his Roman guards (along with
his mother) on 12 March 222.

The new monarch Severus Alexander was a true heir to his
grandfather, indeed he governed at first with the advice of his
grandmother, Julia Mamaea, the sister-in-law of Septimius
Severus. So the meritocratic men of talent who had served
Septimius were now restored to office. The great jurist Ulpian
was made guard prefect, and one of Septimius' old generals
(with direct experience of half a dozen different provincial
commands) was made co-consul with the emperor. As a young
man, like all his family, he was called to the East, because the
revived force of Persia, under the new Sassanid dynasty, was
making itself felt. Just two years after his accession the last king
of Parthia had been killed. By 226 Artaxerxes I had emerged
as ruler of a state that consciously looked back to the ancient
Achaemenid dynasty that had ruled over the vast Persian world
empire before the conquests of Alexander the Great, whose
name the Roman emperor bore. For the next 440 years, the
rivalry between the two superpowers (the Roman and Sassanid

empires) to control the Near East overrode all other issues. Severus Alexander ruled the empire from Syria for two years, before he was forced to return to Rome in order to meet the threat on the German frontier.

Having negotiated a peace with his northern neighbours, rather than leading his army into military victory (which was customarily celebrated with a cash donative), he was killed by his own soldiers on 21 March 235. Thus died the last of the Severan dynasty. They had ruled for forty-two years. With the murder of Severus Alexander, something of the old empire also died, for the series of soldier emperors who plotted and fought for the throne over the next fifty years also brought the empire to its knees. In doing so, their careers spiralled ever further away from the *cursus honorum*, that graduation of legal, military and administrative posts that prepared an aspiring young man to join the Senate, before becoming a consul, then a provincial governor, then one of the legates of one of the twenty-five legions, to rise at last, by hook or by crook, or by adoption, to the throne.

To those who had ears to hear, the knell of an incipient social revolution had already been sounded. The guard prefect Ulpian was murdered by his own men in just his second year of office. When Cassius Dio served as governor of Pannonia, his strict discipline so offended the soldiers under his command that the emperor had to privately warn him to shun the streets of Rome, or else be lynched. The empire was about to descend into a dark age of feuding soldier-emperors who built and wrote nothing, and barely clung to power for more than a year before their murderer replaced them, himself in his turn to be replaced. The currency was debased and the army grew ever more greedy and unprofessional.

After fifty years of licensed anarchy, the era of the Soldier

Emperors, the authority of the empire would be restored, but under an entirely different breed of rulers. Diocletian, Maximian and Constantius were tough, brawny fighters who had joined the legions as young men. Entirely self-made, they climbed to the very top rank (as joint rulers in AD 285) having started near the bottom, the sons of peasant farmers from such poor mountain regions as Serbia and Thrace. Sometimes we know their father's name and village, very seldom anything more. Their university was the barracks. They created a simpler line of direct power, composed of soldiers, tax-collectors and officials obedient to their orders, and which bypassed the old culture of literate, well-educated landowners, proudly engaged in the governance of their own cities as well as the wider empire. How much the bulk of Roman citizens regretted the departure of the old caste system is a moot point. The theatres, libraries, temples and elegant town houses with their exquisite mosaic floors and frescoed walls certainly dwindled in that vast constellation of city-states, but the bathhouses and circus arenas seem to have survived in all the great cities.

9

St Augustine of Hippo

To give some sense of the resonant worldwide appeal of St Augustine, I started to collect together some of his most popular sayings, which I heard whenever I brought him up in conversation – you can check if you type his name into the internet. He is well represented.

On Love

Love is the beauty of the soul.

Better to have loved and lost, than never to have loved at all.

Fear is the enemy of love.

It is love that asks, that seeks, that knocks, that finds, and that is faithful to what it finds.

There is no greater invitation to love than loving first.

I was not yet in love, yet I loved to love, I sought what I might love, in love with loving.

Beauty is indeed a gift of God which he dispenses even to the wicked.

Give me chastity and continence – but not yet.

Love and do what you will.

On Faith

There is no saint without a past, no sinner without a future.

The truth is like a lion. You don't have to defend it. Let it loose, it will defend itself.

Lord, give what you command, and command what you will.

God became man so that man might become God.

God provides the wind but man must raise the sails.

God had one son on earth without sin, but never one without suffering.

To sing is to pray twice.

Do not despair, one thief was saved. Do not presume, one thief was damned.

It was pride that turned angels into devils, it is humility that makes men as angels.

On Virtue

Charity is no substitute for Justice withheld.

The good man, though a slave, is free, the wicked, though he reigns, is a slave to as many masters as he has vices.

Wrong is wrong even if everyone is doing it. Right is right even if no one is doing it.

In the absence of justice, what is sovereignty but organised robbery?

In necessary things unity, in doubtful things liberty, in all things charity.

Patience is the companion of wisdom.

To many, total abstinence is easier than perfect moderation.

The confession of evil works is the beginning of good works.

Since love grows within you, so beauty grows, for love is the beauty of the soul.

On the Quest

You aspire to great things? Begin with little ones.

Bad times, hard times, this is what people keep saying, but let us live well and times shall be good. We are the times; such as we are, such are the times.

One's destination is never a place but a new way of seeing things.

Hope has two beautiful daughters – their names are anger and courage: anger at the way things are, and courage to see that they do not remain the way they are.

Take care of your body as if you were going to live for ever: and take care of your soul as if you were going to die tomorrow.

The world is a book and if you do not travel you read only one page.

People travel to wonder at the height of mountains, at the huge waves of the seas, at the long courses of the rivers, at the vast compass of the ocean, at the circular motion of the stars, and yet they pass by themselves without wondering.

You have made us for yourself O Lord, and our hearts are restless until they rest in you.

∴

This is an impressively humane, pragmatic and eternally relevant treasury of wisdom. It is also one that I would later find out to be based on false attributions, no matter that they have now been carved into tens of thousand of rosaries, or emblazoned on millions of Christian bumper stickers. But this is often the way with St Augustine. His personality cult is a 1,500-year-old magnet that has attracted many ornaments – and some barnacles. Charles Spurgeon made up that phrase 'The truth is like a lion', while 'There is no saint without a past' dates to the 1920 edition of Ahmad Sohrab's *Persian Rosary*, if not the court-martyred St Oscar Wilde. Augustine's even more famous quotation 'The world is a book' (which I once used in an advertising campaign) has also now been convincingly sourced to an eighteenth-century French wit, while 'In necessary things unity' has been traced back to a seventeenth-century mind. Five million words make a whole city of writing, which has been impossible to police and has only been fully penetrated by a few readers. It shelters many opinions, for Augustine is a hero both to Luther and to such Rottweilers of papal orthodoxy as Cardinal Joseph Ratzinger, later Pope Benedict XVI.

∴

So it was to Annaba (ancient Hippo), in present-day Algeria, that I first travelled to find something concrete about Augustine, armed with a bag full of Peter Brown's books about his life and times. I wanted to touch some of the stones that he might have known as I delved into his story. The city he lived in for half his life has gone by many spellings: it was the Ubon (harbour) of the Phoenicians, which subsequently got elided into Ubbo, then Hippo, Bona, Bône, and now Annaba. It still possesses a hilltop kasbah–citadel (occupied by a decrepit army barracks), which overlooks the narrow streets of an ancient Muslim city that less than two hundred years ago was still ringed with walls, its seven gates guarded by Ottoman janissaries. In the nineteenth century the French added an imposing new avenue beside this city whose central pavement is still dense with flower sellers and pavement cafés shaded by a double line of giant West African fig trees. This animation is overlooked by a charming façade of grandiose colonial civic offices, whose magnificent swirls of baroque white plaster have been picked out with blue shutters. At the foot of the avenue is the Moorish railway station, beside which start the docks, flecked with odd fragments of medieval walls and some fish restaurants. For a traveller, it is like stepping straight back into the 1950s, as there are no tourists, just two hotels that cater for the foreign commercial traveller or the visiting bureaucrat, one efficient but a little soulless, the other run down but with a louche bar on its rooftop. There is just one gift shop in the whole city, whose chief monument is the eighteenth-century mosque built by Salah Bey, its handsome arcades raised over an ancient eleventh-century shrine to Sidi Bou Merouane. It sits in the centre of the old city beside an old square, awaiting the traveller like a personal discovery. Annaba is one of the least visited of the white cities, that sisterhood of the western Levant which unites Tunis, Naples, Casablanca, Algiers and Marseille.

The road to the north of the modern city meanders through a succession of coastal villages, while that to the west climbs quickly into the Kabyle mountains. Eastward stretches a vast sandy bay. Walking along this shore there is not a single café, let alone a hotel, just the odd dirt track pushed through the dunes, to allow Algerian families to picnic here in the summer. Of a summer evening fishermen cast lines from the beach, and make bonfires from beached wooden crates with which to roast their catch. You have to pinch yourself hard to remind yourself that you are in the central Mediterranean, for everywhere else that has this much sand and safe swimming has long been slick with suntan oil and buried under the concrete and tarmac tsunami of mass tourism. And yet all the ingredients are here, ready to be ticked off by some future development project. There is a regional airport right down on the shore, miles of virgin sand that fringe the wide bay, an interesting old city complete with an active fishing port, and half a dozen archaeological sites tucked into the southern mountains waiting to serve as the targets for day excursions. There are also the remains of a stumpy French artillery tower, Le Bastion de France, to remind us that Louis XIV tried and failed to rape this land some 150 years before his descendant achieved this. There is also the St Augustine brand name waiting to be attached to this region by future publicists. A genuine label of recognition, ripe and ready for copy-writers, a name pregnant with culture, history and travel, with a whiff of sex and mystic mystery, but instilled with an overriding sense of good. St Augustine also comes with some ready foreign partnerships, be it St Augustine, Florida (the oldest town in the USA) or Santa Monica (named after his mother) in California, let alone Augustine of Canterbury, or dowdy London's Kilburn and Watling Street.

Ancient Hippo revealed itself to be a small boggy archaeological park on the eastern edge of the modern Algerian city of Annaba. Over many visits I have grown to love it, but it is not a prepossessing site on a first visit. The custodians do their best to keep the undergrowth at bay, but it is a constant battle, as the locals take no interest in ruins associated with a Christian bishop, and foreigners have been rare. So over the years I have seen many more snakes, frogs and cats than other tourists. This is most especially true of the towering vaults of the Roman baths, which remain convincingly feral. The Roman theatre, which lies just beyond the archaeological boundary fence, is merely sad. It was hidden under the floor of a nineteenth-century colonial villa until Allied bombing ripped open the evidence of these ancient foundations in 1941. The theatre benches were then tidied up and exposed for general admiration. They are now used by local drinkers, who park their vans nearby, drink their beer and then smash the green bottles on the stone benches as a last testament to a melancholic tendency. An old brewery and bottling plant stands on the western edge of the excavations of Hippo, hopefully preserving a vast expanse of the ancient city under its cavern of warehouses.

But we must be thankful for the small slice of the ancient city that we do possess. It seems to have been the gift of Erwan Marec, a French naval officer who turned himself into an archaeologist. He was allowed to work the ground below the state prison and employ the better-behaved convicts. Marec's patient removal of centuries of river mud revealed a fourth-century church and the impressive expanse of the city forum, and so saved the site from development. His finds, including a series of vivid mosaics and an astonishing intact bronze Roman victory monument, gradually overwhelmed the prison compound, which eventually gave up the struggle against the past and was converted into the site museum. When I first visited this colonial courtyard, it was under the directorship of a brilliant Algerian archaeologist, my first and best guide, who had specialised in the study of the very earliest historical levels of Islam on the edge of the desert in southern Algeria. 'Which is why,' she laughingly told me, 'the ministry sent me here, to look after a late Roman–Christian site on the coast.' She pointed out with amused authority that there is nothing of Islam at Hippo, for the medieval city of Annaba – Bône – shifted across the river from the ancient ruins to occupy the better-drained, less malarial land to the north-west.

The greatest visual tourist draw at Hippo does not lie within the fences of the archaeological park, but presides on the hill just behind it. Here stands the glitteringly romantic hilltop cathedral of St Augustine. This cluster of orientalised domes fringed by palm trees is a little like Montmartre's Sacré Coeur transported south to glow under the African sun, its interior a fascinating mix of cultures. French heraldry vies with a Kabyle cedarwood dowry chest turned into a Berber altar. A panoply of colour spilled from the stained glass washes over the marble interior. The high walls around the altar are lined with scenes from the life of this world-renowned saint, while near the front door the cathedral walls are studded with votive plaques from French and American soldiers thanking St Augustine for answering their prayers during the Second World War. Behind the altar is a raised reliquary, containing the elbow bone of the saint set within the recumbent statue of a mitred bishop. Here lies St Augustine, one of the Four Doctors of the Roman Catholic Church. He is one of the four intellectual cornerstones who forged the armour of Christian orthodoxy, but who also inspired the leading lights of the Protestant Reformation, such as Martin Luther.

Looking at the statue on my first visit, I found that two stories, taught to me by a father who was a Roman Catholic and an officer in the Royal Navy, came bubbling from out of my childhood memories. I remembered that the good St Augustine was more concerned to complete the conversion of one more soul than to help resist the sack of his home city. For as the walls of his Roman city were being breached by German barbarians, he steadfastly remained at his post, talking one of his congregation into making that last leap of faith and profess Christianity. He died because of this selfless act, but a soul was saved for eternity.

The other anecdote from my childhood had a similar home-spun virtue. St Augustine decided that it was his duty to give the last rites to a pious old lady in the hills, and so missed the chance of going down to the docks to meet a young intellectual who brought letters of introduction from well connected Roman friends. My father went on to explain that though this was the act of a worthy priest, yet it was a wasted opportunity for a bishop. For bishops, like admirals, are no longer free to think about the safety of just one ship, but must keep the whole fleet's safety in their hands. It was in this way that St Augustine missed meeting the only great early Christian thinker to have emerged from the British Isles. Wind and tide wait for no man, and by the time St Augustine got home, Pelagius had been swept onward into the eastern leg of his journey, rather than hold up his voyage. Hence St Augustine lost the chance to listen to some good old British common sense. My father thought highly of Pelagius because (A) he had some good ideas (like babies not being damned for eternity just because there was no priest at hand to give them baptism), and (B) he was British. And so because the two men never met, we would have nonsense to hear from the pulpit from our priests.

It was a complex story for a boy to make sense of, but the idea of a saint getting things wrong, let alone the priests, was greatly appealing. St Augustine had lost his one chance to take the measure of a man who would be maliciously lampooned as 'a swine stuffed full of Irish porridge from the swill of heresy'. He also clearly lacked an eye for the wind (a great failing in a man) and showed a lack of understanding for 'those that go down to the sea in ships and do business in great waters'.

I have always loved these two stories. The image of a young Briton, familiar with the hills of Scotland and Ireland and fond of porridge, patiently waiting in the blistering heat of a North African harbour for his letter of introduction to incur a reply, was also one that certainly had resonance for me. Old men are often up in the hills when beady youngsters try to force acquaintance on them.

But like so much about St Augustine, I have also found out that these two beloved tales from my childhood are not true. The line about Pelagius and porridge is borrowed from Jerome (a notoriously disdainful judge of character), and Augustine died in his bed, not hacked to death by Vandal barbarians having just baptised a freshly converted pagan.

Which is also true of the basilica–shrine on top of the hill. This place is not very true either. The site is not associated with any aspect of the saint's life, let alone a church or a Christian tomb. It was simply chosen for its commanding height, which would allow the nineteenth-century monument to dominate the view of anyone leaving or approaching Hippo by train or on the road. During Augustine's life this hill housed the water cisterns of Roman Hippo, uncovered in digging the church foundations.

And on closer inspection the church pays tribute, not to a North African spiritual visionary of the late Roman empire, but to the power of France. It is a fifty-year victory monument to her 1830 conquest of Algeria, a marble totem pole placed on a conspicuous hill in the 1880s. In its pomposity and style (Byzantine–Mauresque) it can only be compared with another triumphant Roman Catholic cathedral that was then being built on another historic hill of North Africa, the Byrsa citadel hill of ancient Carthage. This cathedral was named after St Louis, a French crusader king. Naming your church after a dead, white, male, royal French terrorist steeped in the blood of innocent medieval Muslims does of course trump the offence of founding the colonial cathedral of Augustine at Annaba. St Augustine's elbow was not extracted from a dig into a native North Africa church, but was sent down from Northern Italy in the late nineteenth century on a battleship.

St Augustine's bones have had an afterlife quite as well travelled as his own corporeal body. They were first smuggled out of Hippo during the collapse of Vandal rule, to ornament the basilica at Bari, in Sardinia, before being acquired by purchase by a wealthy prelate to accompany the royal Lombard tomb of his uncle in Pavia, and then transferred by Augustinian monks to the safety of Milan for two hundred years. So once it had been agreed that the bones were to be returned to Pavia in the late nineteenth century it was a comparatively simple matter for an elbow bone to be selected from out of the marble ossuary and shipped further south. It was inserted into a recumbent statue of a Roman Catholic bishop that certainly gives the casual visitor the impression that this towering figure of Western culture was of and from the West.

It has been my happy task to strip away all of these disguises and to attempt to restore Augustine to his North African identity. To use his life, not to excavate Christian theology, but to illuminate Roman North Africa in the late fourth and early fifth century, by following the career of an ambitious, articulate member of the traditional middle class. A Berber boy from the North Africa hills who made good.

∵

St Augustine is the most famous North African of all time – when viewed from the West. In his homeland he is a footnote from ancient history, but he is also the real thing: not a half-breed from the coast but a native Berber who was born, bred and educated in the mountains of the interior.

He is also the most known man of the ancient world, for he left behind him five million words, embedded in a library of 300 letters, 400 sermons and 33 books, including a soul-searching autobiography, *The Confessions*. These works have never been left forgotten on the shelves but have been continuously written about, taught and commented on over the last 1,500 years. Even if you are a militant atheist bored by the evolution of Christian theology, you have to grant Augustine's key role in the intellectual development of the West. He is one of the Gang of Four, the Four Doctors of the Latin Church, as well as one of the fountainheads of the Protestant Reformation. So St Augustine studies have become a self-sustaining academic discipline in itself, complete with conferences, journals, and rival traditions of scholarship. More material keeps being added to the canon, including four new sermons discovered as recently as 2007.

Despite this, his character remains fascinatingly elusive, which draws forth a tribute of biographies, for as Oscar Wilde reminds us, every saint has a past and every sinner a future. St Augustine, like Winston Churchill, was also determined that history would look kindly upon him, and so became the chief chronicler of his own past. Even by the evidence of his own words, he was a complex fusion of saint and sinner, fully infected by his past actions as an ambitious place-seeker in the Roman empire, a heretical Manichean (better known to the modern reader as a Cathar) who openly lived with a series of concubines.

But it is easy to pardon him for this dichotomy, which was inevitable for a man whose life spans such a decisive period of cultural transformation. For St Augustine's life stood on the cusp of the ancient and medieval worlds. He was a living bridge between the tolerant, careless paganism that predominated in his childhood and the new state-defended and defined compassionate Christianity in which he died. Even in the cradle, he grew up with a foot in both cultures, his father a sensual carefree pagan Roman, his mother a pious Christian.

This duality was quite normal, for the pagan and Christian worlds had coexisted out of kilter for three hundred years before his birth. The flames of the temple altars had blazed and the ancient myths been enacted in our theatres whilst Christians worshipped secretly in cemeteries and private houses. Now and then the two worlds collided, as when Christians became the bloodstained exhibits in the arena of the amphitheatre, their dreadful deaths witnessed by tens of thousands as an entertainment. Then for a period of a hundred years came an interval of tolerance, a time of equality, when a set of newly legitimised Christian churches stood with their doors wide open on the main streets, competing for attention with sensual processions of the goddess of love and beautiful, opera-like enactments of the old myths. This interaction, three generations long, is defined by two legal milestones, opening with Constantine's Edict of Milan (313) and ending with Theodosius the Great's closure of the temples in 390.

Augustine's life was always united by one great passion – an enthusiasm for reading and learning. He was a man obsessed with books and with the power of ideas, as well as in how best to articulate them in both the written and spoken word. Like most intellectuals, this love of ideas was poisoned by a commensurate desire to win an argument, or to start one up if there was no immediate cause to engage in and enrage upon. Even if you dislike his ideas and become haunted by his restless ambition, it is impossible not to admire his energy. He seems to have been driven by a genuine lifelong quest to know God and to understand what is good. He was deeply troubled by the source of evil in the world, and the spiritual blindness that swallowed a man like himself when in rut. All his life he carefully masked his ambition, and tried to keep a check on his pride. He never lost his sense of genuine compassion and responsibility for others.

Over his long career as a public Christian (first as a priest in Hippo, then as bishop of Hippo in his native North African Church) he helped develop the concept of a broad, inclusive

Church open to all mankind. This Church was to be governed by the collective spiritual authority of bishops in council obedient under their chairman, the bishop of Rome. Paradoxically he also articulated such key doctrines as original sin, eternal damnation and divine grace, which effectively demolished the reality of the universal Church and replaced it with a circle of the chosen elect. It was as if he wanted to have his cake and eat it: to keep the passionate sense of an ethical community of the righteous (that came with the first Christian communities and comes bubbling out of the text of the gospels and Acts) but also to win the street battle against the rival faiths within the empire, and wrap his chosen Church in its mantle. His effect on the development of Western Christian civilisation is incalculable: on the one hand sin-obsessed, exclusive and judgemental, on the other individualistic, energetic and inclusive. Arguably it is this restless paranoia embedded within the soul of the Christian West that has made us so demonically creative.

10

Augustine – Aurelius Augustinus, son of Patricius

Aurelius Augustinus was born in the mountains of North Africa in the winter of AD 354. His homeland is untouched by the Sahara desert, and far too cold in winter for either palm trees or camels to survive. His horizon is filled with limestone hills whose lower slopes have been planted out with olive groves but whose summits are clad in native forest. The valley floors have been tilled by the farmer's plough for centuries. It is a land dominated by horse, donkey and cattle, sustained by the two regular crops of wheat and olive oil, eked out by vineyards, orchards and flocks of goats. Climatically and geologically it is the same landscape that can be found in the interior hills of Spain, Italy, western Turkey and Greece. Augustine never visited the desert or saw so much as a glimpse of the sea throughout his childhood. His was a youth filled with scenes of the wheat harvest in the summer, the olive harvest in the autumn, and the pine-scented hills.

Whenever I pass through his home town of Thagaste I stop and have a coffee, so that I am free to scan the faces of the locals. There is, as everywhere in Algeria, much variety. There are thin aquiline faces that could have come from out of a Delacroix canvas or a sketch of windswept horsemen by Fromentin.

There are darker hues blended in from sub-Saharan Africa, and paler hues that might have come from an exiled Moor. There is a world of difference in how the schoolmaster and the pharmacist occupy a table with their newspapers, educationally set apart from farmers dressed in worn green jackets surrounded by television hubbub. It is the faces of the farmers that draw me: strong and weather-tanned, framed by self-tied keffiyeh turbans from which escape thick mops of black hair. Marble portraits of the Roman world brought to life by lively brown eyes. To help this flight of fantasy there is a plaster-cast copy of a young Roman boy, found in the nearby town of Madauros, placed beside the café tables. Nothing convincingly classical has been excavated from this town, which does not have an archaeological site. Thagaste offers something equally precious, which is a sense of organic continuity with the Berber past. It remains a scruffy provincial town dominated by hill farmers. An attempt was once made to create a location associated with its most famous son, by labelling an ancient olive tree as dating from St Augustine. But nowhere does Augustine write about an olive tree, let alone a wheat field, which then as now must have dominated the conversations of so many of his neighbours. The one tree in Thagaste that Augustine does mention (as part of a childhood escapade) is a pear tree, which once again reminds us how much his town is part of the Mediterranean.

I have never found the face of Augustine in this throng of male faces at Thagaste, but I have often identified his father. Patricius was a joyful, open-hearted character, somewhat crude, but in love with his wife, the land and the life of a farmer. He was a native landowner and so he was a member of the town council, the *curia*. This would have met in a hall in the town square beside the Capitoline Temple. The members of this group had front-row seats in all the places of public display in

Thagaste: be it the theatre, the circus racetrack or the amphitheatre. On such occasions, a waist-high stone balcony (the pulpit) partitioned them from the rest of the population. Entry to this class traditionally required possession of landed property worth 300 gold solidi, which would produce an income of 25–30 gold coins a year. Patricius could feed himself, his family, his workers and slaves from the produce of his own freehold land, which had to be at least 20 acres in extent. He almost certainly owned his own team of oxen to plough the land, but we don't know the extent of his acreage, which was the normal state of affairs amongst the resident class of Berber landowners, for they augmented their own freeholdings by taking leases of land from the great imperial and senatorial estates. So an efficient hard-working small landowner could yet amass a considerable fortune, by proving himself a competent manager for others. We know from a verse tombstone inscription found in the North African hill town of Makhtar that even an itinerant reaper (way down on the social pecking list) could rise to great wealth in this way, by becoming an efficient subcontractor to the great estates. The 'Makhtar Reaper' could have come straight from the pages of Thomas Hardy, a classical mayor of Casterbridge who rose up in the world by the sweat of his own brow to become an honoured *curialis*, a town councillor, proudly watching over the elevated status of his grandchildren.

This superior social status was codified, for a *curialis* was defined as a *honestior*, an honourable person who could not be flogged by an official or tortured at the instruction of a judge. His word was respected in the public law courts without the routine verification process of torture, but in return he was expected to serve his turn as one of the administrative officers of the town. Collectively the *curia* also had the responsibility for collecting, inspecting and delivering the town's tax assessment of corn to the state granaries. In times of local dearth, this could literally bankrupt them, but the empire had need of such responsible men, and once entered into the register of the *curia*, it was virtually impossible to get yourself removed. The heir to your lands would inherit your place.

For though the exotic imports of the Roman empire might command our imagination (such as the trade in Yemeni incense, Chinese silk, Indian pepper and Saharan gold, ebonies and ivory), it was the staple produce of the farms that dominated the economy. At least 60 per cent of imperial revenue came in with the annual harvest, which employed 80 per cent of the population to gather it. Yet there was also financial risk entailed in this orderly system, for the price of corn could double between one year and the next as the yields varied by as much as 50 per cent. Likewise there were huge variations in the price of wheat between the different provinces, depending on the state of their own harvests. In a good year, a working farmer was left in possession of about a third of his harvest after rent in kind had been paid to the landlord and tax remitted to the state.

The imperial tax budget was fixed on the first day of January, but this assessment could be appealed against if the province or city could field an effective team to state its case, especially if barbarian raids had ravaged the lands. But the costs of sending a smooth-talking ambassador to the capital, complete with gifts to their senatorial patrons at Rome, as well as to bribe open the doors of the various chancelleries, could be as expensive as the tax itself. Collection of the tax by the local assembly of town councillors on behalf of the state was one of the foremost contracts that underwrote the rule of the empire. It allowed for self-governance while keeping administrative costs to a bare minimum.

To be invited to sit on the *curia* was the vital first step up the social pyramid. There were roughly 2,500 self-governing towns and cities in the Roman empire, a fifth of which lay in North Africa. This galaxy of five hundred communities each had its own agricultural hinterland, sometimes in view of each other, but seldom more than a day's walk apart. The size of the towns varied enormously, but on average the resident urban population was between two and five thousand, of which only 1 per cent would qualify to sit on the council. So in North Africa this *curialis* class numbered 25,000 individuals, with about 65,000 for the whole empire. Of this group only 1 per cent would be wealthy, well-established and clever enough to take up a seat in the Senate of Rome, made up of between 600 and 2,000 senators.

By chance we have a wonderfully exact example of how this worked on the ground, for in the *curia* of the North African city of Timgad an inscription has survived that lists all the town councillors in order of precedence. This, the so-called Album of Timgad, was carved in 368 when Augustine was a boy. Timgad was about four times the size of Thagaste, and was altogether a much larger, wealthier and much more magnificent place. Ten men receive top billing, rated as *viri clarissimi* (most brilliant). It seems that half of them were outsiders but the other five were local men who were other Roman senators or Roman knights. How much time they spent in Timgad we cannot tell, but these were the veins of a network of relationships that connected their city to the provincial capital of Carthage and onwards, ever upwards, towards Rome. We can glimpse the scale of their wealth in the Timgad house of M. Plotius Faustus Sertius, which occupies two blocks of the city just above the forum. It has thirty rooms laid out around two internal courtyards, each with its own pool. There was a monumental bathhouse just across the road, but Sertius' villa also boasted two private bathhouses of its own. Sertius had paid for the construction of three of Timgad's most impressive monuments: a vast temple, a fine triumphal arch (dedicated to the ruling imperial family), and an impressive brand-new market courtyard ornamented by eight statues, dedicated to himself, his wife (Cornelia Valentina Tucciana) and his ancestors.

Beneath such fabulously wealthy individuals as Sertius, the Album lists thirty *principales*. They would be the city's leading residents, who between them shared most of its offices and honours, especially the college of priests associated with each temple. Again we have an example of how this sort of man might appear in the townscape of Roman North Africa, for one of Timgad's listed *principales* is Vocontius, who showed off his taste and patriotism by presenting a number of votive statues to his home town. The lettering for their bases is carved in the flowing forms of uncial script, otherwise reserved for the pages of a codex. The first time I stumbled across them, I wondered what on earth I was looking at, for this lettering suggests the age of Charlemagne, not that of the Caesars. Vocontius was clearly an exceptional man. From another inscription we know that he was a leading member of a local philosophical group called the society of brotherly love, who met in the Baths of Philadelphus.

In the third rank of the urban pecking order, the Album lists 150 town councillors, the *curiales*, also known as *decuriones*. Typically they owned a modest courtyard house in the city as well as their freehold farm in the surrounding countryside. Many of the *curiales* can be traced back through five generations of ancestors, 150 years, for their family names have been found recorded on other inscription lists, due to Timgad's exceptional state of preservation. Half of this body of men had acquired some sort of post within the imperial civil service, which allowed them to escape service from the town council (and the dreaded liability for gathering in the right amount of tax), but this left seventy individuals legally grounded to attend the council of their hometown.

This was the position occupied by Augustine's father Patricius at Thagaste. He stood on the bottom rung of the group of leading citizens who ran his tiny community: not wealthy, but with honourable status, and free of any anxiety about his daily bread. He occupied his own house, ran his own farm, ruled his own household. So we can think of Augustine's father as the Franklin in Chaucer's tale: impulsively benevolent, quick-tempered and rejoicing in his love of wine. He was good-natured to his wife and was known to have never raised his hand to strike her, but then she was careful never to challenge his dignity as paterfamilias of a household that here included his own mother and any number of compliant slave girls. Patricius was also well connected. His cousin Cornelius Romanianus was the wealthiest of the *principales* in Thagaste, a man who could afford to pay for troupes to come to the town theatre, as well as to bankroll the gladiatorial teams that staged wild bear fights in the local earth-banked amphitheatre.

So Augustine grew up in a town where everyone knew exactly where he belonged, which was very near the front row. The first memory he gives us is vividly modern in its sensibility, for he describes a child watching a younger sibling happily guzzling milk at the breast, but recalls the 'bitter look' of the watcher, who is himself 'avid for the breasts'. But this mental image is also part of a happier stream of recollections, for Augustine remembers how he learnt Latin, literally at his mother's breast, beside his brother and sister. The family fluency in Latin was all part and parcel of their elite status, for in the mountains all around them the Berber dialects survived, as well as a degraded form of the old Punic language of Carthage.

Augustine totally adored his mother. She is known to history as Monica, a name that may have been derived from the cult temple at Thibilis where the mother goddess was worshipped as Mon, or from Ammonica – a reference to the oracle temple of Ammon in an oasis of the western desert of Egypt. Despite the pagan origins of her name, Monica was a professing Christian all her life. She was also alive to the sacred in the landscape, for she saw visions of angels that she could distinguish from demons by their smell. Some have suggested that her Christian beliefs might have come through her old slave nanny. Another of the household slaves who helped bring her up gave her the nickname of *meribula*, little boozer, and Monica in middle age appears to have shared her husband Patricius' fondness for wine.

The church she frequented in Thagaste has not been found, and was almost certainly a small rustic affair, built from rammed earth supported on a foundation line of stones. Such simple structures have been found all over the region, typically ornamented with simple pious inscriptions painted in ochre on whitewashed walls. Through her tears, prayers and entreaties she eventually managed to get her husband interested in the life of the church, though he never advanced beyond a catechumen, listening to the chanted psalms, the sermons and prayers. He resisted baptism and so never attended the sacred feast of communion. He may not have thought his role in the church much different from attending any of the other temples in his homeland, where it was customary for the congregation to use the outer courtyard (to listen to the sacred chants and watch the processions), as the temple shrine was reserved for the priests.

At seven years old, the young Augustine attended the local primary school, which taught reading, reciting and writing. He learned grammar and pronunciation, and a knowledge of the classic texts, assisted by the plays he witnessed in the theatre. Even as a boy he developed an absolute passion for the language of Virgil and Cicero, and a fondness for the writings of the North African playwright Terence. He came to the study of Greek later, but this was badly taught in this highland town by an irascible schoolmaster who did not spare the rod. As a man Augustine could make his way through a Greek text, but he never read the language with any enthusiasm.

In Latin, however, he remained an inspired student, and was talented enough to be sent on to Madauros, which was the most intellectually stimulating town in the Numidian highlands. It was a place of absolute loyalty to the old beliefs, with not so much as a single Christian on the entire board of town councillors. Augustine remembers the forum of Madauros ornamented with statues of the war god Mars, one in full armour, one in heroic nudity, and a prominent statue of a local dignitary spreading his hands in an oratorical pose. This latter statue was almost certainly of Apuleius, the town's most famous and flamboyant citizen. Apuleius was a proud member of an ancient Berber family of Numidia. He had been wealthy enough to tour the empire, studying at the great university cities such as Athens, Antioch and Alexandria. Apuleius lived life to the full. His inheritance was consumed by his profligate lifestyle but entirely renewed by marriage to a wealthy North African widow – who was the mother of his best friend. He was accused by her jealous family of witchcraft and defended himself in a brilliant court case, which at last seems to have put his considerable talents to some use. In middle age he wrote the novel *The Golden Ass*, and returned to his home town to teach at its famous academy. *The Golden Ass* is one of the few classical novels that can still be read for pleasure today, for beneath the picaresque narrative of bawdy misadventures it is also a passionate evocation of the worldwide, all-embracing Mother Goddess cult, united with Neoplatonist philosophy. I very much doubt that Augustine actually forgot the name of Apuleius, but he just couldn't bring himself to name such an erudite pagan philosopher in his own memoirs.

You can still walk the pavement of Madauros as it was in Augustine's day, examining the public baths as well as stumbling across innumerable olive presses, which served the olive orchards that once surrounded this city. The most enticingly direct connection between the town and Augustine is the curious small but elegant theatre that directly abuts onto the forum. This is most unusual, and so it is tempting to imagine it as the stage where the scholars of the famous academy at Madauros were put through the paces of public speaking. Aside from continuing with the study of the classics and grammar, Madauros was renowned for teaching fluent speaking – the arts of rhetoric – as well as the far from straightforward task of giving public readings of a text (in the days when these were written with very little spacing between words).

Yet Augustine does not dwell fondly on memories of his old college, for Madauros was linked with memories of a public humiliation. His father withdrew him from the academy after just a year of study, either because he could not afford the fees, or perhaps because he did not think them worthwhile. Once his son was back home, Patricius was delighted to observe that while in Madauros, Augustine had become a man. In his simple bluff style, he openly admired his son's naked body in the public baths, as if he were a young stallion who was ready to be led to the mare. The story goes that he came home that afternoon happily boasting to his wife that, with what he had just seen of his son in the baths, they might soon become grandparents. Patricius may also have been dreaming of passing on the care of the home farm to his son, just as soon as he had fixed him up with a good local woman, of landowning stock, as his wife.

Augustine spent a year at home with his family in Thagaste. It was remembered as a time of idleness, but also of passionate feelings, where in his own words 'he burned, he boiled, swept over the cliffs of desire'. We are left short of erotic details, and it may be that he just hung out with other frustrated young men in the public baths. They would flirt with each other and any available women, go hunting in the fields, and got up to some escapades that included the theft of some ripe pears from a prized fruit tree. As an older man, he looked back with disfavour on this period of his life, but whatever the nature of his sexual experimentation, be it with compliant slaves, merry widows or other boys, it seems not to be so much the acts themselves that he struggled to remember and confess, but the fact that his sexual longings displaced all other thoughts, interests and ambitions from his mind. As a bishop he certainly imagined that young men would whisper wicked and indecent things to married women, if they were allowed to brush too close to them in a church doorway.

It may also be that the failing health of his father kept Augustine in Thagaste. Once Patricius was dead and buried, Augustine would find a welcome in the household of his wealthy cousin Romanianus, who not only agreed to support him in his studies, but continued to do so for the next sixteen years. Augustine publicly and repeatedly thanks his kinsman for taking in 'a poor little young man' and furnishing him with a house and expenses, and 'what is even more with the backing of your mind'. This might sound sycophantic to our ears, but it was standard practice in the Roman world, where you did well to pay court to your connections. Patrons for their part had good cause to invest in the career of a promising young kinsman. There was no knowing how far a man of talent might rise in the service of the Roman empire, and at the very least an educated cousin could assist you in later life, be it with paper-work, in the law courts, or opening up the door of patronage to an even more influential household. Cornelius Romanianus might be the leading *principalis* of Thagaste, but it was just a scruffy Numidian hill town. A grateful, well educated Augus-tine would at the very least help make his life more interesting.

In 371 Augustine had established himself in the city of Carthage with funds enough to enjoy life and the university. In his own ebullient words, 'I came to Carthage and round me crackled a dangerous cauldron of outrageous loves. I was not yet in love but I was in love with love.' You can still climb the steps of one of the city's principal Roman theatres, which the keen-eyed young student must have visited countless times. The contrast with Thagaste would have been immense, for at this stage in its evolution the Roman theatre had reinvented itself.

The theatre season was essentially seasonal, from the festi-val of Cybele on 4 April to the people's games in September. Single actors now dominated the stage, and would sing their way through a famous scene like the modern star of an opera. Pantomime and balletic dances were used to fast-forward the leisurely pace of a classic in order to reach one memorable sequence. This stage management could be reversed so that a single star of the ballet interpreted a dramatic scene, talking with their mute eyes to the audience, while ever-bigger choruses pro-vided clamorous backing and in the process climbed right out of the orchestra pit and up onto the stage. Ever more spectacu-lar staging allowed perennial favourites such as the love of Dido for Aeneas in Carthage to be expanded. For instance one of the favourite ways of working up Aeneas' choice between duty and love was to create an historical pageant of all the great Romans who were destined yet to come. In this same period, Terence's plays were trimmed down to create soap-opera dramas of everyday life complete with protracted courtship and deathbed scenes, clad in contemporary dress with no elaborate masks or costumes.

Of course it appalled the purists, but they and the professing Christians were free to stay away, just as they could avoid the fantastic duels and hunts staged in the amphitheatre, and the packed calendar of sacred dances, ritual dramas, musical processions and public feasts that emerged from out of the city's temples. But not even the sternest killjoy could resist the centripetal draw of the Carthage circus, which hugged a whole internal section of the city walls. The 500-metre track of raked sandy gravel had become a place of obsessional urban energy. Twelve sets of four-horse chariots – four teams of red, white, blue and green – raced seven times around the central spina that was ornamented with fountains, dolphins, flagpoles and giant egg cups (all used to signal the progress of the seven laps of each race). The track in Carthage could seat 80,000 spectators, passionately divided among rival clubs of supporters, some of whom grew so partisan that beneath the gravel they buried lead curse tablets (which have subsequently been found), so that we can read their desperate appeals to the spirits to freeze their adversaries in the starting gates, or else entreating them to cut muscles, sever hamstrings, block hoofs, do anything to 'take their victory from them'.

It also helped to stoke up local interest that the best chariot horses in the world were bred in the southern steppelands of North Africa, which brought out strength and stamina as well as speed. In some cases a team of horses might be collectively owned by a small city, which redoubled the partisan fervour around the track. It was also a passion that united every section

of society, from the slaves who stood for free in the upper galleries to the 'most brilliant' nobles who sponsored the day and
sat in the central royal box right above the track. In most of
the opulent Roman villas that have been found in North Africa
there is some permanent testimony to a victory at the races lovingly laid out in a mosaic floor. Either the track is portrayed in
all the mid-contest excitement, or a team of four horses will be
proudly labelled with their names. Sometimes the victory lap
with its prize-giving ceremonies will be recorded in stone, when
both owners and the charioteer were rewarded. Eastern Libya
had been the nursery of some of the greatest charioteers of all
time, for there are ancient victory dedications from Cyrene
found at Delphi and Olympia. The fame of the two great
charioteers of Cyrene (Karrotos and Antikeris) was assured for
ever, or so they thought in 380. Generations later they would
both be eclipsed by another Libyan superstar charioteer, Por-
phyrius, whose life would be commemorated by seven marble
monuments and 34 poem–songs – that we know about. The
city bars, what baths you frequented – these would often be
dictated by team loyalty, as were the hairstyles worn by the rival
street gangs.

The tradition of seven circuits by four teams, linking the
image of the seven moving planets with the four seasons,
recalled the ancient origins of the chariot race. The Roman tradition of sacred chariot races was specifically linked to the successful gathering of the harvest, especially with the two seasonal
festivals, the Consualia (18 August and 15 December), which
celebrated the safe storage of the harvested corn, the closing of
the underground silos, and then their opening. In this mythic
reading, all the colours of the four teams were involved in the
protection of the stored corn. The white team represented the
Lares, the household spirits and the good drying wind; red

was for Mars in his role as the protector; green was the Great Goddess Mother Earth; and blue stood for the Lords of the Heavens. Rome in its imperial heyday had sixty-six days of the year when the chariots ran, culminating in festival days when twenty-four different races were staged in one day.

For Carthage, indeed for the whole of Roman North Africa, one of the most important annual festivals was that dedicated to the Mother Goddess Ceres, from 12 to 19 April. At the other end of the year, the season climaxed with the festival of the Imperial Cult, running from the last week of October to the 1st of November. Here the very richest, most powerful men in the province gathered as priests of the Imperial Cult and gave of their all. They sponsored a series of public events, over which they presided wearing stylised golden crowns adorned with iconic images of the ruling emperor. The week began with *venationes*, wild beast hunts staged by professional gladiators in the amphitheatre, followed by a series of theatrical events, and were concluded by chariot races. In each and every celebration, the presiding priests bestowed expensive robes or bags of golden coins on the stars and heroes of the arena, amid the roars of popular approval. So the working-class heroes of the city – charioteers, gladiators, singers, dancers, actors – were publicly honoured and rewarded by the very rich in the name of the emperor.

Augustine would spend over ten years in this city of Carthage, so rich in entertainments, with its university, its rival teachers and professors, and its raucous student clubs. He was so well supported by his cousin Romanianus that he could afford to buy a concubine, a slave girl, in his second student year. This was cheaper and safer than visiting the whores in the cemeteries beyond the city walls, or ruining yourself with an expensive courtesan. It was also more homely and affectionate, for a concubine could cook and keep house for her young master, as well as entertain him in bed. Perhaps the example of the good relationship between his mother and father helped to guide him in this. Augustine also knew that he had to make his way in the world. As a young intellectual of the established middle class, with a career to make, two paths lay open: as a teacher or a lawyer. Both required a sharp mind, and a man who could think on his feet, and could dress up the cut and thrust of argument in the elegant language perfected by Virgil and Cicero. These were his two masters, and detailed analysis of his later work has revealed tens of thousands of references, whether in style, vocabulary or allusion, to these beloved role models. They were also appropriate heroes for Augustine: men risen from the ranks of the middle class to hold the centre stage of Roman life through their talent with words.

What has always fascinated me about reading Augustine's autobiographical *Confessions* is the complete absence of any political or historical references. (He shares this much at least with Jane Austen, when she explores the shades of moral choice among individuals, but pays no heed to the broader canvas of the Napoleonic wars that were transforming her world.) Such is the force of Augustine's character that his biographers often fall prisoner to his mindset, but to understand his life we must not allow this powerful myopia to blind us to what he could not help seeing and assessing. I firmly believe that as an intelligent, ambitious young man, keen to get on in the world, he must have found his world-view influenced by events in the empire. They began in a distant province, but came right on home, literally passing his door.

As a fourteen-year-old boy learning Latin in primary school in his home town, Augustine must have heard something about the Great Conspiracy on the island of Britain. It was of interest to any peace-loving provincial who thought he was being protected by the legions. For it appears that in 367 the professional Roman army that garrisoned Hadrian's Wall was in secret negotiation with the barbarian tribes beyond the frontier. They were not talking to just one barbarian tribe, they were talking to them all, to the north, west, east and south. So when the Roman army in Britain mutinied against their commanders, they were aided by Saxon, Frankish, Pictish and Scots–Irish armies. The two senior officers, Admiral Nectaridus (commanding British waters as Count of the Saxon Shore) and Count Fullofaudes, were killed and the whole province overrun by this powerful alliance between barbarians and a mutinous (maybe even revolutionary) legion. A year later, the Roman empire prepared its counter-attack. This was to be led by Count Theodosius, acting under the instructions of the Emperor Valentinian I, who had dispatched two intelligence missions to check out the state of affairs. However, in this hour of imperial vengeance the only troops considered to be tough enough for the task were four auxiliary regiments, which is to say men who were not born Roman citizens but were recruited from the barbarian tribes. So there was no great difference between such a Roman legion and the barbarian tribes they were to fight. Two of these regiments, the Batavi and Heruli, shipped out of Boulogne in the spring of 368.

Though Theodosius proved a brilliant commander, his actions were arguably more diplomatic than military. He issued an amnesty to all deserters, but also saw to it that the ringleaders of the mutiny were executed, and then patched up a series of deals and reorganisations that soon put a legion back on duty on Hadrian's Wall. He was acclaimed Count of the Britons, and promoted to general (*magister equitum*) once he returned to make his report to the court of the emperor. In 370 he campaigned successfully to repair a breach of the Danube frontier. This was all 'foreign news', but in 373 Count Theodosius would have made himself very conspicuous to any young student in Carthage, such as Augustine. For in that year Theodosius was placed in military command of all of North Africa, his authority backed by Symmachus, an impeccable senatorial aristocrat of the old Roman tradition, who was serving as proconsul of Africa at Carthage.

Theodosius had a brief to sort out that had echoes of recent events in Britain, for in Libya a Berber tribe of the sub-Sahara, the Austuriani, were raiding the cities of Tripolitania. They had been led north to avenge the death of one of their tribal leaders, Stachao, who they believed had been unjustly condemned and then burnt to death at the stake. In the words of Ammianus Marcellinus:

> the Austoriani rushed from their haunts like mad beasts ... and encamped for three days in the fertile region ... they slaughtered the peasants, of whom those who were not paralysed by panic were driven to take refuge in caves, burned a quantity of household goods which they could not carry off, and withdrew with a huge load of booty, taking with them as their prisoner a leading local councillor of Leptis called Silva whom they had caught with his family in his country villa.

The citizens in Leptis Magna had called upon Romanus, then serving as the military count of Africa, to come to their defence. Count Romanus stayed in Leptis for forty days, but refused to pursue the Austuriani into their desert lands if he was not provided with 4,000 camels. To those who know how quickly the country south of Leptis turns into the Sahara desert, there may have been tactical grounds for this, but to the citizens of Leptis it was a bizarre request, seeing that their herds had just been stolen and their farms devastated. In their hour of need, they looked for protection from the army of imperial Rome. When instead they faced a punishing supertax, they felt sufficiently aggrieved to petition the emperor about the behaviour of his commander. This set them on a collision course with Count Romanus, who used his influence at the imperial court to bury the subsequent investigation and undermine their story.

The subsequent lack of military action encouraged the Austuriani to return the next year, where Ammianus records that they once again 'overran the territories of Leptis and Oea, killing and plundering, and then withdrew with enormous quantities of spoil. Many local officials lost their lives, of whom the best known were the former high-priest Rustician and the aedile Nicasius'. After which the Berber tribe assailed the very walls of Leptis, though they had no experience of siegecraft, and after eight days of ineffectual assault abandoned the idea.

Count Romanus may well have been corrupt and incompetent, but he no longer had a Roman legion under his command. The professional core of the Roman army didn't exist any more. For just like Roman Britain, which had only been reconquered by using barbarian auxiliary regiments to fight off a 'barbarian invasion', the same state of affairs now existed in North Africa. In a province as poor as Mauretania, it appears that the auxiliary regiments were recruited from Berber tribes under the command of their own native princes. That placed these Berber commanders in a very powerful position, for in effect they had evolved into hereditary Roman generals, and so were courted and charmed. So much so that after the death of Prince Nubel – one of the Berber chiefs of the Kabyle mountains who also doubled as a Roman military officer – there was an unseemly squabble amongst his children not only for possession of his wealth and lands, but also for the command of his men. Zammac was the first of Prince Nubel's children to seize this patrimony, and he had acquired the official stamp of approval from Count Romanus. But when his half-brother Firmus took power in a family coup, the row between two brothers over an inheritance escalated into a trial of authority between Firmus and Count Romanus. Although some romantic historians like to see it as a quixotic Berber rebellion against the Roman empire, it is more straightforward to read it as a faction fight between two powerful and ambitious Roman officers. In any case, this new dispute for power in Mauretania, on top of the failure to restore security at Leptis, ended Count Romanus' military career. He was recalled to the imperial court (housed at the time in Milan) and replaced, as we have seen, by Count Theodosius in 373.

So from 373 to 375 Count Theodosius ruled North Africa, simultaneously conducting an inquiry into the errors and corruption that thrived under his predecessor's rule. He governed from Sitifis (now Sétif), a Roman city that sits in the middle of the high Numidian plateau. It was an excellent base from which to direct the campaign against Firmus, which is why the ex-governor Ruricus was sent there to be tried and executed, while some of his junior staff were tried and executed at Utica, just north of Carthage. It was a dramatic turn of events for Roman North Africa to see its highest officials brought down to such a public humiliation. Augustine would have been in his third year as a student at Carthage.

Theodosius must have had troops assigned when he was sent to command North Africa, but the empire, hard pressed on all its northern frontiers, had few men to spare. The supression of Firmus' rebellion took some time, especially as Firmus contrived to use a split within the Christian Church in North Africa to give him some added militant support. Enlisting the local Donatists as his factional ally allowed the Berber chief to seize control of one of the seaports (the old Punic harbour of Rusucurru, modern Dellys) immediately north of his family's tribal territory, which was the Kabyle mountains. But Theodosius picked up his own factional trump card when he got the backing of Firmus' brothers against his usurpation, which soon started to split his solid support amongst the tribes. Mascezel, Mazuca, Sammac and Dius are the given names of Firmus' brothers, but the one who got Theodosius' full backing was Gildo (almost certainly a Romanised corruption of the Berber title Aguellid – King). And to entrench this new connection, Gildo's daughter Salvina was married to the nephew of Count Theodosius' wife. Firmus died in custody, just before he was handed over to the other side by one of his chief supporters. Once again a shrewd use of diplomatic tactics as directed by Theodosius seems to have been more effective than boots and camels on the ground.

The crowning of the Berber chieftain Gildo rounded off Count Theodosius' work. It was his third successful operation. He came from an old Roman family, long settled in Spain, which traced its bloodline back to the same Julian family that included Caesar. The Emperor Valentinian whom he served, though talented, was descended from Serbian peasants. 'He was of a violent and brutal temper, and not only uncultivated himself, but hostile to cultivated persons ... he hated the well-dressed and educated and wealthy and well-born.'

In November 375 the Emperor Valentinian died, felled by an apoplexy. He was succeeded by his son Gratian, ostensibly ruling with his young half-brother Valentinian II, who was but a boy. There was no anxiety about the succession, for they were both acclaimed by the army, and further protected by their tough old uncle Valens, who ruled the eastern half of the empire.

But a sealed order went to North Africa. Count Theodosius was arrested, taken to Carthage and there put to death. Such an order, disposing of such a man, could only have come from one person. The Emperor Gratian had made one of his first decisions as ruler. Theodosius, a thrice-proven hero of the empire – 'that superb general', in the words of Ammianus – was never brought to trial or accused of treason. His success had combined with his birth to make him a marked man. His son, who had accompanied him to North Africa and served on his staff in the three-year campaign against Firmus, survived, but only by resigning all his offices and opting for a form of internal exile, by retiring to run the family estates in Spain.

Augustine could not fail to have known of these events. The sudden arrest and murder of Count Theodosius must have shocked the entire city. It bore out the last hundred and fifty years of Roman history, in proving that supreme power had fallen into the hands of soldiers. The only people qualified to rule were tough, brutal men who had forced their way up through the ranks. Being born into the well-educated class of town councillors was a block to any future authority, as you were much more likely to ascend to the throne if you were the barely literate child of a poor peasant soldier from Serbia. That was certainly the background of all the founders of Roman dynastic power in the fourth century AD, be it Diocletian, Maxentius, Constantine's father, or as we have seen, the family of Valens, Valentinian and Gratian.

And this may go some way to explaining why Augustine would become so attracted to the Manichean version of Christianity. For ten years he was a devoted follower of this creed, for he was a Manichean 'hearer'. The followers of the third-century Iranian prophet Mani had a powerful and convincing way of explaining the wickedness of the world. If God is good, why is there such suffering on this earth? How is it that only the most wicked and depraved triumph? The Manicheans could answer this question. They taught that there are two equally balanced powers at work in the universe, and though the good must ultimately triumph in the world of spirit, evil yet triumphs over our created world. To help explain this duality of good locked into conflict with the bad, light against dark, spirit versus matter, the truth against the lie, they inherited a rich mythology from the ancient Iranian Zoroastrian faith. So they taught that within every living thing, animals and vegetables as well as man, there is a divine spark of spirit trapped within the flesh. It is our task whilst on earth to enliven this spirit through good living and in death help it return to the source of good. The Manicheans revered the Gospels, the pacifism of Jesus and his self-sacrifice, but considered that the Old Testament, rife with unedifying stories of wars, battles, murder and power, belonged to the dark power.

A true practising Manichean believer was a vegetarian who avoided all bloodshed, be it of man or animal, and thought God was best served not on the altar but through a pure heart. The truth could be taught in many ways – through song, preaching, music and art. The prophet Mani had revealed this in his short life before he, like Jesus, was slow-killed on a tree. The lie, the dark power, could never stay hidden for long, for it always betrayed itself through persecution, authority and force. Manicheans primarily honoured Jesus and Mani, but they also revered other prophets of truth and light, such as St Paul, Zoroaster, Buddha, Hermes, Enoch, Seth and Adam.

Many of the Manichean faithful chose to become merchants, teachers, bankers and traders, deliberately choosing a life that allowed them to cause the least possible harm and to travel and disseminate their faith. Their most controversial teaching was to discourage parents from breeding, for each new child diminished the universal spirit by trapping more light in the flesh. They aspired to celibacy, but considered non-reproductive sex a lesser evil than sex that led to the conception of a child. Their enemies accused them of sperm-drinking and buggery.

To become a fully practising Manichean was impossibly demanding for most humans, for it required you to embrace the life of a celibate, nomadic vegan. So two classes of believers emerged: the mass of hearers and a tiny minority of the Elect. The Elect were governed by a council of seventy-two itinerant bishops, who followed seven important texts and treasured a collection of seventy-six letters written by Mani to answer the questions of believers during his lifetime. They also inherited from Mani a book of pictures and a list of ten theological proofs, divided into twenty-two sections each led by one of the initial letters of the Aramaic alphabet. The Elect loved to list virtues in catalogues of five, such as light, air, wind, fire and water, which were linked to five appropriate mental powers and five supporters. There were also five opposites, five caves of darkness and five trees that represented the princes of darkness.

The Manicheans perceived the Milky Way as a caravan of glory, a vast number of souls liberated from the flesh into pure light and migrating their way towards God, imagined as a vast emanation of light. The influence of the seven planets and the twelve signs of the zodiac was acknowledged, but they could also serve as barriers in the journey towards the light. The most pious of the Elect washed before prayers, working their way through a liturgy of seven prayers that were offered up seven times a day. They fasted two days a week and lived off simple gifts such as bread and olive oil, given to them in the late afternoon. They also sang hymns, fasted for twenty-six days a year to recall the starvation death of Mani, and practised public confession. Their great annual festival was the spring–easter festival where the prophets Mani and Jesus and their writings were honoured on a platform raised up on five steps, garlanded with the scent of roses and bowls of violets set about with oil lamps.

A neutral source describes them thus: 'They venerate the sun without offering blood sacrifices; They chastise their natural desires; They consider their last day as their gain; They are everywhere but they are only few in number; They harm nobody but are harassed by some people.'

Even at this distance, the Manichean faith (which we chiefly know only through the texts of their enemies and persecutors) smells holy. It is little wonder that the well-educated Augustine was a passionate supporter, though an early slip in the arms of his concubine debarred him from attempting to become one of their Elect. For the couple conceived a son, whom they named Adeodatus (Gift of God) and whom they both adored. There were other social problems about being an educated gentleman of the curial class as well as a Manichean. The Manichean community detested the hunting of wild animals (foremost delight of the Roman ruling class) and turned their backs on any relationship with the dark rulers of this earth, while the chief ambition of the Roman upper class was to get as close to the throne as possible.

Fortunately for Augustine's peace of mind, he had a brother, who ran the family farm and had taken up the burden of the family's obligatory seat in the town council of Thagaste. When Augustine returned home to Thagaste in 374, aged twenty, he lodged not with his own family but in the more spacious villa of Romanianus. There he gave free classes in grammar and rhetoric as a guest of the house, freely returning his patron's hospitality. He also started to teach people about the prophet

Mani's version of the Christian message. We know that two years before this Augustine had become fascinated with Cicero's dialogue *Hortensius* (only fragments survive), in which a group of clever friends talk and debate among themselves about the merits of poetry, history, oratory and philosophy. Augustine seized his chance to try this out in real life, and in Thagaste he was a dazzling success. He seems to have converted half the town to his way of thinking, and made a young conquest, a friend 'sweet to me beyond all the sweetness in that life of mine', though this beloved young man, Antoninous, would soon die.

This Arcadian period of being honoured in his home town of Thagaste came to an end when Augustine was offered a salaried post as teacher of rhetoric back in Carthage. It was an irresistible opportunity, and although Romanianus was sad to lose the company of this bright young mind, he was also proud that his generous patronage of his cousin should bear fruit so soon.

Once back in Carthage Augustine begins to make his mark. He wins a public verse competition set up by a literate proconsul, Helvius Vindicianus (who translated Greek texts into Latin in his spare time), which opens all sorts of social and intellectual doors to the young Augustine. He goes on to write his first book, a delicate fusion of Manichean and Pythagorean thought, which he dedicates and sends to a well-known thinker in Rome whom he had probably met at a dinner party in the governor's palace at Carthage. He also makes two new friends, fellow intellectuals from the North African hinterland. Alypius, who comes from another landed family in Thagaste, will serve as Augustine's trusted deputy all his life. Nebridius is more reserved, but also more questioning, and rich enough to be building up a personal library on his landed estate just two days' ride from Carthage.

In 382, Augustine finally gets a chance to engage with one of the seventy-two bishops of the Manichean Church, unapproachable till now. Bishop Faustus comes from another small town in North Africa: Milev in Mauretania. He turns out to be refreshingly empty of cant or the pomposity of office, and makes himself freely available to answer questions at a series of daily sessions whilst in Carthage. Here he is fluent and well educated, and able to reference the text traditions of Orpheus, the Sibyls and Thrice-Great Hermes alongside the gospels. He denies rumours that the Elect also worship the dark god of power in secret rituals, and is emphatic in condemning the violence, ambition and sexual depravity found within the pages of the Old Testament. When questioned about the hidden Gnostic readings embedded within the gospels, he is quite clear:

The gospels are nothing other than preaching and precepts of Christ. I have nothing of gold and silver, and carry no money. I am content with daily bread. You see me poor, meek and a peace-maker, pure in heart, hungry, thirsting, bearing persecution and hostility – yet you still doubt my belief in the Gospels?

He also proves himself modest about astronomy, astrology and the movement of the heavens, and refuses to answer questions on issues he can claim no knowledge of. But the emperors and their spies were notoriously touchy on matters astrological, so it may have been wise to hold his tongue about the mandates of heaven. Indeed, the net of imperial suspicion will soon be cast over the Manicheans. Four years after his meeting with Augustine and other Manicheans in Carthage, Faustus will be exiled to an island where he will write his *Capitula*, another of the lost documents of the Manichean faith, destroyed by centuries of relentless persecution.

Augustine may have been disappointed by Bishop Faustus, who was intellectually and socially his equal. After ten years of waiting for such an encounter, he may have built up unattainable expectations of meeting an all-knowing sage (the sort of person he will ultimately want to turn himself into). He may also have harboured an ambition that the Manichean Church might want to recruit him into its inner circle, but that invitation was never issued.

However, he does not yet abandon the faith; indeed he seems to have been warned that he should leave Carthage before he is persecuted for being a public Manichean, and he uses the links within the secretive community to get him introductions to the Big Apple, the city of Rome. He may also have had enough of the situation at home, for like every North African man that I have known, he was being emotionally torn apart by the rivalry between his mother and his lover. His adored mother, Monica, who had moved into Augustine's small house in Carthage, was using her prayers and tears to weaken that concubine's emotional hold over her son.

In 384 Augustine and his friend Alypius take the boat to Rome, that city of half a million, with the best of everything at its fingertips. Even compared with Carthage it is a place of extravagant bustle and wealth, the streets filled with grand curtained carriages driven post-haste through the streets in the quest for urgent social engagements. Rome seethes with strident ambitions and vast complicated social networks based on the presence of two thousand senators, ambitious knights, imperial prefects and spies. Men who venerate the Latin classics patronise the shining lights of mime and ballet and the swaying of the newest young topless dancing girl. Even the 100,000 plebeians of Rome are a privileged minority at the head of their own social networks, with free access to 1,500 chariot races a year and their dole of bread.

Augustine was still a member of a heretical faith, and too much a new face in town, seeking his way as a freelance teacher of rhetoric, to strike up lasting friendships. Here in the city we know that Bishop Damasus was pursuing his passion for spiritual archaeology, identifying, then quickly monumentalising, the graves of the early Christian martyrs, which then became swamped by midnight picnic parties. Jerome (not yet accused of seducing a rich virgin heiress) and Pelagius were the celebrity preachers of the moment, treading the earliest steps of a lifelong rivalry.

The imperial court had shifted north. In the aftermath of the catastrophic destruction of seven Roman legions by a Visigoth army at the battle of Adrianople (modern Edirne) in 378, the Emperor Gratian had decided to move his military headquarters to Milan. The experiment had lasted just three years, and anyone who mattered was keeping a foot in both doors and running two households, one each in Rome and Milan.

And a momentous break impended, for after a hundred years of tolerant coexistence between pagans and Christians, the Christians had gained the upper hand and were on the point of suppressing the pagan establishment. The Emperor Gratian had refused to appoint a chief of the college of priests, a *pontifex maximus*, while the rich inheritance of pagan temple endowments was being nibbled at by the clerks of the imperial estate. The Roman Senate was secretly furious that the emperor had disbanded the Vestal Virgins and halted their ancient vigil over the sacred fire. The emperor had also ordered the Altar of Victory to be removed from the Senate House, even if the statue of Nike had been allowed to remain.

The case for clerical celibacy in the Church was a very new trend; no one knew if it was going to be considered heretical or not. In the meantime the hot doctrinal potato of the moment was the recent success of the Nicene Creed against the more rational Arian understanding of the humanity of Christ, which was being forcibly backed by certain well connected princesses of the imperial household. Nothing, however holy, was allowed to stand in the way of the city's absolute passion for the circus racetrack, exemplified by the brand-new Church of St Lawrence the Martyr morphing into the unofficial clubhouse of the Green faction of the circus.

The greatest surprise for the court gossips was that Gratian, who had ordered the killing of Count Theodosius, had clearly had some crisis of faith after the news of the destruction of the entire Roman army at Adrianople. In a kind of atonement, he had summoned the young Theodosius, son of the murdered Count Theodosius, from out of his self-imposed exile in Spain and put him in command of the Roman army of Illyria in an attempt to stop repercussions of the disaster of Adrianople affecting the western half of the empire. With each passing year, Emperor Gratian had continued to confirm and strengthen Theodosius' authority, raising him up to become the acknowledged emperor of the East, and then the spiritual and moral powerhouse of the whole empire. In contrast Gratian himself had spiralled downhill to become a boozy old sot before leading an army west to oppose Magnus Maximus, the self-proclaimed new emperor of Britain.

Augustine meanwhile was embellishing his social contacts. In the autumn the magic of a powerful patronage system, well oiled by frequenting waiting rooms and dinners, writing deferential letters, and presenting choice tributes of words and thoughtful presents, at last worked its magic in his favour.

Symmachus, that opulent and magnificent presence who stood at the summit of Roman high society, had been prevailed upon to write a fulsome letter of recommendation of Augustine to the city prefect of Milan, with whom he shared a passion for the old ways. Augustine's link with Symmachus may have started with Symmachus' proconsulship at Carthage, but also depended on various Manichean connections.

Augustine was rewarded with a peach of a job, when the city of Milan selected him to become its public orator. This not only brought him a salary, but ushered him into the presence and the household of the emperor himself. He was soon instructed with his very first task, to be delivered that November. Augustine had to compose and deliver a panegyric speech to the co-emperor of the western half of the Roman empire, Valentinian II, who was celebrating his tenth anniversary as an Augustus. (He had been acclaimed aged two, and was now a mature twelve-year-old.) This speech must have been a delicate task, because the pagan faction of senators had hopes that the young emperor would reverse the Christian trend, while at the same time everyone knew that Theodosius now held all the real reins of power and was a passionate Nicene Catholic, and yet that the boy emperor's influential mother, the Empress Justina, was a virulent supporter of Arian Christianity.

Next year, the subject of Augustine's major public oration was to be the Frankish general Flavius Bauto, barbarian by descent, but who had become a thoroughly Romanised character. He remained an important military presence and had a secret passion to uphold the pagan traditions. As Augustine himself wrote of this period of his life, his job was to 'tell many lies and be approved by people who knew that I was telling them'. Fortunately for his spiritual reputation, none of these sermons in cant have survived.

The principled Manichean Christian within him, cleaving to the God of truth and light, must have been tormented by the role he was playing, even if he shone in performance. Fortunately in this moral quagmire, Augustine stumbled upon a near-perfect role model, for the bishop of Milan in this period was the future St Ambrose. Ambrose was then in his mid-forties, and a dedicated member of the Roman establishment. He had served in the Senate, and risen to the rank of consul, then of consular prefect, as governor of north-west Italy. This high office had propelled him to become bishop of Milan (he personally quelled a riot in 374, and found himself named bishop in the process). It was a post he had filled for the last ten years, and which he expanded and amplified with all the authority and experience of a senior Roman official.

Ambrose seems not to have had a mystical bone in his body. He loathed all the allegories, interpretations and hidden meanings expounded by the Greek- and Aramaic-speaking scholars in the East. What he aimed for was a return to Roman order, a clear moral structure and a system of obedience. He therefore created a whole schedule of new services to keep his congregation on their toes: a system of daily prayers, a diet of straightforward readings, with communion offered at noon as well as night-time prayer vigils. His articulate sermons helped shape a dutiful, honest, respectful Christian, obedient to what the Church council had decided was the faith under the chairmanship of the Emperor Theodosius. Nor was Ambrose plagued by scruples about persecuting anyone who stood outside this new order, be they pagan, Jew, or the wrong sort of Christian. Backed by Theodosius, he even refused to lend one of his churches in Milan for the use of the Arian soldiers who guarded the Dowager Empress Justina. Indeed Theodosius treated Bishop Ambrose as if he were still a Roman prefect, and asked him to lead an embassy to the usurper emperor Magnus Maximus, who had advanced his authority beyond Britain and had set himself up in Trier. Ambrose was to try to retrieve the old Emperor Gratian's body for a decent burial, ascertain the strength of Magnus Maximus' army, and also establish a truce and a recognised frontier.

Professional curiosity prompted Augustine to hear Ambrose speak in the basilica of Milan a number of times. He was clearly impressed by the confidence, authority and clarity of the man. At some level he must also have seen that the example of Ambrose resolved almost all of his personal dreams, anxieties and aspirations. Here was a man of the traditional intellectual class, building himself a platform of authority by using all the skills of a traditional Roman: oratory, legal precision, administrative efficiency and architectural order. Yet he was clearly not deemed a threat by the ruthless military regime, nor as an expendable civil servant with only a year or two in office. Ambrose had been bishop for ten years, could oppose the will of an empress, and seemed to be growing ever more authoritative.

Every new church had to have a set of martyr's bones planted beneath its altar, so when he was ready to construct a new cathedral for Milan, Ambrose required a saint to consecrate the place. A dream instructed him to dig in an old Christian cemetery, and he recorded how:

I found the fitting signs, and on bringing in some on whom hands were to be laid, the power of the holy martyrs became so manifest, that even whilst I was still silent, one was seized and thrown prostrate at the holy burial place. We found two men of marvellous stature, such as those of ancient days. All the bones were perfect, and there was much blood.

The bones were identified as belonging to two martyred saints, Gervase and Protasius, who soon proved their presence by means of miraculous healings and impressive exorcisms that forced demons to speak deep inside the bodies of the possessed. A biography unfolded. The new-found saints were declared to be a pair of male twins, and given the added dignity of being the only children of another pair of early Christian martyrs, Saints Vitale and Valeria. Their cult spread fast across the empire, and they picked up some of the attributes of the Dioscuri, the Heavenly Twins, from a credulous laity. Gervase and Protasius were placed in charge of the hay harvest, and if it rained on their saints day, 19 June, it was known that forty days of rain would follow. They also gained social promotion: although we know that the early Christian community was filled with rootless urban intellectuals, Hellenised Jews, freed slaves and wealthy widows, St Vitale was made a Roman senator, then a consul who had been killed during the reign of the wicked Nero.

Ambrose was a powerful role model, but there were barriers to cross if Augustine was to follow his example. Augustine's position at court had aroused his social ambition, or rather his ageing mother's. Monica had now rejoined her son's household, and her long feud with the concubine was settled at last in her favour. Augustine's girlfriend of thirteen years, who had shared his life, his bed and his beliefs, and was the mother of his only child, was dismissed and sent home. We do not even know her name. Their ten-year-old boy stayed in the household of his father and grandmother. A fresh new concubine was bought to keep Augustine warm at night, and he had also become engaged to a ten-year-old heiress – though she was left to mature into a bride at her own home. He was now wealthy enough to repay the many debts of hospitality he had received as a young man, and became the patron to a group of young friends, formed from students of his rhetoric classes and cousins from Thagaste. He created a contented life for himself, working all morning and visiting powerful patrons in the afternoon. He also found time to join a discussion group of four other writers then living in Milan.

Augustine had picked up references to the Neoplatonist philosopher Plotinus in Ambrose's sermons, and now had the time to immerse himself in his works. Fortunately a Latin translation of his collected works (the *Enneads* were written in Greek) had just become available. He found it to be in fascinating harmony with his existing beliefs, for according to Neoplatonist teachings mankind had a soul that could be fed by good works and the intellect, enlivening a body composed of inert matter. The discursively thinking soul must resist identifying with bodily life and the body's immediate desires. Instead, it could be nurtured to rise to the level of the timeless, self-thinking Intellect. To achieve this required the courage to try and 'know thyself', to exercise self-control and to make an intelligent contemplation of the wonders of the world. At last, turning oneself towards the One and the Good, the philosopher might even hope to return to this perfectly simple and transcendent source of all. Plotinus had been given four brief encounters with the infinite during his own life, which instilled him with 'tranquil confidence and peaceful gentleness'.

Augustine yearned for this sense of calm, and started rereading the gospels, the letters of St Paul and the life of the hermit monk St Antony with new zeal. He was particularly affected one afternoon when, as he sat in his garden beneath the shade of a fig tree, he distinctly heard a voice command him: 'Pick it up, gather it in.' It was not quite Plotinus' vision, or the blinding of Saul into St Paul on the road to Damascus, but Augustine was moved by this experience. For although it was probably just a neighbour shouting out an order to a slave, it might yet also be a command from the Holy Spirit. So he picked up what lay beside him and opened it at random, and read Romans 13, from the epistles of St Paul. The memory never left him.

Two weeks later, all work in the city of Milan came to an end for the summer holiday. From July to August 386, Augustine rented a villa in the cooler foothills of the Alps, 20 miles north-east of Milan. There he renewed the happy memories of the intellectual house party at Thagaste, immersing himself in reading and discussing philosophy with his trusted core group of family and friends. His mother joined in, and for the first time in his life Augustine began to appreciate the clarity of her thought, despite her bad grammar and provincial accent. He also plunged into a fresh reading of the Psalms, which as a Manichean he had always ignored, as part of the corrupt Old Testament. He pulled all these readings together and started to write the *Soliloquies* (which King Alfred would translate in his old age, as an act of piety).

By the autumn term he was ready to transform himself from a Manichean Christian into a Catholic one. At the feast of the Epiphany he attended the Lent series of twice-daily lectures given by Ambrose that prepared a Christian catechumen (a hearer) to become a professed believer through the mystical rite of baptism. They renounced sex, adopted a diet over Lent, and were taught to recite all the most important prayers and creeds to the faithful on Palm Sunday. A two-day fast and all-night vigil was started on Good Friday, to conclude at dawn on Easter day when the catechumens were dressed in white. As they entered the locked doors of the baptistery chapel complex they were anointed by a deacon, then by a priest, after which they turned to the west to renounce the devil. They were then led to the east, where they stripped and were anointed with oil

– just like an athlete – then submerged three times by the presiding bishop in the baptismal pool. On leaving the pool their heads were anointed, their feet were washed, and they resumed their baptismal white robe and gathered once more as a single choir. As they processed from the baptistery chapel into the main body of the church they sang a psalm, and then joined the assembled body of professed Christians in the central nave of the basilica for the service that culminated with communion, the sacramental eating of holy bread and holy wine. It was an impressive ritual, the details of which were kept as a solemn secret by believers – in something of the style of the Eleusinian Mysteries. There is little doubt that Bishop Ambrose personally baptised Augustine, but there is no evidence of any special friendship or spiritual exchange between them.

Four months later, Augustine and his mother Monica were lodging in Ostia, the port of Rome. They were just looking out of the window, when both he and his mother were touched by a wave of heavenly peace, which Augustine would later look upon as one of the greatest blessings of his life. Certainly, whatever conflicts had existed between them were over, his concubines had been dismissed, Augustine had a powerful job and was now a normal Catholic Christian. He may still have been formally engaged to his Roman heiress child bride. Monica was waiting at Ostia to catch a boat home to North Africa, but five days later she fell sick, and gently commanded her two sons: 'Bury me here, for nothing is far from God.' She was buried in the cemetery enclosure of the martyr St Aurea.*

This affecting tale is well known. It can be read as a

---

* In 1430 her remains were discovered. They were placed in the church of Sant'Agostino, and in 1820 some of them were moved to Santa Monica in California.

grandstand story of personal destiny unfolding after a miraculous conversion. The avuncular St Ambrose, the holy bishop of Milan, ordains the intellectual Augustine, after the miracle of the conversion in the garden has blessed his questing mind with peace. Then we pause for a Jesus and Mary-like scene at Ostia, a lovely last lingering moment between a holy mother and her devout son, before he heads south to fulfil his destiny as the great saint of North Africa. But once again Augustine, like Jane Austen, has neglected to provide us with any of the background details, about wars, revolutions and the interesting careers of his employers.

When we last looked, the usurper Emperor Magnus Maximus was sitting in the palace at Trier, as if to watch the Rhine frontier. Magnus Maximus had been recognised as de facto emperor of the far west in 384, when he received Bishop Ambrose as Theodosius' ambassador. Magnus' rule had begun with a military coup in Britain (in 383), which he had augmented by seizing control of France and Spain. The Emperor Gratian's attempt to destroy him at the head of an army had backfired badly. Gratian seems to have fled from the battle before it was fully lost, soon after to be murdered in Lyon. This gave Magnus Maximus some useful breathing space before the inevitable confrontation with Theodosius. He boosted the size of his army by granting independence to the princes of Wales (and probably Brittany and Cumbria as well) in exchange for the loan of more barbarian regiments.

In 387 he led this army into northern Italy, seizing control of the imperial capital of Milan. The young Emperor Valentinian II escaped to the East, to the protection of Theodosius, and together they returned with an army that won the battle of the Save, in modern Croatia, in 388. Magnus Maximus tried to negotiate a truce, but instead he was extracted from the fortress of Aquileia (near the river Po where it flows into the Adriatic) and put to death, while the Romano-Frankish general Arbogast, acting on behalf of Theodosius, rode north and personally strangled his son and heir Victor at Trier. A couple of years later, in 392, Arbogast would arrange Valentinian II's death – he was found hanging in his bedroom.

It was an ugly time. We simply do not know if Augustine tried to keep hold of his well-paid and prestigious job as a hawker of state propaganda, which would have made for arduous ethical choices. Did he owe his loyalty to the city of Milan that employed him, his patron, or the imperial paymaster of the moment? Did he stay loyal to the refugee boy emperor, or try to bend with the wind? The empire had plenty of powerful men whose awful deeds needed the gloss of a panegyric.

Augustine eventually fled to the safety of the walls of Rome, and in 388 got passage back to the haven of North Africa. Whatever his political footwork over these years, there was actually very little chance of keeping his old position, for those Christians tainted with a Manichean past were now being actively persecuted by Theodosius: round one in his campaign for a state-enforced orthodoxy. Between 389 and 393 the emperor issued a series of laws that closed down all the ancient temples and cults, the sacred gardens and public altars, and banned any public celebration not organised by the Catholic Church.

It was a dangerous time for Augustine. The memories of the professor of rhetoric's long Manichean past were even stronger in Carthage than in Italy, so he stood no chance of recovering his old teaching post in the city of Carthage. Instead he retreated right back home to obscure Thagaste. The Emperor Theodosius had also recently banned the selling of landed estates, so that there may have been a double reason why Augustine (no longer enjoying the immunity of imperial service) had to fly home.

The emperor was very insistent that the class of town councillors should not escape its obligations, though there was a new exemption option opening up for the embattled members of the rural gentry, if they joined the hierarchy of the Catholic Church.

Augustine spent two years in his house in Thagaste. It must be considered a form of internal exile, but it was also a highly productive one, for he was thrashing out his own system of beliefs in a series of fluent, well argued letters. Fifty of these, and some twenty-one formulated opinions, survive from this period. They are filled with an almost equal number of references to Christ, Plato, St Paul and Plotinus. Sometimes his biographers claim that during these years he made a first start at creating a monastery. I cannot believe this. He was licking his wounds, scorched by the ordeal of working too close to the Caesars' bloody throne.

He also had a task to perform, which was to explain his new Catholic identity to all his old friends, most of whom he had personally converted to Manichean Christianity only a decade before. He had a flair for this sort of thing, and his letters from this period are some of his best, working out problems with his correspondents, not lecturing or winning on points. Evil is no longer defined as an eternally equal force, but rather the absence of good. Paradise is a state of mind, not a definable place in the heavens. God does speak to our soul, but through clouds of scripture, which require of us both toil and labour, but also love, before the final revelation can be discerned. This highly productive period, of the hermit thinker touched both by the truths of Neoplatonism and by Catholic Christianity, would come to a sudden end with the death of his son. Adeodatus, Augustine's only child, was seventeen when he died. He seems to have had a bright, inquiring mind, and to have been trusted by his father both as a soul brother and as a clerical editor of his works.

Over the winter of 390–1 Augustine spent much of his time in the city of Hippo Regia, the big port of Numidia, which was a quarter the size of Carthage. Hippo had a rich agricultural hinterland that stretched for 20 miles along the banks of the docile waters of the Seybouse River. You can grow anything here, but the city was also the channel for all the grain and olive oil of Numidia, which entered the Mediterranean through its docks. Hippo had often functioned as a younger sister to Carthage, with a resident legate, working as a deputy to the governor there. It was also aware of its royal past: in Punic it was the Ubon, 'the harbour' of the Numidian kings and their successors in power, the Roman proconsuls. One of these had paid for the enlargement of the forum, which bore his name set in polished bronze in the stone. Among the hundreds of votive statues in this place was one to the historian Sallust, alongside the bronze victory monument raised by Julius Caesar. (This urban monument miraculously survived the centuries and now stands in the local archaeological museum.)

Augustine might have been grieving for his son, but he was a breath of fresh air for Valerius, the elderly Catholic bishop of Hippo. Valerius was a Greek-speaker from the Eastern half of the empire, and so was out of touch with the cut and thrust of North African provincial life, for he didn't speak Latin fluently and had no grasp either of the old Punic language of Carthage or of Libyan Berber. The city boasted several churches, and it seems that Valerius' was the least well attended. Augustine, the ex-rhetorician from the imperial city of Milan, was not only supremely articulate, but amounted to a ticking intellectual time bomb, striving to sift his personal beliefs.

Lacking a son to connect him with his ancestral land,

Augustine was ready for the next step. Month by month, year upon year, Theodosius was transforming the Catholic Church into a powerful new arm of the empire. It offered Augustine everything he wished for: protection, a future, a position in society and the full employment of his restless mind, not to mention escape from the glittering dead end of his official career in Italy.

It seems that the incident that made Augustine a priest took him distinctly by surprise, though the elderly Bishop Valerius seems to have been in on the plot. For one day, after communion was over, the congregation physically led him towards the bishop's chair, where Valerius placed his hands on Augustine's head and blessed him as a priest. Much the same thing had happened to Ambrose in Milan, and would happen to many a promising gentleman whom a town wished to claim for its own. But for whatever reason – maybe he was heckled by members of a rival church congregation as both a Manichean heretic and a place-seeker from the toxic politics of imperial Rome – Augustine made a bolt for his hills.

He would spend six months at home in Thagaste, sorting things out with his friends, and writing to the bishop about the how, where and when of his new life. If he hadn't already done so, now was indeed the time for him to formally settle his lands on the local church at Thagaste, and dismiss and provide for old servants and friends, along with his siblings. He must also evolve the right frame of mind to respond to personal abuse. He needed to be able to quote back from the Gospels to the hecklers, not just reference Plato, St Paul and Plotinus in his letters.

When he came back to take up his post in Hippo, he seems to have had everything worked out. He was going to combine the ideal of the villa retreat of the philosopher with the active life of an urban rhetorician. So he took over a garden courtyard beside the Catholic church and set up a cottage there, which was to be the home of a small community of like-minded intellectual friends. To begin with, they were all friends from Thagaste. Thus was the institution of the Augustinian canons invented, living a communal life, but also engaged within a living community. Old Valerius remained officially in charge, but within a couple of years had anointed Augustine his deputy, then his episcopal heir (in 395), before he died in 397.

We are well used to the idea of a community of friends holding everything in common and devoted to trying to understand what is good and then practising it together. Indeed, after two thousand years we are so filled with the glorious examples of the Christian monastic and teaching tradition that we almost take it for granted that this is intrinsic to Christianity. Certainly there can hardly be a more compelling roll call of Christian heroes than those five men, St Antony, St Benedict, St Basil, St Francis and St Augustine, whose rules and example have inspired thousands of Coptic, Orthodox and Catholic monastic communities that would spiritually colonise the old world.

But no such communities appear in the gospels. Nor do the remembered sayings of Jesus or the writings of St Paul afford a model for them. There was however a communal tradition within the Mediterranean which had dominated everyone's imagination for centuries. It led straight back to the Greek mathematician–philosopher Pythagoras. It was he who was the first to establish a community of friends, to declare that 'Friends have all things in common' and that 'Friendship is equality.'

Pythagoras is a man who remains as fully relevant to our own time as he did to Augustine's. He is one of the very few heroes who can separately and equally be honoured as a scientist and mathematician, philosopher and mystic. His ethical vision also embraced animals, not just humans, the past as well as the present. He encouraged, but did not enforce, vegetarianism, and correctly first taught that the sun stood at the centre of the circulating body of the planets. He believed in the punishment of evil, the reward of good, and the slow cleansing of our immortal soul through the transmigration of souls. One of the first wonders of maths is Pythagoras' theorem, while he also began the mathematical notation of music, by working out the proportionate pitch of the different notes. He believed that the disabling passions of fear and rage, the egotistical appetites, the narcissistic emotions, as well as slothful self-pity, could be cured through melodies and introspection. He is the moral and ethical force that inspired Plato, and all the Neoplatonist thinkers after him, finally summarised for us by Plotinus (born in Egypt) and his biographer Porphyry (born in Tyre).

Pythagoras is customarily labelled Greek, for he was born on the Greek island of Samos. He was the son of a migrant, a travelling Phoenician merchant, the gem-carver Mnesarchus, who came from the city of Tyre. Pythagoras grew up on the island of Samos, but his university was Egypt, where he spent twenty-two years travelling from temple to temple along the valley of the Nile. In particular, he revered the memory of two teachers, Soches and Oenuphis of Heliopolis (the so-called Plato of Egypt), who taught in the ancient city of the Sun which stood just outside modern Cairo. After the Persian conquest of Egypt by Cambyses, Pythagoras was swept further into the East, to Babylon, and spent another twelve years of study among the wise men of the many temple-cities of Mesopotamia. So it was said of Pythagoras that he learned his knowledge of geometry in Egypt, his arithmetic from the Phoenicians, his astronomy from the Chaldeans, the principles of religion from the magi of Persia, and his ethics from the priestess Themistoclea of Delphi.

He did not return home to teach in Samos until he was fifty-six years old, but left after a few contentious years in order to try and establish a community of friends in one of the prosperous colonies of the West, the city of Croton in southern Italy. Here his entire community of ethical followers got caught up in a civil war – it seems that their learning drew suspicion. Their communal meeting house was burned down with all of them inside. So no authoritative collection of the writings of Pythagoras survived, let alone a successor community. Instead his teachings were shared out to the world, sparks that inspired endless attempts to create a religion out of knowledge, one that was bound together by number and moderation, bloodless rituals, and a respect for ethical behaviour, music, proportion and friendship.

To this ancient and holy heritage the Christian hermits of the Egyptian desert had added their own experiences. They desired solitude but knew they needed the support and direction of a spiritual father. So the early Egyptian monks added constant confessional scrutiny to the communal regime of friendship centred on fasting, the chanting of psalms and reciting of prayers. The conquest of sexuality was a prime task, which they documented through a regime of six stages, beginning with the waking hours but aspiring to control the demons of the night, morning erections and wet dreams – which prohibited a Christian monk from taking communion the following day.

Many of the Christians in Hippo were bewildered by Augustine's community. Where was the authority for such an institution in the scriptures? Was it not part and parcel of Augustine's heretical past? Did it not reek of the distorted sexuality of Manichean Christianity, that body of sexless men living a communal life?

Augustine was guarding his back. He was planning a very

public, irrevocable break with his Manichean past, but in the meanwhile he settled down to becoming the very model of a parish priest. He wore dark robes and deliberately travelled at a peaceful gait on a horse, not using the stirrups of soldiers, the imperial post or huntsmen. Food is always a political decision in the Mediterranean, and though for his own part he seems to have favoured a vegetarian diet, he made certain to join in with any public meat-eating, so as to further distance himself from the Manichean and Pythagorean ideal. The prohibition of pagan sacrifices had at last made meat-eating permissible for pious Christians who in previous centuries had much preferred not to eat meat that might have been sacrificed to the gods, of which there was a great deal on offer in the ancient world. Fish was never offered up as a sacrifice to the pagan gods, and so had always been a safer dish for a Christian to consume. There are many fish-eating references in the Gospels, while a good number of the apostles were lake fishermen.

Augustine now took over the dowdier of the two Catholic churches in Hippo. All churches in this period were based on the layout of a Roman law court, a basilica. They were built with a wide central aisle leading up to the apse, where the bishop, or presiding priest, sat on a wooden throne, just like a Roman judge. And just like this Roman official, he would be surrounded by his staff – secretaries, deacons, readers, ushers – seated on a low bench at the foot of the semicircular apse, ready to step forward to perform some task.

Apart from the bishop's throne, the interior of a church was dominated by a stone altar, a monolithic table on five stone piers. The bones of a martyred saint were usually inserted into the central pier, which was hollowed out to receive these holy contents. In early Christianity the altar could be placed right in the centre of the church, but it would later join the bishop's throne before the apse. Above the altar, four slender columns supported a dome-like canopy, and a waist-high screen kept the congregation away from both apse and altar. There was usually a large flat offerings table by the entrance, whose shape was borrowed from those used in the ancient temples. In the wealthier churches the offerings from this table could be taken up to the altar in a formal procession of deacons who acclaimed the gift and named the giver.

Aside from the bishop's wooden throne, there were no other chairs or pews. The congregation stood, or swayed gently as they sang, or spread their arms wide open to recite a prayer, or stooped down low over the ground in supplication. Unlike all other Roman public spaces, the first churches lacked the marble statues that elsewhere peopled the forum, theatre and public baths. There was already a rich tradition in painted plaster, so that past heroes of the Christian faith (especially the holy martyrs) could be painted just above the dado level (covered in stone or matting) and would seem to stand on a level just above the living, staring straight out above the heads of the congregation, like a spiritual witness to each gathering of the Church. Higher spiritual concepts were not yet depicted in human form, though symbols were popular.

Christianity had developed its own complex code of symbols during the long period of persecution. It reflects the overwhelmingly Greek-speaking nature of early Christianity that all these secret early symbols are based on Greek letter forms. The sign of a fish was a Christian symbol because the Greek word for a fish, '*ichthys*', could be decoded as an acrostic for 'Jesus Christ, Son of God, Saviour'. Alpha and Omega was another very popular symbol, the first and last Greek letters, and by inference the beginning and the end – a phrase applied to Jesus in the book of Revelation. The Chi-Rho symbol (which is a P shape entwined with an X) depicts the first two Greek letters of the word 'Christ', just as IHS is the Latin version of another Greek acrostic for 'Jesus Christ'. The number 318 when written in Greek was another recognised symbol. These signs could be set in a floor mosaic, daubed on a plaster wall or stamped into clay to form tiles or an oil lamp. What was lacking was any prominent cross in a church (let alone a crucifixion scene), though making the sign of the cross over head and body seems to be an ancient tradition.

Lettering was everywhere, either painted red on the white-washed walls, or red script set against white marble on the floors, recording the date of death of a believer, or the dedication ceremony with which the building was opened. Early Christian mosaic floors can have an eclectic charm, for different patches will have been paid for by different members of the congregation. Once again the town's curial class was at work making sure it was included in any inscription: teachers and lawyers would set aside three solidi in their wills for such work. As the church rose in wealth these would be gradually replaced, or overlaid by a single coherent geometric design, or some enrichment from the symbolism of the liturgy, like a wine harvest. In Egypt, the dry soil and air has preserved some fragments of church curtains, which we know from other sources were a significant element in the furnishing of a church. Curtains were used to screen off the three public doors from the gaze of the vulgar pagan public, and could be drawn shut when hung between columns to separate the central aisle (reserved for fully initiated members of the cult – those who had been baptised) from the catechumens, the hearers and listeners, restricted to the side aisles. From the few tapestry-like curtains that have survived, one can see that these hand-woven and embroidered fabrics in linen and cotton brought a strong female identity into the interior of a church, to supplement, humanise and domesticate the stone, marble and brick elements of its architecture. No one can yet tell for certain whether flowers were permitted in the churches of Roman North Africa. We know they were used in Italy, but must have had overpoweringly strong pagan references to the sensual festivals that united the Great Goddess with her resurrected young lover, be he Adonis or Tammuz or a hundred other resurrected heroes.

The most elaborate churches would gradually expand their width, the capacity of their interior space, by throwing out ever more side aisles, so that from the canonical three they could grown into five-, seven- or even nine-aisled spaces. They had much more in common with the forested interior of an early mosque than with anything that a Christian is likely to experience in a modern church. The richest late Roman churches were set back from a street-front in order to create an outer courtyard furnished with a basin. This allowed worshippers to wash (or have their feet symbolically washed) before entering the church. The same area could be used by beggars and penitent sinners from among the congregation, who had been banished for a while from the church interior.

Enormous energy was put into the construction of a late Roman Christian baptistery. In some church complexes, this will include a suite of baths and an enclosed processional corridor that links a purpose-built meditation chapel with the baptistery font. The font was covered by a domed baldachin, paved in mosaic and sunk into the floor to permit space for both bishop and initiate to stand naked in this basin of holy water. The cathedral complexes at Djemila and Timgad are particularly striking and moody examples of Roman churches built during the lifetime of Augustine. The ruins of Hippo also contain a splendid example of a church of similar age. This has been enthusiastically labelled the Basilica of St Augustine, though pinpricks of academic doubt have intervened. (The current consensus is that it probably belonged to his Donatist rivals.) At the very least, it is one of the churches he must have known about and set foot in at some time in his life.

It is within interiors like this that Augustine followed the example set by Bishop Ambrose, performing his new priestly tasks with vigilant sincerity. He catechised the new set of Christian seekers in Hippo, where various local rituals had developed, such as physically searching the faithful for traces of the Devil. The breath of the priest could exorcise resident demons from the body, and the use of goatskin prayer-mats symbolised the triumph of the spirit, trampling over the coarse vices.

That summer of AD 392 Augustine organised a public debate with a representative of his old Manichean Christian community. The debate was held over two days in the Baths of Sossius in Hippo. These have never been located, but it shows the comparative wealth of this Roman city that the colossal walls of the bath complex that stands in ruin on the edge of the archaeological park were only one among many such structures in the city. It may seem odd to stage a theological debate in rooms customarily filled with naked bodies and heroic nude statues of gods and men, but many bath complexes included courtyard gardens, libraries and debating rooms, and Christians might very well prefer them as a more neutral space than the theatre or amphitheatre, which could seat many, but were incorrigibly linked in their mindsets to the pagan demonic world. A church, on the other hand, was a place of fixed authority, not a chamber for debate.

To keep things fair, the first two days were spent on debating a prearranged set of principles, which both Augustine and the Manichean representative Fortunatus had time to prepare for. So they would both talk about the nature of evil, the soul and sin. Fortunatus went out of his way to stress how much the Manicheans shared with all other Christians, such as the concept of the Trinity, the way they honoured the gospels, the nature of Christ's suffering and his redemption of our sins. He was also able to quote St Paul with powerful effect, when he asserts that 'the mind of flesh is the enemy of God, for it is not subject to the law of God, nor can it ever be so' (Romans 8: 7) and writes: 'for the desires of the flesh are against the spirit, and the desires of the spirit are against the flesh, for these are always opposed to each other' (Galatians 5: 17).

Augustine, the former professor of rhetoric at Carthage and orator to the imperial court at the city of Milan, was a trained master of word craft. He also had the enormous advantage of having spent years both believing and then questioning the Manichean doctrines inside his restless mind: he knew their weak points in forensic detail. So when Fortunatus let slip a remark about the good God working under 'necessity', Augustine pounced on this dualist confession and opened up the debate in favour of a single, monotheistic, source of good. In official Catholic circles he became the hero of the hour, and of course for him it was a double victory, boosting his standing and separating him from his old friends. He needed this.

By the end of 397 both Bishop Valerius of Hippo and Bishop Ambrose of Milan were dead. The men who could have testified for him, who formed some sort of paternal role model, were both gone. It is thought that Augustine may have had some sort of physical collapse that winter, possibly bedridden with an attack of haemorrhoids. He used this time of pain and immobility to dictate his *Confessions*. It is an autobiography which charts his spiritual progress, not his public career. It concerns itself with his soul, not his life and times. In Roman law a public confession allowed the judge to cut through all tiresome procedure and proceed straight to sentencing. Augustine's may well have been first composed for the ear of God, not of man, an act of atonement that also stood side by side with the full confession required before the celebration of Easter. It is an extraordinary soul-searching document, the like of which would not be re-created for another 1,400 years. It alone of his books can be read with interest by a non-theological audience.

In June 1918 a testament of another kind was found in a cave some 60 kilometres south-west of Tébessa. The Codex of Tébessa provides rare textual proof of the North African Manichean Church of Augustine's youth. It is the remnants of a partially destroyed book, reduced to twenty-five leaves and four loose fragments, that was examined and conserved by a French bibliophile, Henri Omont. He recognised that the pages, with their neat two columns of thirty lines of semi-uncial script, might date from the time of Augustine. It is a fragmentary text, but enough can be read of it to see that it consists of a series of questions and answers. It explains the role of the Elect, the hearers and non-believers, and is filled with references to the gospels and St Paul, and to the 12 teachers, the 72 bishops and 360 presbyters of the Manichean community. It is tempting to imagine this document, the Tébessa Codex, as a crib that a delegate of the Manichean Church might have used to help him prepare for a debate with Augustine in the Baths of Sossius.

This is the only Latin Manichean document to have survived the centuries of comprehensive book burnings and inquisitions organised by the Catholic Church. In other places and at other times this community, variously known as the Paulicians, Messalians, Euchites, Marcionites, Banat Bulgarians, Bulgari, Patarenes, Albigenses and Cathars, were hunted and tortured into extinction.

Fortunately there was another much bigger and visible enemy close at hand for Augustine to engage with, and that could lead him to even greater triumphs, promotions and important friendships. This opponent was one that, just like the Manicheans, he knew all about, for to an extraordinary extent his mother Monica, that lifelong champion of Christianity in his household, was probably one of them. North African Catholics had been split for the last three generations into two rival camps. Much recent academic ink, and even more ancient blood, has been spilt about the differences between the Caecilianist Catholics and the Donatist Catholics. There were no doctrinal differences, and despite centuries of work on this subject, no archaeologist or art historian has been able to identify a single difference in the way they built or decorated or used their churches.

The schism was about moral behaviour. It concerned the difference between heroes suffering for their beliefs in a time of danger, and trimmers who submit but then bounce back once it is safe to do so. The Donatists were the Church of the North African heroes, the native Christians who had refused to compromise their faith during the time of the pagan persecutions. They had chosen imprisonment rather than to sprinkle a little incense on a public pagan altar in order to qualify for a *libelli* certificate. They had refused to surrender their gospels for burning and had often suffered martyrdom as a consequence. As a group they were characterised by strong local pride, and were especially dominant in the agricultural hinterland among the Latin-speaking Berbers of Numidia. They were the natural majority.

The Caecilianist Catholics were the trimmers. They were outwardly the bad guys, the priests who had made a deal with the ruling power at the time of the pagan persecutions, surrendered gospels to be publicly burnt (which may or may not have been old copies about to be replaced), and made symbolic sacrifices to the cult of the emperor in order to survive. They tended to be townspeople, associated with the *curiales* class and the imperial administration, and might have important connections with Italy and the Greek-speaking East.

There had been three crisis points for North African Catholic Christians to look back upon, and recall which side of the fence they stood on. The empire-wide persecution of Decius (249–51) had been the first to introduce a positive test of active respect for the deified emperors and the fortunes of Rome. I have seen one of the *libelli* documents that survive from this period, a passport-sized piece of paper, signed and countersigned. They were issued by local committees, as statements to testify that 'we have sacrificed to the gods all along, and now in your presence according to orders I poured a libation and sacrificed and tasted of the sacred offerings'.

Seven years later, the persecution under Emperor Valerian in 258 was a much tighter and cleaner operation. It focused on the curial class, targeting the known Church leadership, and was able to reward local prosecutors out of confiscated resources, such as a house church. One of the most celebrated casualties was Bishop Cyprian of Carthage, who had been a lawyer and a professor of rhetoric before he converted to Christianity aged forty-six. He was a thoroughly good and moderate man (his thoughts are preserved in fifty letters), and much admired as a local leader. When he was led out to execution on 14 September he was escorted by a crowd of well-wishers.

Not long after that, the first Edict of Toleration, issued by Emperor Gallienus in 260, ushered in forty years of peaceful development of the Christian community. So when the last of the three official persecutions struck – under the Emperor

Diocletian in 303 – there was a highly visible community to be attacked. The emperor had also reformed the structure of provincial governance, so North Africa was one of the eight super-provinces of the empire, then known as dioceses. Carthage remained the seat of the governor, but there were now seven sub-provinces.*

These frontiers suddenly became a matter of life and death for Christians, especially those living in Numidia, for the governor was determined to prove himself reliable in the eyes of the emperor. So in his province, we hear that not only was Felix, bishop of Thibiuca, executed, but an entire congregation of humble farmers were dragged off to court. Fundanus, the bishop of Abitinae, had submitted and handed over the holy scriptures to be burnt, but the local priest, one Saturninus, had remained steadfast, along with the core of his congregation. So forty-nine obdurate Christians from Abitinae were tried before the governor and sent to their execution. They became renowned throughout North Africa as the forty-nine martyrs. Governor Annius Anullinus had proved his zeal, and achieved much higher execution statistics than any of his colleagues. He earned his reward. The Emperor Diocletian promoted him to become prefect of Rome.

In Carthage, under a different governor, the persecution was directed by gentler hands. Bishop Mensurius had been persuaded not to follow the example of St Cyprian. He had instead bent with the wind and handed over some copies of the gospels to be publicly burnt. Many others followed their leader's

---

* Starting from east to west: Tripolitania (western Libya), Byzacena (southern Tunisia), Zeugitana (northern Tunisia), Numidia Cirtensis (north-east Algeria), Militana (southern Algeria) then Mauretania Sitifensis (middle Algeria) and Mauretania Caesariensis (westernmost Algeria).

example and made the required oath, but then later sought forgiveness, especially from those martyrs who had suffered and were in prison. For St Mark 13:11 seemed to offer special authority: 'But when then shall lead you and deliver you up, take no thought beforehand what ye shall speak; neither need ye premeditate. But whatsoever shall be given you in that hour, that speak ye; for it is not ye that speak, but the Holy Ghost.'

The archdeacon of Carthage, Caecilian, saw the potential danger of these hotheads believing themselves to be possessed of the Holy Spirit. He tried to halt the stream of guilty Christians bribing the prison guards to be allowed to give presents of alms to the prisoners and then proceeding to seek their advice, make their confession and beg a blessing. For in a bizarre bureaucratic twist, the official *libelli* certificates which had testified to the minimum performance of a public pagan sacrifice (to the genius of Rome and the deified emperors) had inspired the imprisoned martyrs – especially those waiting for execution on death's row. They now offered up a counter-document, a *libellum pacis*.

The full storm of persecution launched by Diocletian in 303 did not last more than two years. The initial fury lapsed when the emperor retired in 305, and had completely ended by his death in 311. This was the year that the formal Edict of Toleration was published by his political heirs.

In North Africa, however, the memory of the persecution did not wither. The extraordinary differences in experience, between the martyred Christians of Numidia and the temporising bishops from the coastal cities would not go away. Numidia was now strewn with the tombs of the martyred faithful, while the bishops who had turned traditor (traitor) remained in office. This included the most senior bishop of North Africa, Mensurius of Carthage, who was despised as a completely unworthy successor to St Cyprian.

The key issue was this: had a traditor forfeited his right to be a member of the Church, let alone a priest or a bishop, without formal forgiveness from those who had remained firm in the faith? The gospels did not provide a clear answer, especially with the equivocal example of St Peter's three acts of denial. This issue might have dwindled with time, except that Archdeacon Caecilian was hurriedly elected bishop of Carthage after the death of the despised Mensurius in 311. Because of his activities during the time of persecution, Caecilian was a highly contentious choice, and though not considered a traditor himself, his apostolic blessing was given by Bishop Felix, who was one.

The persecuted body of Christians were so disgusted that they elected their own candidate, Majorinus, who ruled for a few years before he was succeeded by Donatus Magnus, the charismatic and heroic bishop of Casae Nigrae, an oasis settlement on the edge of the Sahara in southern Numidia.

The issue of who was the right bishop of Carthage was sent to Rome. The investigation favoured the establishment candidate, for Miltiades, the bishop of Rome at this time, had not himself been one of the martyr heroes of Christianity, but a trimmer. The contrast between the two candidates was also all in favour of the principled Bishop Donatus, who impressed the Emperor Constantine with his moral authority and saintly demeanour. A retrial was ordered (at Arles), but this also found in Caecilian's favour, who celebrated his victory by organising a persecution of his rivals in 316 with the assistance of the Roman state. It was a hugely ill-advised policy, for in Donatus' telling phrase, 'the true church is persecuted, not persecuting.'

By the time this persecution had been called off, the Christian population of North Africa was wholeheartedly behind Bishop Donatus. They would have been highly vexed to be called Donatists, for in their eyes they were the true Church, not a schism. Thirty years later, the establishment Caecilian party of the Catholic Church (under the command of Macarius, bishop of Jerusalem) launched a second persecution. The establishment had become obsessed with the dangers of Circumcellions, wandering bands of Berber harvest labourers whose passionate support of the Donatist Church was ignited by mass pilgrimages to the shrines of the martyrs.

This was the period when the church in Thagaste, which included Augustine's mother Monica, was forcibly handed over to a Catholic priest, though the congregation remained unchanged in its beliefs. The Donatists recovered their position under the Emperor Julian as the true Church, where they enforced their doctrine that sinners (members of the establishment Church party) required a second baptism from the true Church if they wished to take communion. There are also descriptions of them washing away the impurity of the Catholic priests by scrubbing the church floors with salt. So by the end of the fourth century, the whole of Christian North Africa was divided into two antagonistic communities, with the vast majority in favour of the example set by Bishop Donatus rather than Archdeacon Caecilian.

The reign of Valentinian I (364–375) was a period of toleration, ushered in by the earthquake of 365, which toppled most of the buildings in North Africa – which due to the wealth of the province were rebuilt.* Augustine grew up in a society where practically every major city in North Africa had at least two cathedrals that were locked in neighbourly antagonism. The

---

* The vast temple at Timgad had been toppled by the earthquake of 365, but was speedily rebuilt at the suggestion of the governor of Numidia, Publius Caeonius Albinus. Just twenty years later a Donatist cathedral was being raised a five-minute walk to the west of this temple, with a 200 by 50 foot basilica entered through a processional courtyard.

suburban churches, many of them built over the actual tombs of martyrs, were also divided between the two factions. To make matters even more contentious, every Christian church had to possess the bones of a martyr before it could function. There was intense competition between the two factions as to who possessed the true bones, and a corresponding literary industry in providing a local saint with the acts of their martyrdom. Some of these incorporated local myths, others rested on well documented recent legal history.

Saints were venerated on the day of their death, which was the day they had been transformed into a spiritual force, transmuted from a mere mortal to a martyred saint in the heavens. These annual celebrations acted as a lodestone that brought together pilgrims from all over North Africa, such as St Cyprian's feast at Carthage in September and St Crispina of Theveste's (Tébessa) in December.

St Crispina is an interesting figure, who was ranked beside St Thecla and St Agnes. Her death was well documented, for she was a mother who had been executed on 5 December 304 during the Diocletian persecution. Her hair had been shaven off, and she had resisted even the desperate appeals of her own children to submit to the regime, and so died a true martyr. The vast cathedral complex that stands just to the north of the walls of Tébessa, complete with its own exterior walls and courtyards, domed side chapel, baptistery complex and row of pilgrim cells, is one of the great monuments of the late Roman empire, an exquisite, if seldom visited, Romanesque jewel. The only things to match it in integrity and scale are the saintly shrines that would rise in Syria: St Sergius at Resafa and St Simeon at Qalaat Semaan.

Augustine had been able to stand outside the passionate storm of this divisive North Africa schism all his adult life, for as a Manichean he would have been indifferent to the claims of both these houses. But having been ordained a priest in the Caecilian-establishment wing of the Catholic Church at Hippo, he now turned his agile mind to what could best be done. There was no shirking the issue, for a rival congregation of Catholic Donatists was near enough to his own church for their vigorous psalm singing to be heard during his sermons. He recognised that the moral high ground had always rested with the 'Donatists', and that the establishment must work very hard to be seen as more godly.

Fortune was on his side, for the very admirable leader of the Donatist movement, the theologian Parmenian, had recently died, and the movement had itself just fissured into two wings. On 3 October 393 a small Church council was held in Hippo, which under the discreet chairmanship of Augustine led the way in clerical reform. It had been attended by only twenty bishops, but they worked with a will, tidying up the liturgy and establishing rules of precedence and procedure in the Church. They also started defining which books of scripture were canonical and suitable to be used in church for readings. Priests and bishops were advised not to go into taverns, unless they also doubled as wayside inns that had to be used on a journey. They were also instructed that they must not just be good, they must be seen to be above suspicion, so that when in the company of a widow or virtuous young nun it was always necessary for even a bishop to be chaperoned.

Augustine, from long experience of his mother's habits, also knew how to attack the Donatists. The council framed a letter about suppressing the excesses of the cult of the dead, which was addressed to Aurelius, the current bishop of Carthage. All over the Mediterranean, the cult of the dead had been seamlessly inherited by the Christians, who like their pagan neighbours loved to picnic beside the graves of their ancestors on anniversaries and important festivals. Throughout North Africa you can find gravestones from this era fitted with a horizontal stone, with recesses neatly cut into the decorative stonework to allow ritual bowls of wine, milk, bread and oil to be offered and shared with the dead. It was a charming custom, which stressed the connection of kinship and a vertical loyalty to an ancestor. The Donatists were especially embedded in this tradition, as it bound them up with the cult of the virtuous martyrs who had preceded them. Augustine's mother had followed these traditions all her life, happily sharing wine with her neighbours and ancestors. These ceremonies took place in cemeteries, the often very lively cities of the dead. Wine is a prelude to music, and wine with music can progress to dancing.

Augustine realised that this close fusion between rural traditions and the cult of the martyrs (shared by all Christians, but taken to an emotional extreme by the Donatists) gave the establishment party a tactical advantage. He explained his mission to a council of Catholic bishops convened at Carthage on 26 June 394, so the next year he had doctrinal backing before taking the extreme step of cancelling the annual party for one of the martyr saints of Hippo, St Leontius. He was standing in the way of two days of wine-sodden joy from the 2nd to the 4th of May with which the anniversary of Leontius' death was habitually celebrated.

Augustine had done his research impeccably, for he had established that Leontius, though he was buried beneath the altar of his church, was not a sainted martyr but was just an early bishop. His suppression of this annual May party of all-night drinking and singing was deeply unpopular with his congregation, but he had prepared his ground well. In sermon after sermon he made a passionate call to follow Christ in cleansing the temple, and not to repeat the sin of pagan drunkenness before the Golden Calf in the time of Moses. So when it came to the May festival his own church was the scene of godly all-night vigils and sober chanting of the Psalms, whilst the neighbouring Donatist church went ahead with two days of boisterous, wine-fuelled celebrations.

The contrast between the two churches was a personal triumph for Augustine, which was reinforced by a season of strongly argued sermons, denouncing such excessive cults of the dead as sharing the Eucharist with them, and retrospective baptising. And to keep the momentum up, he had started a scheme to popularise his readings of the Old Testament Psalms. Line by line, phrase by phrase, they were forged into both a prophecy and a commentary on Christ's life. The church he had inherited, a club for lonely establishment widows, grew into one of the most popular places in the city, packed out to hear a master wordsmith proclaim the directions for a godly and goodly life. The rich started tasking their secretaries to take down his sermons, if their church attendance clashed with more pressing social needs.

Augustine also had a gift for popularising: for creating graphic phrases and numerical listings that his congregation could recall. So he made up the Seven Gifts of the Holy Spirit from his reading of Isaiah, just as he turned Matthew's Beatitudes into a programme of seven steps towards God. He then transposed these virtues into that memorable list of the Seven Deadly Sins. His stock as the intellectual champion of the Catholic Church was rapidly rising, and he made certain that his best sermons and letters of advice to the faithful were copied out, and sent to the great and the good all over the Roman empire.

The little community of friends in poverty that he had established beside his church evolved into a highly efficient secretariat. They created file copies of Augustine's correspondence, requesting the loan of new books to be copied whilst also functioning as a training ground for future priests and bishops. By comparison the Donatists proved very bad at propaganda, while some of their favourite quotations, such as 'What has the Church to do with an emperor?', or – quoting Daniel – 'May your gifts remain with you, O King' could be made to sound treacherous to a Catholic emperor.

Augustine by contrast always kept a weather eye for gently incorporating the upper-class *principalis* and *viri clarissimi* into his Catholic community. This required considerable ingenuity, for the Gospels put it bluntly: 'It is easier for a camel to go through the eye of a needle than for a rich man to enter the kingdom of Heaven.' But Augustine started morphing this in his sermons, explaining that 'Get rid of pride, and riches will do you no harm' and that the active challenge was to be 'rich in good works'. In the city of Tipaza we can read how these new Catholic maxims were set in stone by Bishop Alexander, who placed in his new church the line: 'The highest pitch of righteousness is to wish for martyrdom. You have another like it: to give alms to the best of your ability.'

It was not always easy to strike the right balance. Augustine's own congregation could sometimes lose their sense of the equal dignity and spiritual fellowship of all Christians. They tended to fawn on wealthy Christian visitors who had come to meet Bishop Augustine. Pinian and Melania were just such a celebrity couple: young, beautiful and both hugely wealthy (think of a Getty married to a Rothschild) and determined to do good with their inheritance. Augustine's congregation virtually lynched these celebrities, dragging them to the altar to make them swear that they would spend their money in Hippo as deacons. It was very embarrassing.

The turning point in the Caecilian Catholic–Donatist Catholic rivalry happened by chance, or rather through the murderous politics of the Roman court. You might recall that Gildo had become recognised as the Roman-approved Berber lord of the Kabyle mountains after he had helped subdue his brother Firmus. During Theodosius the Great's long reign, Count Gildo was an untouchable. He was a confidant of the old emperor, for they had served together as young men in the army under his father and the bonds of friendship had remained strong. Gildo was also related by marriage to the emperor's wife. (His daughter Salvina had married Nebridus, the nephew of Theodosius the Great's first wife, Flacilla.) So Gildo under the reign of the Emperor Theodosius had become the strongman of North Africa, for he had been made both *Comes Africae, Magister utriusque militiae per Africam* and the acting legate in charge of the vital African grain shipments to Rome. (In this period the Egyptian harvest had been switched over to supplying the New Rome of the East, Constantinople.)

But after the death of Theodosius the Great, Gildo's political star, which had shone so bright, inevitably waned. He fell under the suspicion of the Gothic general Stilicho, who had effectively become regent of the empire. Gildo was accused of treason, and so his younger brother Prince Mascezel was lent an army of 5,000 Frankish soldiers from Gaul to overthrow his brother and place himself on the throne. Gildo tried to raise a local Berber army to defend himself, which in no way can be considered a national rebellion against Rome, for it was just the third round in a murderous dynastic game of thrones between brothers. But in recruiting his own army, Gildo looked around for any possible local ally, and struck up a quick and easy alliance with some charismatic Donatist bishops, including Optatus of Timgad – the man who had built that splendid

Donatist cathedral whose ruins one can still admire just west of the enormous temple. But even when assisted by bands of Donatist zealots, the outcome of the battle between the two brothers could never be in doubt. With two legions at his back, in 398 Mascezel defeated his brother Gildo, who tried to escape by boat but was driven back by the winds into the Tunisian port of Tabarka. Having executed his nephews, he had every reason to fear the vengeance of his victorious brother Mascezel, so he hanged himself from a dungeon window.

In the aftermath of these troubles, in 399 and 405 the empire passed a series of anti-Donatist laws, which were almost impossible to enforce on the ground. Soldiers could march in and place a Catholic bishop on the throne of a Donatist cathedral, but they could not guarantee his safety there. This even happened in Augustine's city of Hippo. The Donatist bishop was expelled from his cathedral, but in 409 would be triumphantly reinstated at the head of a procession of thousands of Circumcellions, chanting *Deo laudes*, Praises be to God, as they carried old bishop Proculeianus on their shoulders and placed him back on his throne.

In rural areas, the scenes could be even rougher. A Catholic bishop was imposed on the town of Bagai, but he was nearly lynched by his own congregation, who then went on to burn down their own church. Other Catholic priests were humiliated and permanently mutilated, with the loss of a finger, an ear or an eye. The murder of the regent general Stilicho in Italy in 408 allowed a moderate voice to briefly prevail in the imperial court.

Count Marcellinus (whose elder brother Apringius was the ruling proconsul in Carthage) began to correspond with Augustine about what might be peaceably done to end this dangerous schism. Augustine had now been a force for renewal within the North African Catholic Church for twenty years, fifteen as bishop of Hippo. He would never be made bishop of Carthage, but his intellectual leadership of the Catholic Church in North Africa had long been accepted by all the other bishops.

In January 411 invitations went out for a formal debate to take place in Carthage in June, in the private 600-seater hall of the Baths of Gargilius (once again not the vast bath ruins that one can visit in Carthage, but somewhere else that has never been discovered). All the bishops of North Africa were invited by name, and after twenty years of missionary activity by Augustine and his allies, the number of active Caecilianist Catholic bishops now for the first time equalled their Donatist Catholic rivals. But it turned out to be an especially busy social year, as hundreds of wealthy refugees poured south out of Italy to spend that summer in North Africa. They were escaping the three-day sack of Rome by the troops of King Alaric, largely Gothic but also Christian. Augustine stayed at his post in Hippo for the important Easter celebrations and baptisms, before travelling to Carthage to give a key address–sermon in May and complete his discussions with Count Marcellinus.

In June the conference opened. It was well organised, for seven bishops from each side were to speak, with seven more acting as an advisory board for each side, and another four composing a secretarial board to agree on the written transcripts of all the speeches. No one had thought how the various bishops were to be positively identified, and any vote-rigging impostors sieved out, so somewhat bizarrely the two factions of the Church stood as mutual surety. The rival bishops of each town could guarantee to identify each other – some with animosity, though Augustine and Macrobius of Hippo managed to finesse it. The final tally was 286 Caecilianist bishops against 279 Donatists, with 120 abstentions and 63 vacant sees.

The Donatist position had hardened: the good and the bad might mix in the streets, but not in the basilica. They were also open to the charge that the mystery of communion ought not to depend on the moral purity of the priest, but on the grace of God. Their long-lived watchword, 'The true church suffers persecution and does not inflict it', had also been weakened by the lynching of Catholic priests. But whatever the arguments that echoed through these halls, the result of the conference had been fixed. Count Marcellinus was the only one seated. He was the judge, surrounded by over five hundred elderly clerics on their feet. Once again a Roman court found that the election of Archdeacon Caecilian as bishop of Carthage (exactly a hundred years ago – back in 311) had been valid.

However, in order to sugar this bitter pill, Augustine had negotiated an effective tactical compromise. All the Donatist clergy would be left in possession of their churches. There would be no confiscations, no expulsions, no need to suffer the humiliation of a second baptism at the hands of your rival. He also seems to have done his best to turn the annual gathering to honour St Cyprian, held in the Basilica Restituta (a site as yet unknown) that September, into an occasion for unity and forgiveness. The sack of Rome must surely have helped to fix the minds of the feuding bishops of North Africa on the comparative good fortune they all shared. In the autumn Augustine journeyed back home to Hippo, calling at the port of Hippo Diarytus (Bizerte) to attend the inauguration of a new basilica.

Once back at home he started writing *The City of God*. This started as a rebuttal of the charge that Christianity had weakened the eternal City of Rome, which had been sacked in 411 for three days by the Vandal army because it had abandoned the old gods. It grew into a much greater project, a definition of contemporary Christianity, which was engaged in the construction of a truly eternal City. Everything of worth from the old empire was to be preserved within the newly triumphant Church. Time would prove him right: after the fall of the last Roman emperor of the West, Latin language and literature, Romanesque architecture and history would be conserved through the stewardship of the Roman Catholic Church.

The conference of Carthage was the apogee of Augustine's career, both as a Christian peacemaker and as a Roman politician. Not since his days in the court of Milan had he come so close to the empire's real power: his young patron, Count Marcellinus, had been very impressed by the conduct of the old bishop. But this useful friendship was not destined to endure. Just two years later, Count Marcellinus was arrested in his palace, taken outside the walls of Carthage, and abruptly executed.

His death was due to the intrigues of Count Heraclian, the military commander of North Africa. Heraclian had risen to power as a trusted officer of the Gothic general Stilicho, who had become regent of the western empire. Then Heraclian had murdered his master Stilicho on behalf of the young Emperor Honorius, who had grown jealous of Stilicho. Heraclian now needed to remove someone as decent as Marcellinus before he could make his own bid for the throne of the Caesars, its steps, as ever, slippery with blood.

Augustine stayed away from the tainted atmosphere of Carthage for three years after Marcellinus' murder. Once again the brutal, deadening reality of serving a Roman emperor in any capacity must have made his choice of a career within the Church a thoroughly reasonable and rational decision. Once again the issue of why a good God permitted the criminals to prosper, and the good to die young, must have tested Augustine's belief system.

I think it was experiences like these, reiterated time after time, throughout his life, that helped beget his ultimate theological position. Augustine gave rise to a belief system that turned its back on Origen's conception of a loving Christian God who allowed for all creation to be saved and find eternal happiness. This kindly doctrine stood as an heir to the Neoplatonist philosophy that united the pagan world.

Instead, Augustine in his old age argued himself (and much of the Western world) into a doubtful, depressive, anxious, lonely, troubled spiritual vision. He agreed that the soul was immaterial, intellectual but immortal. But he also argued that it was deep-dyed in evil through the inheritance of original sin. It could only be saved by the gift of divine grace.

The only blessing of this position was a life full of anxious hope that the Holy Spirit might be at work amongst us, bestowing this divine grace – though through a detailed reading of his own *Confessions* (which he updated and revised towards the end of his life) Augustine seems to record this sense of divine peace descending upon him on just two occasions: once in a garden in Milan, and once beside his mother in Ostia, many years before he became either a priest or a bishop. Those long clerical decades with their millions of emotive words had lacked the slightest hint of divine peace.

He had fought hard for an all-inclusive Roman Catholic Church, and had helped suppress two of its rivals, the Manichean Christians and the Catholic Donatists. To do so he permitted persecution, but he must not be judged by the standards of our day. The sort of persecution he had in mind was simply the legally ordered beatings and torture commonly applied by any Roman judge to a court case. Augustine did not authorise execution. But there is an essential contradiction to all this relentless activity. He energetically expanded the human compass of his Church, while at the same time he argued that this community of humans had no effective power to do good. For no individual could save his soul merely through living a long life filled with good deeds. We were all damned by original sin, and only a few of us sinners could be saved. A Christian could not earn salvation through good works: he must just be content to pray for the miracle of divine grace.

Augustine would spend the rest of his long life intolerantly and aggressively attacking Pelagius for daring to suggest otherwise. Nor was Pelagius a wishy-washy liberal cleric, preaching the presence of an endlessly compassionate, all-forgiving deity. Pelagius preached that most of mankind was doomed to eternal damnation, but not through a decree of heaven, but rather through their own moral failings and inertia. He also refused to accept that unbaptised infants would be sent to hell for eternity.

Augustine would have none of this. He pursued Pelagius in an unedifying intellectual vendetta, which would involve the calling of another North African Church council to condemn him. When the Pope of Rome did not immediately agree with these proposals, an opportune gift of eighty prized Numidian stallions was sent to the imperial court at Ravenna in an attempt to outflank the moderate position taken by Pope Zosimus. It was a clever bribe derived from knowing just how much a win at the circus track mattered to the ruling class of the Roman empire. In the words of his pre-eminent biographer, Augustine's writings against Pelagius 'deter affection, they are weary and dispiriting'. The vendetta against Pelagius brought Augustine closer to Jerome, the irascible but brilliant scholar from the Balkans who was translating the Greek scriptures into Latin in the holy land. The two saints never met, though they engaged in a waspish, watchful, prickly correspondence all their lives, but both buried the hatchet of their mutual rivalry in order to attack the 'serene, optimistic, cultivated' Pelagius.

But the central dichotomy remains. Why did Augustine fight so passionately for a universal Church, when the mass of humanity that was to be so energetically included within these walls of authority were to be damned for all eternity? Augustine was a much more natural fit as a Catholic Donatist, where he could have usefully enlarged their concept of a Church of the saved, standing safely apart from the corruptions of the political Roman empire. His central doctrine of original sin (especially as the wellspring of the spiritually corrupting sin of lust) seems to have been acquired during his many years as a Manichean.

Was Augustine just an intellectual Rottweiler who assaulted all the doctrinal groups that he had a natural affinity with – first the Manichean Christians and then the Donatist Catholics – in order to build some position of authority for himself within the tattered fabric of the imperial administration, as represented by the Church? Looked at in this light, we can chronicle the champion attack dog assaulting three enemies in turn: round one, the Manichees, 392–404; round two, the Donatists 400–412; round three, Pelagius, 412–430.

At other times I like to focus on Augustine, that earnest young man who set up summer holiday discussion groups from among his friends and relations. The man who tried to balance the conflicting demands of affection between an adoring mother and the warmth of his concubine, the man who befriended his own son and had a genius for maintaining hundreds of friendships through correspondence. Who all his life long tried to balance his own questing ambition with the search for what is good. A man who travelled to know himself better, but returned to his own North African homeland to give of himself. Who threw his intellect behind a passionate series of sermons, letters and debates, not weighed on the merchant's scale but freely given to the world. It has been calculated that he delivered six thousand sermons, some of them two hours long, between the years 396 to 430.

For it was not Augustine and Jerome who made the Church triumphant, but the Emperor Theodosius the Great's edicts of 390. Arguably Augustine was just doing his duty as a member of the traditional curial class in enforcing these orders over his community. He did this through public argument and voluntary conferences. His long residence in Thagaste and Hippo speaks volumes for this inherent sense of local responsibility, and the passionate attachment of a Berber to his native land.

He certainly loved the language of Cicero and Virgil, and at the end of his life, his own store of words. Like many writers, Augustine would spend his dotage checking that his cathedral library at Hippo had copies of all his letters, sermons and books, that they were all safely filed and catalogued and duplicated by gifts to other holding libraries elsewhere in the empire. His last work, *Retractationes*, was essentially an annotated bibliography. We have absorbed 5 million of these words into our culture. He died at home with the walls of his bedroom pasted over with extracts from the Psalms. He died 'disdainful, remorseful and hopeful'. He was buried before the city of Hippo fell to the Vandal 'barbarians'. Aged seventy-five years, eight months and fifteen days.

But the barbarians who broke through the walls of the city of Hippo were not illiterate savages. They were Roman 'auxiliaries', a tribe of Christian Vandal soldiers, initially working in alliance with the commander of the Roman army in North Africa, Count Boniface, who had loyally supported the accession of Valentinian III after the death of his uncle, the Emperor

Honorius, in 423. In the process Boniface had assumed total command of the grain supply of North African corn to Italy. Augustine admired his physical courage and in a letter rated his wealth and rank 'as a gift of God'. Four years later a small army was dispatched from Italy in order to dethrone this over-mighty regional governor, but Boniface defeated this force. When threatened by a second invasion from Italy, Count Boniface called upon a Vandal auxiliary regiment (who travelled with their women) to come to his aid. This they did as mercenary allies shipped across the western Mediterranean to the ports of North Africa from Spain.

While this auxiliary regiment was in transit, the political crisis had passed. Count Boniface had no need of their services and attempted to send them back home, dismissing them without adequate pay. Instead they held their own ground. Outside the hill town of Calama (just inland from Hippo, from where the Seybouse River comes pouring out of the hills to water the agricultural coastal plain) Count Boniface was worsted in battle against this Vandal auxiliary regiment, so much so that he decided to throw it all in, and take a boat for Italy. The Vandal auxiliary regiment was left in command. Their military commander effectively stepped into the shoes of the legate of the legion, indeed in due course we find them occupying all the customary barracks and forts of the resident legion for the next hundred years.

One of the only cities that they had to fight their way into was Hippo. When they marched on Carthage, the citizens of that city had seen far too many coups and counter-coups to be much impressed. In fact the citizen body preferred to watch the chariots on the circus track than spend their time watching another band of soldiers march into their barracks. They would not have noticed the difference between the Vandal auxiliary regiment and their own field army, for the fourth century had witnessed not only the slow triumph of Christianity, but also a subtle revolution in dress. The toga of the senatorial class and the leather-strapped kilt of the legionnaire had not been worn for a hundred years. Instead the Roman army and upper class had taken to wearing the uniform of the militarily victorious auxiliaries, which we sometimes continue to label as barbarian. Heavy cavalry cloaks were suspended from the right shoulder with a golden fibula of barbaric gem- or enamel-studded magnificence. The cavalrymen's trousers, borrowed from the Parthian and Persian wardrobe, were worn below a belted tunic, with a coloured long shirt, the shirt sleeves and creases of trousers embellished with panels of embroidered cotton and silk. The civilian officials everywhere copied this martial style of dress, which we can still see vividly depicted on mosaic panels in lively hunting scenes from the fourth and fifth centuries that stress the ideal of manhood, the mobile, restlessly busy cavalrymen. Ceremonial occasions now concentrate on explosions of highly coloured mounted horsemen in procession, for the season of the reverend fathers, sitting in solemn conclave in their white toga robes in the Senate house, overlooking a forum of architectural splendour, has long been gone. Mosaics and frescoes will concentrate in decorating the interior of the holy places, replacing the old world's concentration on marble exteriors. Carving in the round, both statues and columns, will soon be forgotten for a thousand years. The free-standing marble pillar is replaced by the arch of brick and stone.

Edward Gibbon wrote of Augustine that he possessed 'a strong capacious, argumentative mind. He boldly sounded the dark abyss of grace, predestination, free will and original sin ... His learning was often borrowed, his arguments his own.'

Augustine helped create the strong outer walls of a universal

Church that had the authority to define, police and punish the minds within it. It was a tougher, more resilient, more compassionate and elastic formation than the brittle old Roman empire that it replaced. The dark inner chamber of the mind that he also helped create, powered by strong and contradictory urges, of original sin and divine grace, of free will and a jealous, ungenerous God, may have borne the stamp of the times that he lived through.

11

The Oasis of Ghadames

The only legal way in to Gaddafi's Revolutionary State of the Masses was through a single frontier post in Tunisia. In 1992 Libya had been placed under international trade sanctions. It was exhilarating to watch the effect this had on an otherwise bleak stretch of Tunisian steppeland. Imagine a totem pole composed of a million dollars stacked 300 feet high, then multiple this by 50,000 to create a forest of money. This is what Libya was then earning every year by selling its crude oil. As a boy I learnt that you may be able to dam a river, but you can never hold it back, however well you lace the stones with driftwood. The most you can expect to do is build up some back pressure, then watch which way the river flows next.

This was one of them, for a happy traffic jam now stretched for mile upon mile on this salt-flat arid plateau on the eastern edge of Tunisia. Large Libyan cars with their green and Arabic number plates dawdled their way back and forth across this vast drive-by black marketplace. It was fed by an irregular supply line of white Peugeot farm trucks with their stock professionally tied down with rope, bouncing slowly over the desert tracks. Plump middle-aged drivers, clad in the blue cotton Anti Cher jackets of Tunisian traders, tried to look glum and serious, but their angular sons and nephews could not but grin at the windfall profits of this never-ending fair. At either entrance to the traffic jam there was a brazen black market in notes, run by young men in leather jackets, gently waving fans made out of wodges of cash, Libyan pounds in one hand and Tunisian dinars in the other, with bulldog clips of the other useful market currencies cascading out of their pockets. There were mountains of brightly coloured Tupperware, entrenchments of rice and flour sacks, box castles made of bright tins of olive oil, sardines and harissa, whole supermarkets of clothes strung along lines that swayed with the desert wind, masses of garish plastic toys, as well as freshly butchered meat and the sweet smell of burning fat dribbling off grilled kebabs. It was utter animation, but unless the Orientalist traveller screwed his eyes up tight to make an impressionist vision of the thing – blurs of bright colour blotching the dun environment – there was nothing elegant for an heir of John Frederick Lewis to paint. Not a single carpet, no camels, no dates, no worked brass canisters to hold gunpowder, no cascades of embroidery or displays of jewels. Yet even so, it still managed to be undeniably exotic, even if the close-up details were composed of spun nylon from Japan, Korea and China, and the caravans that edged their way through this souk were not draped with madder-red saddlery but with sunscreen filters and mashallah stickers.

I came upon these streams of bottled Libyan cash, flowing in curious tributaries, in other places. There was the sudden emergence of local Tunisian airlines that specialised in flying oil engineers from Tunis to Houmt Souk (near the frontier), as well as a daily fleet of ferries that connected the harbour of Tripoli with the grand harbour of Malta and a palace guest house that could be used by the Gaddafi court just across the Algerian frontier in El Oued. These existed for just as long as America cared to enforce the 'UN-mandated trade sanctions', and could be paused for a whole week if a US embassy sent out an outraged cable to where it mattered. Even so, there were always ways of embedding a material fly in the amber of a diplomatic protest. Such as the time when the Tunisians closed their land frontier obediently shut, but then were forced to open it again, on compassionate grounds, for the dozens of US oilmen stranded in the no-man's-land between the two sets of customs posts.

Less than a year after I had first witnessed these exuberant desert black markets, I came back. I was part of a group that had been invited by the Libyan government. We were led by a journalist who was making a film about the children of mixed marriages (between Libyans and Britons) who had been unwittingly separated due to the sanctions. Our credentials as observers of the distress caused by international sanctions had got us permission to use a Saharan frontier post that was otherwise kept firmly closed. We were stopped at least a dozen times at various Tunisian roadblocks that inspected our paperwork and warned us that we would be turned back (despite our valid paperwork) by the Libyans. It was a matter of faith with all Tunisians that their eastern neighbours were over-excitable, overpaid, and dangerous drivers. The Libyans wanted only to drink and to play with women and cards, once allowed out of their puritanical country, and were treated as hillbillies on a spree. Though once they had spent all their cash and sobered up, it was agreed that they were all good men at heart, if not blood cousins.

Tunisia is a governed country – most especially the dissident-inclined south and east. So a traveller becomes a uniform-spotter, trying to sort out all the different organisations and uniforms that are entitled to stop you, be they the internal customs, frontier guards, road police, immigration officials, rural militia, the army or the town-based cops. Despite the delays at all these officious roadblocks, with their neat red- and white-painted poles and guardhouses, we remained in excellent temper. The checkpoints multiplied as we got closer and closer to the frontier, and it was clear that it would be well after midnight before we arrived at the crossing.

This was a good thing, for arriving at the Libyan frontier at two in the morning was like waking into an Alice in Wonderland dream world. Despite the billions of dollars of spend, the frontier of the nation was a roadside shack made from a couple of abandoned containers pushed together, over which was stretched some tattered canvas, all illuminated by a series of powerful arc lights fed by a noisy generator. The officials on guard were young soldiers, with no discernible badge of rank, but sporting an eclectic array of green turbans, desert boots, T-shirts and locally made waistcoats. There were lots of automatic rifles, discarded tins, jeeps mounted with twin machine guns, smiles, and an Arabic banner that translated: 'We have no frontier other than friendship to all peoples, Welcome to the Jamahiriya.' This last word could be translated as 'Libya', or 'the revolutionary-state-of-the-masses', and the lack of an imposing built frontier post had a political purpose to it. The borders of Libya had been dissolved and were now open to all the peoples of Africa and Arabia. A new capital city had also been declared.

The hotel had been expecting us for weeks, but not to the extent of preparing any of the rooms. It proved to be a homely brothel used by Libyan soldiers and garrisoned by Tunisian, Moroccan and Egyptian women. There was no food on offer, and what was eventually found was sealed in small, homogenised catering packets that had been smuggled in from Holland. Condoms and razor blades decorated a chipped pink washbasin that provided no running water, and so the drains were whiffy.

It is at rare moments like this that the emergency travel supplies I like to pack come into their own. An incense stick stuck into the edge of a nightlight candle, and an impromptu midnight feast of oatmeal biscuits garlanded by a tin of sardines soon had us relishing the humour of the situation.

Two of our travelling companions had added to the confusion. They were of Jewish descent (so theoretically forbidden in Libya) and though both bright, clever and successful, they had taken against each other and had begun to snipe. 'No I wouldn't wear that hat, it looks as if you are a rather aggressively assimilating Anglophile, circa 1902, origin Odessa' countered by: 'You can speak some Armenian can't you? I mean with a nose like that, I don't think there's any other hope.' My wife was pregnant, and an old girlfriend was part of our group of half a dozen travellers, as well as two artists who wore long skirts with their hair massed up into a bun interwoven with silk scarves.

Our mission was to reach Ghadames, an austerely beautiful Saharan oasis town. We had heard that the population had been provided with brand-new houses in a new district complete with running water, drains and tarmac roads, so the old city was deserted and empty of the seven thousand citizens who had once packed its narrow streets. But it was not unloved. We found that all the old houses remained in private ownership, and though one or two roofs had fallen in to reveal a rib-cage of palm-trunk beams, the locks and doors were all in place. We fell in love with the dreamy light that diffused through the narrow covered alleys, complete with benches set into the walls, and the twisting warren of passages, here and there framed by an arch that led past secretive bolted house doors and gated side alleys. Every now and then our guide would lead us into a sun-drenched open courtyard, where the power of the midday Saharan sun was instantly tangible. Though empty now, these had once been the central hubs of the trading city, spaces to market and make festivals in, as well as functioning as town squares for the civic parliaments, bordered on one side by an austere mosque. The streets were everywhere covered in fine golden Saharan sand, and the walls had an organic softness and curve to them, where centuries of limewash covered walls of sun-baked brick. Nothing could be bettered – neither the scale, the sense of mystery, nor the feel of an ordered hive assembled out of hundreds of self-contained family units. The covered streets were designed to act as wind tunnels, funnelling faint breezes past anyone who sat on the public benches. And like all other visitors to this empty city, we always found that our walks concluded with an invitation inside one of the secretive houses to eat a communal lunch, a series of round dishes heaped with fresh-baked round loaves, mutton stew, couscous and a cascade of fruits.

I know it is a historical fallacy, but for me the interior of a Ghadamsi house is sure to reek with ancient history. It is as if I have been invited into one of the houses of ancient Carthage that have been excavated below the Byrsa hill. The same intimate space, the same cascade of levels with niches, stairs and cupboards built into the thickness of the walls. The same alcoves to hold, protect and reflect an oil-fed lamp, whilst the decorative details familiar from textiles, embroidery, basket-weaving and female tattoos have been splashed in bold red against the whitewashed walls. The rooftops of Ghadames were the female-only space, abuzz with washing, the cleaning of grain and the drying of foods, and were interconnected by aerial walkways, counterparts to the male-dominated streets below. Many of the houses are embellished with acroteria – sharp, rather modernist-looking fins that project up from the four corners, which might originate from those crow-stepped machicolations that would seem to be a naturally occurring flourish for anyone with an eye for decorative brickwork, but are one of the tell-tale signs of the ancient, brick-derived culture of the Middle East. You can spot them all over the place, be it at Petra, carved by the Nabateans in the red sandstone rock walls, as well as in the decorative coronet that until recently crowned the flat roof of the central shrine of Bel at Palmyra, and ornamented the domed tombs of Sidon. They are a song line that leads back to the first forms of the mud-brick architecture of Mesopotamia, their shape suggesting both the high terraces of a stepped pyramid and the profile of a stylised cedar tree.

Another aspect that unites this Saharan architecture to our antique past is the lack of the rigid furniture that so possesses a modern house, that studied arrangement of table, sofa, bed, chests and chairs that announces the preconceived purpose of any room. In the recent past a room became a dining room only with the entry of a succession of laden trays, or a bedroom when a mat and blanket was unrolled, or a sitting room with the spreading of a carpet, cushions and guests. This lack of permanent clutter on the floor space gave an added glow of importance to the objects that defined how a room was going to be used, be it metal plates or basket-like trays arrayed in the walls, or the wooden coffer that held textiles when not in use.

What I found most fascinating of all is that this community, completely isolated on the edge of the Sahara, with its own dialect, musical traditions and material culture, had been riven by innumerable social stratifications. Ghadames was composed of a seething set of castes, clans and rival communities. So although an outsider might have viewed the Ghadamsi as an isolated people all companionably locked together in a dense mass of housing behind a fortress wall, this was not at all how a native would view things. To start with there was a political and physical fissure that separated the central walled town into two rival factions, the Beni Ouazit and the Beni Oulid. Like Cain and Abel, Romulus and Remus, Seth and Osiris, it was the rivalry between a pair of brothers that was the legendary heart of this ancient animosity. Ghadames is not alone in this fracture, indeed most North African communities seem to exist with an inbuilt bipartite tension to them. Medieval Fez was divided into the Andalusian and Kairouan quarters, while the rivalry between the Kabyle and Shawia Berbers continues to empower faction fights within the army of modern Algeria. To put it into a British perspective, it is as innate as the rivalry between Glasgow and Edinburgh, married to the internal tension within both these cities, which can be triggered by the question 'Hearts or Hibs?', 'Celtic or Rangers?' So, just like the Montagues and Capulets of fair Verona, the Beni Ouazit–Beni Oulid rivalry within Ghadames fuelled a bitter but poetic harvest of doomed love affairs and blood feuds. It also meant that the whole region was hard-wired for civil strife, so that some distant piece of palace chicanery, be it in the court of a medieval Hafsid Emir or the thirty-year Bachiya–Hussinya war (a mid-eighteenth-century war of the roses in Tunisia), could fan out like a forest fire to engulf this distant oasis. The Beni Ouazit chose one side and so the Beni Oulid chose the other. So did their allies among the tribes.

If you had the wit to look still closer, this division was further dissected. For the Beni Ouazit was an alliance formed from the self-governing oasis villages of Tferfera, Tinguezine and Djerassen, while the Beni Oulid embraced the Beni Derar, Teskou and Beni Mazigh clans. Each of these subdivisions traditionally maintained its own market, its own mosque, and its own gateway into the town – or at least aspired to. The entire adult male population of these urban clans, when gathered together in their own mosque, effectively formed a 'parliament' that set up a committee of elders who appointed such officials as a teacher, the gatekeeper and the water watchman.

To add a further edge to the social life of a Ghadamsi, every community was also stratified into two classes who in theory could not marry each other: the noble and free-born families, 'the Ahrar', standing apart from 'the Homran, Atara and Oucif'. The latter were theoretically descended from slaves and protected clients, though this division was muddled up by wealth creation. There is a whole cycle of legends (that sings of the love of Antar for Abla) clustered around this division. Antar behaves with much greater bravery, chivalry and élan than any noble clansman, but our hero is the child of a black slave mother, so he cannot be permitted the hand of his beloved Abla, his noble pure-blooded cousin. Elements of this prolonged love affair also get fed into the Abu Zeid story cycle, which pits a wily Bedouin Arab warrior against a Berber chief. In addition to all this complex social life, the people of Ghadames had at various times to absorb the physical presence of a garrison that occupied a fort on the edge of the oasis, be it Turks, Italians, Byzantine or Romans coming from the north, or Garamantian, Tebu or Tuareg clans coming from the south. In Gaddafi's day, the military camp was one of the training areas where disaffected Tuareg from Mali and Niger and Moors from Western Sahara were trained into his own foreign legion.

The most insistent fissure of all was the one that existed between the society of men and women. There was the happy limbo land of childhood, when boys and girls played together, but as sexual maturity approached around the age of ten, the adult frontiers were imposed. Girls were veiled and secluded, whilst the ceremony of circumcision transformed a boy. He was expelled from the happy memories of his grandmother's rule over the female quarters and had to join in the society of men, be it in the palm orchards, the caravan trade, the mosque, marketplace or hammam. They lived in different spaces, performed different tasks, wore different clothes and inhabited separate command structures. As a general rule, the higher the class, the less likely that a woman would need to leave her house, except for such great annual festivals as the celebration of the Prophet's birthday – Mouloud (Mawlid).

What united all these different forms of humankind, and drew them together at the oasis of Ghadames, was water. The Ain el Fras, 'the spring of the mare', used to pour 3 cubic metres of water every minute into a large basin just outside the town walls. You can visit other springs in the region, but most of them are contaminated by either salt or sulphur. The water from Ain el Fras was sweet, and so four channels reached out from this precious basin to supply the rival villages and their fields. The flow of water was monitored by a measuring bucket with a hole in it. Each empty bucket was recorded by a knot on a string, and so the right to irrigate the neat interconnected maze of furrows in the gardens and palm orchards was assessed by 'so many knots of time'.

In the past the palm orchards were considered a place apart, so that things considered inappropriately Islamic in the town environment could be performed by the descendants of slaves to an African beat and intensity. Hence many of the fun things in life – music, dancing, bonfires, pit-roasts, palm-wine drinking, flirting and kissing – happened outdoors under the forgiving shade of palm trees. Date palms have to be married and the male flowers smell of spunk. In some Saharan oases, to add to the already highly complex social geography, there was an additional strand of legalised homosexual relationships that were permitted under the shade of the palm groves. This lost world of tolerance is supported by what a learned social historian once told me about pre-modern Europe: forget about our modern obsession with sex on beds, they were for huddling together as a family to keep out the cold, and as theatrical stages for child-birth and death. All the real action happened outdoors, in the woods and meadows. I found this take on reality was backed up by the confessions of a seasoned female traveller who had converted to Islam and settled down as a teacher, who told me the same thing about the reality of village life in the North West Frontier of Pakistan and Afghanistan. A very strict moral-ity ruled the street and the home, but providing that public decorum was maintained, when the fields grew high enough the crops sheltered many a passionate embrace. And despite the blame we heap on the monotheistic morality religions, I doubt that things have ever been very different.

Ghadames had a Christian bishop in the sixth century. Two hundred years later, through the near-legendary vortex of the conquering Arab missionary warrior Sidi Oqba ibn Nafi (sometimes spelt Uqba ben Nafi), the oasis was converted to Islam. The actual process of Islamic conversion has everywhere been mythologised, and Sidi Oqba is still very much in the air of the oasis of Ghadames. The oldest Islamic building, the cem-etery–mosque just to the south of the city, Sidi Oqba El Badri, bears his name. His fame was such that an ancient foundation legend was amended to include him. One version of this story has it that Ghadames was a desolate desert camping ground the first time that the great Oqba passed this way at the head of his army, on the way to conquer the oasis of Tuat, deep down in the Western Sahara. On his way back, he paused to examine his old campsite, where some food had been almost miraculously left intact. He exclaimed *Tidamensi* – 'yesterday's lunch' (which is also an Arabic pun on the word Ghadames) – upon which his mare's hoof broke through a crust of rock to miraculously release the spring, the Ain el Fras, giving birth to the oasis. It is an enchanting story, which has pleasing parallels to the tale told about his uncle, the heroic warrior Abu Al'As (a Companion of the Prophet), who created the city of Cairo around his old campaign tent which he found standing after a year's absence and being used by a pigeon as a nest. The tale of Sidi Oqba at Ghadames has other resonances, with such magical horses as Pegasus creating springs, and the old linkage of horse and sea gods (such as Neptune) with springs, which were once imagined to be fountains that tapped the great Oceanus body of water on which the Earth's crust floated.

The ruins of a hilltop *ksar*, or castle, which stand about 7 kilometres to the north of the city, are known as Tegout or El Khoul. It is a place of ill omen, linked with the last stand of some obstinate Christian Roman soldiers against the first Muslim Arabs. I have on subsequent trips to the oasis had time to plan picnic stops here, and potter around the shin-height ruins of this *ksar* set on a knobbly outcrop of rock, but have never spotted any dressed stones or pottery sherds. There are, however, plenty of late Roman and Byzantine fragments to be found in Ghadames, especially in the five old mosques in the centre of the oasis. In the Younes mosque portions of columns and classical capitals have been thoughtfully recycled and then incorporated with layers of limewash. The sunken wash-house off the Ghadamsi square (often introduced to visitors as the slave market or the Place of Mulberries) and that beside the Younes mosque has perhaps the best array of these ancient sculpted stones.

I have never worked out if there is any symbolic gesture behind the re-use of ancient columns and capitals for new Islamic buildings. Italian antiquarians believed that these classical fragments came from a Byzantine cathedral whose foundations were presumed to stand below the two oldest quarters: the Beni Derar and Tinguezine. Fortunately no house demolitions were made to test this theory. I think these antique stones may have been stripped off 'the Idols' – which are the remnants of a Roman necropolis on the edge of town. This antique city of the dead was once overlooked by five towers, for this region of North Africa is still dotted with mausoleums – wonderful, whimsical structures that can look like a stolid temple shrine or which climb up through three storeys that taper into a pyramid spire. Only two of these towers survive at Ghadames today, and they have been completely stripped of their outer skin of carved stonework, so the Idols now stand forth as the mysteriously shaped inner core of these monuments – like a Whitehead reverse sculpture before its time.

No traveller in the Libyan Sahara, ancient, medieval or modern, can avoid passing the oasis of Ghadames, but it has always been a trading way station and has never served as a political capital. The base camp of the first Arab Muslims who conquered the Libyan Sahara was fixed on the oasis village of Zuwayla, which is about 450 miles south-east of Ghadames. The traditions record that Oqba ibn Nafi conquered Zuwayla in 643, and for once the archaeologist's trowel does not beg to differ, for organic matter mixed up with the mud bricks from the ruins of the old white mosque of Zuwayla has recently been sampled. It confirms that it was in use as a place of prayer from AD 671. Other recent archaeological work in this region of the Libyan Sahara has also gone against the expected grain of history, as the desert oases enjoyed an economic boom in the early medieval period (around AD 400–700), just when the maritime trade of the late Roman–Byzantine empire was collapsing. Strong Berber trading links were already in place across the length and breadth of the Sahara: east to Egypt, west to Morocco and south to West Africa. The engineering techniques that built foggaras (underground water canals used in the Saharan oases) were long believed to have travelled in the baggage of the first Arabs, but it has recently been proved that these canals had been in operation since 400 BC, gifts of ancient Egypt alongside the cultivation of linen and cotton. Sorghum and millet cultivation was also brought north across the Sahara by West African traders. This is now seen to be part of a burgeoning trans-Saharan trade, which carried merchandise by mule and camel caravan, contained in sacks of woven textile or worked leather that gradually replaced pottery amphorae as the packaging of North African trade.

So there is every reason to see that the Arabs did not come to this part of the Libyan Sahara as trail-blazing explorers, but were almost certainly guided along well-known roads by their allies among the Berber tribes. Such a policy would have been made possible by the traditional rivalries that fissured Berber communities. So just as we have seen that the Romans succeeded in conquering North Africa by dividing before ruling, I believe the same technique was used by the first Arab armies.

Ghadames is a near-miraculous survival of a Berber oasis community, but it was forced to exist in a cultural limbo after Colonel Gaddafi took power in Libya. For Gaddafi always aspired to an Arabic identity, and publicly stated that anybody retaining their Berber identity 'sucked poisoned milk from their mother's breast'. This was ironic, for he was himself the son of a Bedouin shepherd of the Qadhadhfa tribe, who are ethnically Berber. But like so many of the political leaders of North Africa, Gaddafi needed to feel an Arab, not just on intellectual and spiritual grounds, but to take part in the political renaissance of the Arab world. For the long struggle for Arab freedom against the French, Italian, British and Ottoman empires had been coupled with the dream of creating a strong, unified Arab state. The Arab struggle against the old colonial powers had finally been won in the 1960s (in the bloody independence struggle fought against the French in Algeria, as well as against the British in Yemen and the bizarre episode of the Suez War). But just as the Arabs finally emerged victorious, the 1967 Six Day War and Israel's subsequent settlement of the West Bank provided the Arab people with a brand-new colonial enemy to confront. So Arabic identity was never just a matter of the ethnic DNA in your veins, but part of a 500-year-long struggle for self-determination, with the living cause of the Palestinian people bringing it right up to date. In Gaddafi's case this was also blended with his personal aspiration to lead the Arab world into unity, a task he felt had been bequeathed to him by his childhood hero, Colonel Nasser of Egypt. To a late twentieth-century Arab nationalist, any community that weakened the concept of Arab unity, especially such ancient peoples as the Kurds, the Copts of Egypt or the Berbers of North Africa, was considered to be either an annoying irrelevance or else potential traitors.

This means that the history of the Arab conquest of North Africa often gets the full-airbrush treatment in the classroom. Its storyline only needs heroes, especially if these militant Arabs can be seen as prefiguring the struggle of modern Arab heroes, rescuing their people from the colonial slavery of an evil empire. So Oqba ibn Nafi liberating the oppressed Berbers from the Roman–Byzantine empire ticks all the right boxes.

The facts on the ground were more complicated, for as we have seen the Berber tribes rebelled against their Arab conquerors frequently, but made no objection to the new religion of Islam. They rejected not the teaching of the Prophet

Muhammad, but the tribute-tax of the Arab emperor (the Umayyad Caliph) sitting on his throne in distant Damascus. In North Africa this tribute did not take the reasonable form of a percentage of the annual harvest (as laid down by the Koran and confirmed by the traditions) but instead inflicted the social catastrophe of an annual levy of slaves, destructive to families. In a war waged between 705 and 710 the Arab general Emir Musa ben Nasser re-established the caliph's dominion over North Africa. During this five-year 'pacification' it has been estimated that he enslaved 100,000 Berbers and sent them in long caravans of tribute to the palaces of Damascus.

As ever, it was a military defeat on a far distant frontier (an Arab cavalry army slave raiding deep into France had been expelled at the battle of Tours in 732) that first revealed that this vast empire was defeatable. The flashpoint of the Berber revolt came from two decisions. One was an order to tattoo the veteran Berber soldiers fighting within the Arab army with the insignia 'Slave of', the other was a new poll tax that demanded one Berber slave from every five members of the population. Critically, this assessment treated the Berber allies of the Arab armies as enemies, not friends. Islamic converts and veteran Berber soldiers of the Arab conquest armies were categorised on the same level as the conquered peoples. It was a similar arbitrary decision of Colonel Gaddafi's, to round up the Berber population of these southern hills and pack them off into his depleted army (treating them as no more than militia cattle), that reportedly goaded them into full-scale rebellion. It tipped the balance in the first Libyan civil war of 2011 that would finally reduce him to hiding in a drainage tunnel before he was lynched. The same thing, on an even bigger scale, exploded across North Africa in 739, and ripped the heart out of the caliphate's North African empire. Instead of dividing and ruling, the Umayyads had managed to unite the ruled into a single strong and coherent enemy.

There had always been good Arabic teachers as well as bad slave traders. Arab Kharijite missionaries had worked as merchants, which had allowed them to migrate across the ancient caravan trails that criss-cross North Africa, and quietly convert various communities to their way of thinking. Their doctrine provided the unifying discipline and revolutionary zeal that powered the Berber rebellion of 739. The Kharijite teaching was a highly attractive message to the Berbers of North Africa, for Kharijites argued that race had nothing to do with Islam, only a pure heart. As they saw it, the violent schism between Sunni and Shia Arabs had more to do with a war for political governance than with religion: the true path was that every community must be free to choose the purest and the best as its teachers and sheikhs. This message spread like wildfire across North Africa. It took deep root in the desert-mountains and oases of the Sahara. In the hills of Tripolitania, the Libyan oasis city of Ghadames, the valley of the Mzab (deep in southern Algeria), and in the island of Jerba in Tunisia, this tradition had miraculously survived.

So it was in the oasis of Ghadames that I first stumbled across these medieval figures, still highly relevant to the choices of North Africans in the twenty-first century – my heroes of ancient North Africa.

Suggestions for further reading

I have picked out four works that might provide a useful cumulative introduction to the general history of North Africa. This is followed by several titles for those wanting to tighten their focus on the ancient and classical period of North Africa. A more extensive reading list is available at barnabyrogerson.com.

North Africa

Abun-Nasr, Jamil M., ed. *History of the Maghreb in the Islamic Period* (Cambridge: Cambridge University Press, 1987) – a great and still unsurpassed regional history by a Lebanese scholar working from Germany.

Brett, Michael and Fentress, Elizabeth, *The Berbers: The Peoples of Africa* (Oxford: Oxford University Press, 1996) – an essential first building block for any real understanding of the indigenous peoples, language and traditions of North Africa.

Julien, Charles-André, *Histoire de L'Afrique du Nord* (2 volumes) (Paris: Payot, 1978) – a prime source to be placed right beside Abun-Nasr.

Rogerson, Barnaby, *A Traveller's History of North Africa* (London: Duckworth, 2012) (third edition), the simplest historical survey but the most wide-ranging in terms of time and geography.

Ancient North Africa

Birley, Anthony, *Septimius Severus: The African Emperor* (London: Routledge, 1999) – the standard biography, which will lead you back to the three prime original sources: Dio Cassius, Herodian and the Augustan History – to be trusted in that order. I would avoid the slim biography of Septimius Severus by Peter Green.

Brown, Peter – start with his biography (*Augustine of Hippo*), then read *Through the Eye of the Needle* and *The Cult of the Saints*, topped up Robin Lane Fox's provoking *Augustine* and James O'Donnell's more considered *Augustine, Sinner and Saint*.

Harden, Donald, *The Phoenicians* (London: Thames and Hudson, 1962) – remains a useful introduction, grounded in ceramic types.

Hoyos, Dexter, *The Carthaginians* (London: Routledge, 2010) (peoples of the ancient world series) – a lifetime of knowledge in a deceptively slim volume; excellent reading list for further research, including his other works on Hannibal and his wars.

MacKendrick, Paul, *The North African Stones Speak* (London: Croom Helm, 1980) – slightly quirky archaeologist's eye view of the classical ruins of North Africa but achieved with diligence and honesty; has a copious bibliography.

Miles, Richard, *Carthage Must be Destroyed* (London: Allen Lane, 2010) – a splendidly readable narrative but informed by serious scholarship which will, if you so wish, lead you back to the prime original sources, Plutarch, Polybius, Silius Italicus, Diodorus Siculus, Sallust and the Roman propaganda of Livy.

Picard, G.C., and Picard, C., *The Life and Death of Carthage* (London: Sidgwick and Jackson, 1968) – written by a pair of French scholars (a husband and wife team) who combine the detail of an on-site archaeologist with the overview of a literate historian. Among many other relevant works, they also produced the charming, *Daily Life in Carthage: At the time of Hannibal*, 1961.

Raven, Susan, *Rome in Africa* (London: Routledge, 1993) (third edition) – fluent regional study with a useful book list for those who want to study this period in further depth.

Warmington, B.H., *Carthage* (London: Pelican, 1964) – an accomplished history, satisfyingly well-written for the general reader and innovative enough for the specialist.

Index

BARNABY ROGERSON was conceived on a yacht and born in Scotland. Travel was a vital aspect of his childhood which followed in the wake of his father's career in the Royal Navy with postings to Gibraltar, Malta, Skye and Virginia. A degree in History at St Andrews University proved to be adequate preparation for work as a barman, tutor for a child star in a film made on a Greek island, a pony boy in the Highlands and stints at two determinedly independent publishers which led to a job in the press department of the Afghanistan Support Committee. A chance encounter in the Outer Hebrides led to his first commission to write a guidebook to Morocco followed by Tunisia, Cyprus, Istanbul and Libya. These projects were intermingled with summers spent restoring grottoes and garden temples at Hampton Court, Leeds Castle and Fort Worth, Texas.

Subsequent to the birth of two daughters, Barnaby wrote *A Traveller's History of North Africa* and *The Prophet Muhammad: A Biography*, followed by an account of the early Caliphate, *The Heirs of the Prophet*, and the story of the battle for the Mediterranean from 1415–1580, *The Last Crusaders*. He has made a collection of the sacred numerological traditions of the world, *Rogerson's Book of Numbers*, contributed the text for Don McCullin's photographic study of Roman North Africa and the Levant, *Southern Frontiers*, and most recently written *In Search of Ancient North Africa*.

He has also co-edited a collection of the contemporary travel writing *Ox-Tales* for the charity Oxfam; edited a collection of the travel literature of Marrakesh; a collection of contemporary travel encounters with Islam, *Meetings with*

Remarkable Muslims; a collection of English Orientalist verse, *Desert Air;* and a collection of poetry, *London.* Barnaby is on the advisory board of Critical Muslim, the editorial board of *The Middle East in London* magazine and is a Fellow of the Royal Asiatic Society and the Royal Geographical Society. He has been elected a Fellow of the Society of Antiquaries and an honorary member of The Travellers Club. He is also a lecturer, tour guide, television presenter, journalist and book reviewer with a scrapbook of three hundred articles pasted up at *barnabyrogerson.com*, where you can also find a Book List for those interested in reading more about Ancient North Africa.

His day job is running Eland, a publishing house, which specialises in keeping classic travel books in print, *www.travelbooks. co.uk.*